A NATION WITHIN A NATION

*Texas is a state of mind. Texas is an obsession.
Above all, Texas is a nation in every sense of the
word.*

John Steinbeck, *Travels with Charley*

Kennikat Press
National University Publications
Series in American Studies

General Editor
James P. Shenton
Professor of History, Columbia University

MARK E. NACKMAN

A NATION
WITHIN A NATION

The Rise of Texas Nationalism

National University Publications
KENNIKAT PRESS // 1975
Port Washington, N. Y. // London

TO MY MOTHER AND FATHER

Manufactured in the United States of America

Published by
Kennikat Press Corp.
Port Washington, N.Y./London

Library of Congress Cataloging in Publication Data

Nackman, Mark E
    A nation within a nation.

    (Series in American studies) (Kennikat Press national
university publications)
    Bibliography: p.
    Includes index.
    1. Texas—History—Republic—1836–1846. 2. Texas—
History—1846–1950. 3. Nationalism—Texas. I. Title.
F390.N28   320.9'764   75-34450
ISBN 0-8046-9131-2

Contents

ACKNOWLEDGMENTS

I am first of all indebted to the librarians of the University of Texas at Austin, the Texas State Library, Texas Tech University, Columbia University, Yale University, and the New York Public Library. I regret that I am not able to mention by name all who helped. Conversations with Texans in academe and out were especially helpful and are fondly remembered. I particularly wish to thank Joe B. Frantz, Dorman H. Winfrey, William H. Timmons, Joseph Leach, C. L. Sonnichsen, Rupert N. Richardson, William H. Goetzmann, Seymour V. Connor, Alwyn Barr, Ernest Wallace, Robert Wagner, Stanley Marcus, Lee Bennett, Hallie Stillwell, Barry Scobee, and Tom Lea. I am also grateful to Professors James Shenton, Eric McKitrick, and William Leuchtenburg of Columbia University, Howard Lamar of Yale University, and Carleton B. Chapman of Dartmouth, all of whom took an interest in this study at various stages of its progress.

A NATION WITHIN A NATION

ABBREVIATIONS USED IN NOTES AND BIBLIOGRAPHY

AH	American Heritage
AHR	American Historical Review
ATCC	Austin-Travis County Collection, Austin Public Library
AW	The American West
CO	Chronicles of Oklahoma
EG	Economic Geography
ETHJ	East Texas Historical Journal
GR	The Geographical Review
HAHR	Hispanic American Historical Review
JAH	Journal of American History
JNH	Journal of Negro History
JSH	Journal of Southern History
MVHR	Mississippi Valley Historical Review
NYHSQ	New York Historical Society Quarterly
PSHA	Publications of the Southern Historical Association
PSQ	Political Science Quarterly
QTSHA	Quarterly of the Texas State Historical Association
SHQ	Southwestern Historical Quarterly
SR	Southwest Review
SSSQ	Southwestern Social Science Quarterly
SWC	Southwest Collection, Texas Tech University Library Archives
TLR	Texas Law Review
TMH	Texas Military History
TSL	Texas State Library Archives
UT	University of Texas at Austin Library Archives
WHQ	Western Historical Quarterly
WTHAYB	West Texas Historical Association Yearbook
YU	Yale University, Beinecke Library

Introduction:
Nationalism and the Texan Nation

This is a case study of nationalism in an infant nation. That nation as such no longer exists but the nationalism lingers on. The Texas nation endured for a mere ten years, from 1836 to 1846. During that period the task of nation-building was undertaken in a manner reminiscent of the United States in its first and most critical decade. The Americans avoided war and possessed the resources and productive capacity to survive. The Texans could not avoid war and lacked the means to prosecute it. They had yet to develop their vast subterranean wealth and were doing well simply to feed themselves. Bled by incessant warfare and choked by economic stagnation, they were at least fortunate in having an alternative to abject surrender. They could relinquish their grip on nationhood by bowing to American sovereignty. Nationality would be lost but the country itself might prosper.

The struggle to form a nation left its mark on that and future generations of Texans. Both the struggle and the nation made an imprint. The struggle yielded an *esprit de corps;* the nation gave a memory of nationality and a hallowed tradition of revolution and independence. A common experience of frontier community-building in an inhospitable environment, contact with alien cultures, revolutionary war, and unceasing border defense against both Mexicans and Indians resulted in an unusual degree of interdependence among Anglo-Texans. The fellow-feeling was implicit; it required no articulation or explanation. But the Texans were a sentimental people and could not always refrain from verbalizing it: "I am on my way to New York, shall not see you again soon," said one in 1860. "May you live always — I would not write you as I have, if we had not been raised together on the Colorado, in the dark days of the Republic." Another was less bashful and displayed more of the exuberance Americans had come to expect of Texans. Writing home from Philadelphia in 1846, he reported how he had discovered the name of a *Texas* lady on the list of arrivals at the Exchange:

> I could not believe my own eyes, so I rubbed them up with knuckles & took another look, & sure enough there it was . . . upon which I jumped up, threw my old hat on the floor, gave one yell, three whoops, & two of the d-n-dest biggest huzzas you ever heard; it threw everybody in and out of the room in a panic.[1]

The *esprit de corps* endures to this day. From Brownsville to Amarillo, from Texarkana to El Paso, the Anglo-Texan retains what Karl W. Deutsch calls a complementarity of social communication — "the ability to communicate more effectively, and over a wider range of subjects, with members of one large group than with outsiders."[2] A Texan has more in common (or thinks he has) with his fellow-Texan living hundreds of miles across the state than with his neighbors a few miles across the border in Louisiana or Oklahoma. David M. Potter observed this phenomenon in his study of nationalism. The political state "can employ the concept of a 'common territory' so persuasively as to create the illusion of commonality for geographically diverse areas. . . . "[3] Since the inception of the Republic in 1836, the process has been at work in Texas. It must be conceded that our modern age of high mobility, rapid transportation, and instant communications is taking its toll on this cohesiveness and solidarity. No state or region has been able to withstand the impact. As the United States becomes homogenized, regional character evaporates. The thousands of newcomers brought to Texas by corporations, universities, government agencies, and other bodies cannot be expected soon to feel a bond with the land and its people. The modern Texans who share this kinship are natives with family roots in Texas soil.

If the struggle for a nation produced a group consciousness, the Texas nation itself bequeathed a heritage of nationalism that seems to have survived more than a century of statehood. By nationalism I mean a love of place, a fierce loyalty to the state, and a desire to advance its power and prestige. Nationalism can be both a sentiment and a movement. The movement is political in thrust. It requires territorial autonomy or nation-state status. It seeks to maintain national independence. It may also seek territorial aggrandizement or the repatriation of putative nationals living in contiguous territory. As a movement, Texan nationalism flourished during the early years of nationhood, waned as the financial and military odds against survival became overwhelming, lapsed altogether with the consummation of annexation, revived during the New Mexico boundary dispute of 1849–1850, and rose briefly again in the secession crisis of 1860–1861. It has remained dormant ever since. Successive generations of Texans have grown increasingly reconciled to or enamored of membership in the American Union. If there is anything left of a nationalist movement, it persists only in jest.

Humor is a part of sentiment. While jokes do not make movements, neither should they be entirely discounted. They may have a literal underlying intent. The sentiment of nationalism can easily exist in the absence of a movement. The citizen finds his own identity in the national group, recognizes his membership in the state, and gives his primary loyalty simultaneously to both group and state. Individuals in a nationalistic state may withhold such loyalty or give it reluctantly; not all are enthusiastic. For the nationalist, however, all other group associations – race, religion, class, occupation, etc. – are secondary.[4] "This is my country, hurrah for Texas!" shouted the young daughter of Albert Sidney Johnston as she came across Red River with her mother in 1855. Her voice was echoed throughout the state and the reverberations have come down to the present. "I hope that I shall not be criticized too severely for often thinking and speaking like every other ardent Texan of his splendid country," wrote a German visitor in 1848. "'All for Texas and Texas forever'." As one man put it in 1860, the interests of Texas (as opposed to any other country) are "dear to my heart." "I was born on her bosom, and I love her with a son's devotion."[5] As a sentiment in the past century, Texan nationalism has taken the form of chauvinism – a demonstrative display of excessive pride. Every American recognizes it. There is nothing comparable in any of the other states.[6] To many of us, including the Texans, it is a source of wonderment. From whence does it come? This study will attempt to lay bare the roots of the Texas allegiance.

Texan nationalism, like American nationalism, did not give birth to the nation-state. Both nationalisms surfaced with the creation of the state itself. The Texas nation was from the start a homogeneous one and national unity through social integration was achieved almost immediately. The "nation" spoken of in this study is the "Anglo" nation, embracing white Americans and Europeans. Other racial and ethnic groups on the land – Mexicans, blacks, and Indians – were not assimilated and remained powerless. With rare exceptions, they did not contribute to the political state. Language, religion, and custom isolated the Mexican, race and slavery excluded the black, and a wide cultural chasm separated the Indian. Thus, Texan nationality had little or no meaning for these groups. The Anglo-Americans dominated and enjoyed certain advantages in the quest for nationhood: a common language, religion, ethnicity, and political heritage. Even class differences were slight among the generations up to the Civil War. They made a coherent group and a credible petitioner for nationality. Like all nationalists, they wanted to convince others (particularly other governments) that they were entitled to a nation-state. No one could deny their territorial conquests, least of all the Mexicans. From a cultural standpoint, however, did they truly constitute a nation? To be recognized as a separate and distinct people, they should have certain distinguishing characteristics. Wherein did the Texans differ from the American friends and relatives they had left behind in the States?

I must say at the outset that a separate culture is not a *sine qua non* of nationality. Nor must there be, where there is a separate nationalism, a culture of equivalent separateness.[7] Whether the Zionists of the twentieth century who settled in Palestine and founded the state of Israel became culturally distinguishable from the Jews remaining in their native countries is a moot question. Whatever the verdict, it is undeniable that they considered themselves deserving of their own nation and nationalism was a natural outgrowth of that determination. One might also observe that Americans of the revolutionary era were highly Anglicized. It may then seem paradoxical that they revolted from England at the very time they most resembled their English rulers. Where cultural antagonisms exist (as between the Anglo-Americans in Texas and their Mexican masters), the potential for revolt is greater, but the drive for self-determination does not depend on cultural differentiae. Whether the Texans differed significantly from their American brethren or from other frontiersmen is not germane to the rise of nationalism. But it should be borne in mind that personal circumstances cast them into a similar mold and that their subsequent historical experience departed from the American norm.

Up to 1846, they had this in common: they were all expatriates. The very fact that they had abandoned home and country to settle in an unknown and untamed wilderness marked them as a breed apart. We may ask why any sober individual would choose Texas, a country infested with "wild" Indians and banditti, and threatened continually after 1836 by a hostile Mexico. Why should they volunteer for such a land in preference to their own American frontier, which at least enjoyed the protection of federal laws and a national army? A good many, it seems, were debtors or criminals seeking refuge from economic hardship or the hot breath of the law.[8] Some fancied themselves empire-builders who never blinked at national boundaries, many more wished only for anonymity and a place in the vast landscape to hide from a hounding wife, or creditor, or sheriff. Others, doubtless, were ordinary farmers and businessmen no more ambitious or desperate than their counterparts in Iowa or Arkansas. Or were they? The vexing question remains: why should they take their chances in Texas?

An army wife stationed in Texas in the 1850s encountered an individual whom she considered the epitome of the Texan. This was one Henry Clay Davis of Rio Grande City, who had in a few years established himself as a prosperous ranchero while earning a reputation for fighting prowess as the leader of a local ranger company. "Clay Davis was a true specimen of the Texan, tall and athletic," she wrote. Indeed, Davis's past seemed to fit perfectly into the mold of the typical Texan. Seeking adventure, he had left his Kentucky home at the age of fifteen and while still a youth got into a bloody fight on a Mississippi steamboat, apparently killing a man. He took off for Arkansas, a fugitive from justice, without friends or money. As he grew to manhood, he learned the necessity of self-reliance. His many escapes from danger imparted to him a recklessness which he would put to good use in the Texas Revolution. When he reached Texas, the woman concluded, "He found himself among men of tastes and dispositions similar to his own. . . . Fighting simply for the love of it, he cared less for the result than for the pleasurable excitement it produced."[9]

Many American visitors came away convinced that Davis was the stuff of which the average Texan was made. Whether from the security of the United States or in the nerve-fraying atmosphere of Texas itself, persons acquainted with Texans before the Civil War concluded that a daredevil spirit and volatile temperament were part of their being. Those who got to know them at first hand sometimes felt themselves rubbing elbows in situations too cozy for comfort. "I saw at the breakfast table one morning," related one, "four murderers who had sought safety in this country; and a gentleman assured me, that on one occasion, he had set down with eleven." Another reported that he had once spent the night at an inn where he found himself in the company of fourteen men, "all of whom freely acknowledged that they had absconded from their native country, and were drawn into Texas as a last resort." Samuel E. Chamberlain, whose knowledge of Texans came from what he saw of them in the Mexican War, did not hesitate to generalize: "Take them all together with their uncouth costume, bearded faces, lean and brawny forms, fierce wild eyes, and swaggering manners, they were fit representatives of the outlaws who made up the population of the Lone Star State."[10]

Contemporaries also testified to certain ennobling qualities. "What a race!" marveled the French minister to the Republic in 1839. "What can the Mexicans do against men of this kidney!" An English settler found the country "full of enterprising and persevering people" ("the timid and the lazy generly [sic] return to the States"), and the British chargé in Austin doubted there was anywhere in the world a race of men "more enterpris-

7

ing and energetic." To a traveler from Germany, the Texans fully deserved "all the praises which impartial observers have heaped upon them in the past. Even the really bad Texan is no common, low, vulgar, debased criminal, but in his character and conduct there is still discernible a certain degree of greatness." The Scotch militarist, General Arthur Wavell, had known the men of Texas since the days of the early filibusters. In 1844, he offered this assessment to the British Foreign Office:

> To as much if not more natural Talent, and energy to call it into play, and knowledge of all which is practically useful under every Emergency of the most Civilized Nations, they add a reckless hardihood, a restless spirit of Adventure, resources and confidence in themselves, keen perception, coolness, contempt of other men, usages, and Laws, and of Death, equal to the Wild Indian.[11]

The many travelers who visited Texas during the antebellum years tried to fathom what they felt certain was a distinct Texan character.[12] In doing so, they made the Texans acutely conscious of their specialness. The Texan found himself to be a curiosity, almost a legendary figure in his own lifetime. Half-alligator, half-horse; villain, desperado, Indian fighter, wild man — he personified the exoticism of the far western frontier. Some, like William "Bigfoot" Wallace, enjoyed telling tall tales and yarns to the folks back home in Virginny, and the very dimensions of his physique persuaded his eager listeners that the mythical Texan was real.[13] Texans could not depart the boundaries of their country without being surrounded by curiosity seekers. "What has contributed very much to my daily annoyance is the circumstance of my being a Texian," wrote Sam Maverick to his wife from Charleston in 1846. "I leave it to you to imagine for I cannot describe the fatigue I constantly suffer by continual calls from my very friendly but exceedingly uninformed acquaintance & kindred." From London, the self-effacing Texan ambassador to the Court of St. James related a diplomat's experience:

> I dined a few evenings since, by special invitation, with Sir John Herschell the great astronomer, and Mr. Tytler the eminent Scotch historian. Several other literary gentlemen of distinction were present. . . . I of course was modest and reserved in such company — and yet they would bring me out on the subject of Texas and the U States — we discussed the affairs of the two nations — their prominent men — institutions etc. They listened with much deference to all I said about those countries — but evidently with delight to the accounts of our Indian fights — prarie [sic] life — buffalo hunting etc.[14]

As every historian of Texas will insist, the majority, perhaps the vast majority of settlers were decent, law-abiding folk. Visitors to the country gratefully commented upon their friendliness and hospitality, while admitting to their intelligence, their fortitude, and even their morality. It may have been a goodly flock; nevertheless one is struck by the evident profusion of black sheep in it. Their ubiquity was remarked upon by nearly every traveler who journeyed to the country in the formative years.

Texas generally may with safety be regarded as a place of refuge for rascality and criminality of all kinds — the sanctuary to which pirates, murderers, thieves, and swindlers fly for protection from the laws they have violated in other countries, and under other governments. . . . Many innocent and deluded people are certainly mixed up with this vile population, and some mercantile men of respectability, education, and probity; but, in the main, scoundrelism, under one shape or another, constitutes the larger portion of the present population of Texas.[15]

As early as 1822, *Niles' Register* called Texas "a rendezvous for criminals," and soon the initials "G.T.T." ("Gone to Texas") would become infamous. As an American explained to an Englishman, "When we want to say shortly that it's all up with a fellow, we just say 'G.T.T.', just as you'd say gone to the devil, or the dogs." The place was known as the "Elysium of rogues," and its people as "renegades and ruffians." Anson Jones, who later became a president of the Texas Republic, was living in New Orleans and failing in business in 1833 when he was urged to try his luck in Texas. "My impressions of Texas were extremely unfavorable," he recalled. "I had known it only as a harbor for pirates and banditti." When the fires of the Texas Revolution were about to blaze in 1835, the Opelousas, Louisiana *Gazette* opined that if Texas and Mexico went to war, "The world would lose many bad citizens and the devil would gain some faithful servants — that everybody knew that the immigrants to Texas were vagabonds and refugees from justice."[16] The heroics of the Revolution made Texans world renowned for their fighting prowess but did nothing to diminish their notoriety for plunder and thievery. The widely circulated exposés of Benjamin Lundy, William Ellery Channing, and others stigmatized the revolutionary effort as a land-stealing escapade and a conspiracy to advance the domain of slavery. Purportedly executed by a cadre of audacious adventurers, the Revolution made the names Sam Houston, Jim Bowie, William Travis, and Davy Crockett household words in America and kept Texas in the public mind for years to come.

As a fledgling nation, Texas fared little better with the American press than it had as a Mexican province, particularly as the question of annexation rose and fell. The New York *Sun* remarked in 1839 that few Texans had "the conscience to abstain from plundering whatever they can lay their hands on," and gave the country faint praise by declaring its president, Mirabeau B. Lamar, "the only man in Texas, whether of high or low degree, who possessed a character unstained by villainy of some sort or other." As annexation came to be more and more an issue in the mid-forties, an avalanche of epithets descended upon the Texans. Horace Greeley in the *Clay Tribune* cast Texas as a "den of thieves" and a "rendezvous for rascals of all the continent." At an anti-annexation meeting in New York, Philip Hone was shocked by the behavior of a gang of "prize-fighters and pardoned felons" who riotously broke up the gathering by hissing, groaning, and shouting, "Hurrah for Texas!" The Hartford *Courant* labeled Texas "the land of Bowie knives and Toothpicks." In a scathing editorial against annexation, the paper urged the nation's legislators not to sully America's good name by adding a population "composed mainly of a wild and desperate set of men." The debate over Texas in the 1844 presidential campaign featured a widely disseminated cartoon showing candidates Polk and Dallas wooing "Lady Texas," while a sanctimonious Henry Clay stood to the side with folded arms, saying: "Stand back, Madam Texas! for we are more holy than thou! Do you think we will have anything to do with gamblers, horse-racers, and licentious profligates?"[17]

The leading spokesmen for Texas had for some time deplored the sayings of the "foreign press." "We have been most dreadfully slandered in the U. S. papers," complained Stephen F. Austin to a Philadelphian. "Such publications have injured us dreadfully . . . it is really a cruel & unjust thing to have the best interests of a whole community, and a new & rising one, injured and men jeopardised by a set of silly scribblers." Texans suspected that a conspiracy of sorts existed to discourage desirable citizens and families from emigrating. The Houston *Telegraph and Texas Register* in 1841 accused American publicists of "unwarranted and reckless jibes and taunts," which had darkly colored the image of the Republic. "It is to be regretted, that so many blackguards and grossly ignorant men are still conducting public journals in the United States; while this state of things continues, we must expect to experience the effect of calumny and detraction."[18]

Texans were, of course, aware of the political considerations operating against them. Their stuttering bid for annexation to the United States marshaled an array of forces, particularly in New England, opposed to the extension of slavery. In answer to William Ellery Channing's open letter to Henry Clay in 1837, a modest Texan, George L. Hammeken, allowed that if the Bostonian's denunciation of the Revolution contained merely his objections to slavery and to annexation, he would have left it to "abler pens" to respond. "But no man of honor and feeling, however incompetent to cope in fine language," he asserted, "should remain quiet when the character and motives of his friends and countrymen are so unjustly vilified." Hammeken conceded that Texas was filled with men who had been "unfortunate in commerce, or been ruined by their kindness to swindlers," but he insisted that there were no more than three or four hundred fugitives from justice, and they had no influence on the inhabitants in general.[19]

Still, the Texan reputation was not confined to Northern opinion subserving the purposes of political anti-slavery. Southerners, too, entertained the notion that Texans were, according to William H. Wharton, "a set of adventurers, of young men of desperate fortunes" bent on conquest and glory. "To the contrary," argued Wharton, the first Texas minister to the United States, "the people of Texas [are] generally unpretending farmers and planters from the middle walks of life, [and] all they desired on earth was the privilege of cultivating in peace those fertile lands which they had so dearly earned by the perils and privations consequent upon the colonizing of a wilderness." Other Texans stoutly maintained that theirs was a decorous society, that young men did not come to town loaded down with pistols and knives, and that Texas had no call for an "anti-Duelling and Peace-Making Society" such as had been organized in Mississippi in 1844. Moreover, as Guy M. Bryan grandly announced to his Kenyon College mate, Rutherford B. Hayes, Texas could boast its "circles of beauty & accomplishment & intellect that will vie or bear comparison with the proudest & best of your land." Upon Texas's debut as a state in 1846, local editors implored the voters to exercise discretion in their selection of U. S. congressmen. We should impart to the world, the LaGrange *Intelligencer* admonished, "a just and proper impression of our moral and intellectual character."

It is a matter of infinite moment on our first entrance into the fold of the confederacy, that a gross delusion under which a great many honest and intellectual minds have long labored, in regard to our moral, social, and intellectual condition should be at once and forever removed. We should take a peculiar degree of pride and satisfaction in convincing our sister states, that we . . . possess a large fund of moral and intellectual wealth . . . by sending to the councils of the nation gentlemen who will compare to advantage with any of their fellow members. . . . We should delight to show such puny snarlers [revilers of Texas] , not only that something good can come out of Texas, but some of the most precious and elevating goods which this world may boast.[20]

A Matagorda newspaper in 1844 observed that since the Revolution eight years earlier, "It has been the fate of Texas to attract the attention of the world to a greater extent than was ever done by the same number of the human family in any age."[21] It was a fair estimation. If nothing else, the unwelcomed publicity advertised Texas to an audience far and wide. Foreigners were perhaps more amused than disheartened by the halo of evil surrounding the Lone Star. "When every other land rejects us," the Englishman William Bollaert punned, "here is the land which freely takes us (Texas)." A playful broadside published in Great Britain advised the weary populace to which of several shores they might head:

> The brewers should to Malt-a go
> The loggerheads to Scilly;
> The Quakers to the Friendly Isles,
> The fur-riers all to Chilli. . . .
>
> Hie bachelors to the United States
> Maids to the Isle of Man,
> Let gardners all to Botony go,
> And shoe-blacks to Japan.
>
> Thus emigrate, and misplaced men
> Will no longer vex us;
> And all that aint provided for
> Had better go to Texas.[22]

For all these refugees, Texas became a homeland. Its broad boundaries gave them room to roam and enveloped them in a protective shell. They, in turn, embraced Texas. As a society of pariahs, the Texans could achieve self-respect and self-realization through identification with a virile state. The citizen's supreme loyalty went eagerly to his fellow nationals, and the vehicle of their joint aspirations was the state. The achievement of nationhood, reinforced by such palpable effects as a constitution, a flag, an army, a navy, fired their nationalism. Nationhood gave them security; nationality told them who they were. With the Republic of Texas they became "Texians" and nothing else. No longer need they be men without a country.

CHAPTER ONE

The Awakening of a
Texan Consciousness, 1821-1836

The fifteen years of Mexican rule in Texas, from 1821 to 1836, witnessed a contest for power between the forces of centralism and localism. When the Americans first settled in Texas at Mexico's invitation, they encountered a national government jealous of its authority and anxious to exert centralized control. In the provincial governments, authority was vested in a few select officials upon whom virtually all responsibility for local affairs devolved. Under this system, community initiatives were discouraged and the American emigrants were allowed few opportunities for participation in the political life of their adopted country. The seeds of Texas nationalism were planted in these years: the contrast between Mexican ways and their own, between Mexican people and themselves, gave the expatriate Americans a heightened self-awareness. Neither Mexican nor American, they became Texan.

The star of Texas glimmered at a propitious moment. In America, the Panic of 1819 precipitated an economic depression that gripped the country for the next three years. As prices plummeted, thousands of urban workers lost their jobs, hundreds of businesses failed, and trade slowed to a near standstill. In 1820, Congress revised the land law in an effort to bring Treasury receipts into line with acreage sold. Under the laws of 1800, 1804, and 1817, less than half the value of public land sold had actually been paid for. While the new law of 1820 reduced the price per acre from $2.00 to $1.25, it also removed the generous credit allowances that previously had enabled settlers to acquire land by making full payment in annual installments. For the would-be homesteader, the sudden abolition of the credit system was dismaying. One cannot imagine it happening at a more trying time. The Bank of the United States was already contracting the money supply by calling in loans and restricting the issuance of scrip, and "wildcat" banks in the West were closing their doors by the dozens. The credit crunch and the depression now destroyed the ambitions of thousands who had looked hopefully to a farm and a new start in life somewhere in the West.

In the Adams-Oñis Treaty of 1819, the United States abandoned its claim to Texas under the Louisiana Purchase, and the boundaries of Spain's territory in North America were at last defined. This fortuitous event coincided with America's economic woes and led to the decision of the Spanish governor in Texas, at the prompting of one Moses Austin, to initiate the *empresario* system as a means of bringing American and other settlers to that wilderness region. For some, hope now lay beyond the Sabine. In January, 1821, the cherub-faced Austin secured an *empresario's* permit to settle three hundred families in Texas within some 200,000 acres along the Brazos River. Having experienced the ups and downs of business life in Philadelphia, then failing in a mining and smelting enterprise in Virginia, this Connecticut Yankee eventually went to Missouri (where he again went broke) and finally to Texas in his lifelong search for wealth. He was now sixty years old and in weakening health. Before a single colonist had taken up residence, Moses was felled by pneumonia and died in June, 1821. His son, Stephen Fuller Austin, who only reluctantly had agreed to leave a promising political career in Missouri to help him found the colony in Texas, succeeded to the commission. In December of 1821, the twenty-eight-year-old Austin arrived in Texas with a small party of emigrants and established a base on the west bank of the Brazos, calling it San Felipe de Austin. The age of Anglo-Texas was dawning.

Unlike most other frontier regions of America, Texas under the Austins was founded as a colonization enterprise. Moses Austin was contracted as an agent of the government to bring families and respectable individuals into the country. He would receive as compensation land grants from the government and administrative fees from the colonists. But the ten-year revolution in Mexico that finally toppled the moribund Spanish regime in 1821 threatened to shatter the whole scheme. The new provincial government of Mexico at once repudiated the acts of its predecessor, including the *empresario* program. This was a severe blow to the younger Austin. He had just advertised, in local papers throughout the United States, land grants to settlers of 640 acres, with an additional 320 for a wife, 100 for each child, and 80 for each slave. It was a splendid inducement. The catch was Austin's 12½ cent per acre survey and registration fee, but an immigrant need not accept the whole package; he might take as little land as his finances would permit or, with the *empresario's* approval, he could acquire acreage exceeding the stipulated amount.[1]

What was Austin to do? Already parties of debt-ridden American emigrants, having heard of the prospective bonanza in Texas, were crossing the Sabine or coming ashore at points on the coast. His only hope for salvaging the plan, he realized, was to confront the new regime in person. In the guise of a beggar on horseback (so as not to be a tempting target for bandits), he set out for Mexico City in the spring of 1822 with a Spanish grammar in his saddlebag. He completed the perilous journey in several weeks, and spent the next eighteen months in the capital learning the language and trying to persuade Mexican officials to reinstate his father's contract. Only the Americans, he pointed out, would be willing to enter the wastelands of Texas and fight for survival against bands of wild Indians. If Mexico should ever derive any wealth from its northern province it could come only from the labors of an enterprising people. Austin's tact and sensitivity to Mexican suspicions of the North Americans, together with his persistence, at last prevailed. The *empresario* idea was endorsed by Emperor Iturbide's rump congress and made law in January, 1823.

The first imperial colonization act granted a *sitio* or league (4,428 acres) of grazing land plus a labor (177 acres) of farming land to each family brought to Texas by an *empresario*. Single men would receive one-third of the total acreage assigned to ranching and farming families. Fees to the agents and the government would come to almost $200, but in practice credit was extended and Austin, for one, charged a flat fee of only fifty dollars. Austin estimated that the total cost did not exceed three cents an acre. Thus, the head of a family settling in Texas could acquire with credit nearly 5,000 acres of choice land for less than what 80 acres would cost in the United States. A further incentive to immigrants was exemption from all federal imposts and taxes for the first six years of residence.[2] Austin had reason to be pleased.

The national colonization law of 1824 surrendered to the Mexican states the power to dispose of the public domain within prescribed limitations, particularly that titles be issued to residents only and not exceed eleven leagues. In 1825 the State of Coahuila y Texas passed the colonization measure that would govern land and immigration policy in Texas up to the Revolution. A league of land would be granted to family men who became naturalized Mexican citizens and adopted the Roman Catholic religion, and one-quarter of a league to single men who fulfilled the same requirements. Fees totaling nearly $200 could be paid in installments over six years, beginning with the fourth year. This allowance gave new immigrants a full three years to get their feet on the ground. In addition, state taxes and duties would be waived for the first ten years of settlement.[3]

15

As the news spread in the States that land titles on thousands of acres in Mexico's Texas could be had on easy terms, hundreds of American migrants started pushing westward to the Sabine.

Over the next ten years, under this colonization plan, more than a dozen *empresarios,* contracted by the government, began bringing people into Texas. The government grants defined by geographical boundaries land to be dispensed within six years to a stipulated number of families. No titles could be issued without the agent's approval and he had to meet his quota or forfeit his contract. The grants virtually ignored any possessory rights of the many Indian tribes in Texas. They naturally justified their claims on the basis of prior occupancy. Only a band of Cherokees, who worried enough to send a small delegation to Mexico City, succeeded in getting some government assurance that their property in northeastern Texas would not be alienated. But in practice, any Anglo bold enough to move in on the Indians might secure title to the hunting grounds. As for the indigenous Mexican population, much of it was concentrated in such towns as San Antonio, Goliad, and Nacogdoches, and did not stand in the way of the Anglo-American settlers. In time, the Mexicans would become a subservient minority with little property of their own.

Thus, the Anglos engrossed the vast estate of Texas. Ten thousand of them poured in during the 1820s, and by 1836, their numbers had swelled to about 30,000. In the decade of the 1820s, the great majority departed from the trans-Appalachian states of Tennessee, Missouri, Arkansas, Alabama, Mississippi, and Louisiana, the ones hardest hit by the belt-tightening of the "monster" bank and the collapse of the wildcat banks.[4] Not a few of the new arrivals were men who had fallen deeply in debt during the early twenties and had fled their native states to escape harassment and, in some cases, imprisonment. Many a collector or sheriff in the hill country and cotton belt of the southern states approached the dwelling of a delinquent only to find a hasty note — "G. T. T." (Gone to Texas) — scribbled on the door. That most of the Texas settlers emigrated in financial distress was acknowledged by Stephen F. Austin, the principal promoter of settlement in the province. "The majority of the immigrants to Texas," he confessed in 1828, "owe debts in the country from which they came. . . . "[5] Since his colony contained about half the Anglo population, Austin was in a position to know.

Not all of the Americans arrived under the auspices of an *empresario.* Many who settled in East Texas were enticed by fraudulent land companies offering sections they did not possess or which had not even been located; many more simply stole across the border, taking land as squatters. Several thousands, in fact, immigrated illegally from 1830 to 1834, the period when Mexico prohibited the further entry of American nationals. The Texas borders stretched too far northward and westward to be sealed against intruders by the government in Mexico City.

Under the Mexican Constitution of 1824, which was patterned after the Constitution of the United States, the northern provinces of Coahuila and Texas were combined to form one of the eighteen Mexican states. Texas itself was organized in 1825 as one of several departments within the state of "Coahuila y Texas." The governor appointed a political chief to preside over each department and supervise the municipalities, the units of local government. A municipality consisted of one or more towns and the adjacent territory, and might cover an area as large as several thousand square miles. Its chief officer was the *alcalde,* who governed in conjunction with an *ayuntamiento,* normally a five-man council roughly equivalent to a county court in the United States. No explicit provisions were made for town government. As might be expected, the hierarchy of state governor, department political chief, *ayuntamiento* and *alcalde* did not in practice reach down very well to the villages within the municipality. Inhabitants of Nacogdoches, for example, complained that many had lived in the district for years without political authority or even knowledge of the laws. Only a town as large as five hundred (and Anglo-Texas had none such) was entitled to select a *comisario* to represent its particular interests in the *ayuntamiento,* but that official was not permitted to vote. Nor were the new citizens encouraged to participate in government. Under the state constitution of 1827, a member of the *ayuntamiento* had to be literate in Spanish and a resident of his district for at least three years. Rather than be voted directly by the people, officers were named by electors chosen by a popular majority at annual conventions. Similarly, the *alcaldes* and political chiefs were usually appointed by the governor.[6]

With all legitimate power delegated to a few select authorities, the colonists were largely deprived of whatever initiative they might have mustered collectively. Rather than promoting a partnership of officeholder and citizen, with frequent turnover, an exchange of roles, and a consequent diffusion of leadership, the Mexican system imposed a liaison-type relationship upon the colonists, with the ordinary settler at the bottom of the chain of command. Taking its cue from Roman and Spanish law, Mexican policy differed from American in that authority proceeded from the top downward, a policy conducive to oligarchic rule. Such a state of affairs resulted in passivity on the part of the colonists, an indifference (up to a point) to community problems, and a willingness to leave their resolution to the constituted authorities. As late as 1835, George W. Smyth could cite the symptoms of such feeble local government: "We pay no Taxes, work on no roads and perform no public duties of any kind...."[7]

17

Perhaps the most irritating problem to these Americans was the administration of justice. The *alcalde* listened to pleas and sent the trial record to the state capital, Saltillo, where an *asesor general* handed down a ruling. This procedure took weeks for transmitting documents alone, but the Texas colonists naturally expected trial by jury and resented a legal system where the judge never faced the accused and decisions were based on written testimonies. The want of appellate courts meant that all appeals in important civil or criminal cases were again sent some seven hundred miles by mule to Saltillo, forcing delays which made the system almost inoperable.[8]

By 1830, with a population of about 10,000, Anglo-Texas remained under the jurisdiction of but one *ayuntamiento,* even though the state constitution called for one such municipal government for every thousand inhabitants. Even the constituted authorities were quiescent. The *ayuntamiento* of San Felipe, serving nearly the entire Anglo portion of Texas from 1828 to 1832, met for only two months in its first session, with no other result than that its members were fined for neglect of duty. "They did nothing on any subject that they ought to have attended to," Austin charged.[9] The observable result after the first ten years of the colony's existence was a near-prostration of local government and a marked backwardness in town development. General Manuel Mier y Terán, commenting metaphorically that the American colonists carried their political constitutions in their pockets, "demanding the privileges, authority and officers which such a constitution guarantees," could, on his inspection tour of East Texas in 1828, discover scarcely a civil authority or magistrate in the area — "One insignificant little man," he lamented, "not to say more — who is called an *alcalde,* and an *ayuntamiento* that does not convene once in a lifetime. . . . " For the most part, the small outposts of Anglo settlement stood ungoverned except for the *ad hoc* arrangements, usually militia duty, of the settlers themselves. "The colonists," Mier y Terán warned, "murmur against the political disorganization of the frontier."[10]

By 1830, Mexican officialdom, suspecting the motives of American emigrants and those of the United States government in this period of Jacksonian expansionism, indicated alarm over the rapid Americanization of the province north of the Nueces. Terán's report had exposed the dissipation of Mexican influence in Texas and alerted the government to the possible loss of the territory. Another inspector, José María Sánchez, confirmed that the American immigrants had nearly complete occupancy of eastern Texas, and many were squatting without permission of the authorities. "They immigrate constantly, finding no one to prevent them, and take possession of the *sitio* that best suits them. . . ." That the Americans wished to have all of Texas for themselves seemed obvious to Sánchez. "The vigilance of the highest authorities has been dulled while our enemies from the North do not lose a single opportunity of advancing . . . toward their treacherous design which is well known."[11]

In response to this threat, the Mexican Congress on April 6, 1830 handed down an obliquely worded decree prohibiting "emigrants from nations bordering on this Republic [from settling] in the states or territory [of Mexico] adjacent to their own nation."[12] Nobody missed the point. Simply stated, Mexico was now demanding that *American* emigrants cease coming to Texas.

The pronouncement thundered northward like the roll of funeral drums, and like a shock wave, it rippled through the Anglo settlements. Everyone located in Texas had anticipated a steady influx of immigrants and rising land values. What else could bring prosperity? Less than a year earlier, Stephen F. Austin enthusiastically had reported receiving "a great number" of inquiries from prospective settlers in Lousiana, Alabama, Mississippi, Tennessee, Kentucky, Ohio, and Missouri. "Texas is beginning to create considerable interest and there will be a large emigration this fall," he informed a Pennsylvania correspondent. "The [Mexican] Govt. have offered the most liberal encouragement to emigrants of good character and moral and industrious habits."[13] Before the law became known to Texans, they had made the opportunities in Mexico seem limitless. "The resources of this republic, the soil, mineral wealth, facilities for manufacturing and commerce, the salubrity and diversity of climate," exulted the San Felipe *Texas Gazette,* "are exceeded by no other country under the sun."[14] Suddenly this roseate view was dashed, and with it the expectations of future prosperity. William H. Wharton gave voice to the dimmed outlook of the Texas people:

This law was sufficient to goad us on to madness, in as much as it blasted all our hopes, and defeated all our calculations; in as much as it showed to us, that we were to remain scattered, and isolated, and unhappy tenants of the wilderness of Texas, compelled to gaze upon the resources of a lovely and fertile region, undeveloped for want of population, and cut off from the society of fathers and friends in the U.S. of the North. . . . [15]

Up to this time, the Americans had actually shown some inclination to attach themselves to their adopted country. Except for an abortive revolt in East Texas in 1826, originating over a land titles dispute, few had bothered to complain of their Mexican hosts. "I have never had any views whatever adverse to the true interests of the Mexican Govt.," Stephen F. Austin reiterated in 1830. "I consider that I owe *fidelity & gratitude to Mexico. That* has been my motto, & I have impressed it upon my Colonists." Judge Robert M. Williamson, editor of the *Texas Gazette*, had reassured the Mexican government that there could be no repetition of the 1826 uprising: "If ever there was a people who have reason to be satisfied with their government," the *Gazette* attested ten days before the curtain on American immigration descended, "*it is* WE, *the people of Texas.*"[16]

The passage of the infamous Law of April 6, 1830 marks a turning point in Anglo-Mexican relations. It alienated the Americans irretrievably, convincing them that the parent nation could never accept them as genuine Mexican citizens but would regard them instead as a potentially dangerous class of aliens. Left without recourse to their mother country, these Americans now became conscious of themselves as an anomalous citizenry — as *Texans*. Moreover, they found little in common with their supposed countrymen, whom they generally considered a mongrel race, "ignorant, superstitious & treacherous," passively adhering to a rigid class structure in a church-oriented society. "The Americans and Mexicans are entirely dissimilar," George W. Smyth observed. "Their Education, their religion, their habits, their feelings and prejudices, are different and it is impossible that they should ever amalgamate." Even Terán was forced to admit that the Mexican population of Texas comprised "the lowest class — the very poor and ignorant. . . . It could not be otherwise than that from such a state of affairs should arise an antagonism. . . ."[17]

The rumblings of discontent that began with the federal immigration restriction act of April, 1830 were heard in distant parts of the United States by restless, ambitious men. Ironically, a law designed to lock the gates on a certain national group, who by sheer weight of numbers might reduce Mexican power in Texas to a cipher, discouraged the emigration of law-abiding family men while enticing the illicit immigration of footloose individuals, among them political adventurers, soldiers of fortune, land sharks, and town promoters — not to mention the delinquent or criminal element that had been drifting into Texas from the start. Not content with a parcel of land on which to spend the rest of their lives in quiet repose, certain of these individuals had bolder ideas. It was no accident that Texas attracted its Archers and Travises and Houstons in the wake of the anti-immigration law. What better moment to stir the cauldron of turmoil? Impatient with Mexico's pretensions of republicanism, resentful of the government's hostility to black slavery, disdainful of Mexican citizenship and the state religion, these parvenus, given the chance, would not hesitate to sever the Anglo sector of the Mexican Republic from the body politic. Should Texas strike for independence, the political and economic restraints of the Mexican government would be removed and these men could enjoy an open field on which to satisfy their varied personal ambitions. "We have in Texas too many would be great men," remarked the perspicacious George W. Smyth in 1832, "too many whose ambitions have been unsuccessful in their own country, and have taken refuge in this one, and who view it as their ultimate field of glory, the whole object and design of their actions being to stir up a revolution."[18] For a time, however, they would have to wait.

As Texas embarked upon the decade of the 1830s, a chorus of voices called for home rule. "The cause, and the *sole cause*, of any and of all the little bickerings and confusion that may have existed in Texas," insisted the *Gazette* in 1830, "have proceeded from the want of a proper organization of our local government." There was little likelihood, the paper added, that Texas could ever prosper while attached to Coahuila and the possibility of separate statehood was "beginning to occupy much of the public attention." Not until 1832, when the *ayuntamiento* of Brazoria was created, did the state government show signs of awakening to the needs of the localities. Still, the situation remained far from satisfactory. "The organization of the local government is very defective," complained Jonas Harison at the Texas Convention that year. "The greatest inconveniences and evils may arise from such a state of things; for a large portion of the inhabitants are almost without any local government."[19] The demand for internal autonomy that issued forth in the early 1830s stated the necessity of solving the peculiar problems of Texas at the local level. The Texans had already experienced ten years of indifferent rule from the distant capitals of Saltillo and Mexico City. They had meekly acquiesced in the arrangement, much to their own detriment. They were now determined to govern themselves in their own way.

Tension mounted in Texas as President Anastacio Bustamante's centralist regime erected new garrisons and reinforced existing ones, not for defense against Indians (which the country desperately needed), but to bring the Texans under tighter rein and secure the border against interlopers from the United States. It was a vain ambition. The introduction of convict soldiers to stand guard over the settlers merely exacerbated the immigration issue, and the friction sent sparks flying. In the summer of 1832, organized assaults were launched by local citizens on three garrisons — at Velasco, Anahuac, and Nacogdoches — in which the soldiers were rudely dislodged and forced to evacuate. Stephen F. Austin urged General Terán, the commander of Mexican forces in Texas, to remove the entire army, observing that its presence greatly antagonized the people.[20] A month later, Terán (whom Austin considered sympathetic to Texas) committed suicide.

Tempers cooled late in the summer with news of the accession to power of one Antonio Lopez de Santa Anna, a liberal federalist and champion of the Mexican constitution. The relieved Texan colonists gave unstinting and enthusiastic support to the Santanista forces and seized this auspicious moment to announce their desire for separate statehood within the Mexican confederation. Meeting in convention at San Felipe in October, 1832, they passed resolutions calling for their own state government and demanding revocation of the law of April, 1830 that closed Texas to American immigrants. That measure, John Austin charged, "has entirely paralyzed the advancement and prosperity of Texas," and, he added in allusion to the adventurous spirits recently arrived, "exposed it to be filled with a bad and useless population." The delegates also requested the extension of tariff exemptions for three years, the appointment of a commissioner to issue land titles in eastern Texas, and the donation of government lands for the maintenance of primary schools.[21] Texans had not lost their American habits. In taking their leave, the delegates agreed to form committees of "safety and correspondence" to keep the widely scattered communities informed of Indian troubles at home and political events inside Mexico. Presentation of the resolutions was postponed, however, by the refusal of the people of Bexar to send a delegation, giving the impression that the Mexican population of Texas had no cause for complaint. A petition of dissatisfied Anglo-Americans alone would not sit well with the Mexican Congress, and Stephen F. Austin prevailed upon the convention to await a unanimous declaration.

Over the following months, Austin visited the Mexican settlements to induce their participation; in the meantime, a second convention was called for San Felipe to convene on April 1, 1833, the day Santa Anna was scheduled to be inaugurated as president of Mexico. At this convention, the delegates again petitioned for repeal of the anti-immigration law and the divorce of Texas from Coahuila, pleading that the only solution to the manifold problems of Texas "is to be found in the establishment of a *local state government.*" The marriage of Coahuila and Texas, they observed, was as unequal as it was unnatural. Texas had but one member in the state's delegation to the federal congress and only one of twelve representatives in the state's unicameral legislature. The predominantly Anglo character of the population (Anglos outnumbered Mexicans by ten to one) made it natural that Texas should become a separate sovereignty. Moreover, Coahuila was not burdened by an Indian menace and the wide extent of wilderness between Coahuila and Texas created a physical barrier that prevented the Coahuilans from assisting Texas in frontier defense.[22]

Anticipating the success of their petition, the convention drafted a constitution (based on a 1780 Massachusetts document that happened to be at hand) to accompany their application for statehood. Austin was elected to deliver the document to Santa Anna and urge its acceptance. Upon his departure from San Felipe, he confided to his cousin, Henry

Austin, that Texas could not survive without home rule. "Things have been so disjointed ever since the military authority began to interfere with the civil, and with citizens, that nothing can set them to rights again but a state Government." In an ominous mood, he judged that should his mission to Mexico City fail, the consequence "will no doubt be war."[23]

Austin reached the capital in July, 1833. At first, he could not get an interview with Santa Anna and met stubborn resistance to the convention's proposals from the General's front man and puppet, Vice-President Gómez Farías. In exasperation, Austin scribbled an ill-advised message to the *ayuntamiento* at San Antonio, urging the immediate organization of a state government for Texas. Perhaps without realizing the implications of his act, Austin had come close to advocating revolution. As Texans awaited word of the outcome of his journey, Ira Ingram of Matagorda articulated the general malaise in a letter to his uncle living in the Michigan territory. Santa Anna, he reckoned, offered some hope for civil government in Mexico, as he appeared to be reducing the privileges of the priests and the influence of the military. But who could be sure? "The ordinary laws of domestic and national strife, afford no barometer by which to calculate the incantations of a nation of semibarbarians," he commented. "If they will listen to the claims of Texas, and receive her as a State . . . all is safe. But if not, Texas must go for herself, and stand or fall, *alone.*"[24]

When Santa Anna finally granted an audience in November, he greeted Colonel Austin cordially. He agreed to have Congress rescind the anti-immigration provisions of the 1830 law and promised necessary reforms in Texan local government. But he stood adamant against the creation of a new Texas state government. Before returning to Texas, Austin witnessed the act of the Mexican Congress which ruled that by May, 1834, immigrants from the United States would again be welcomed. Altogether, he could be satisfied with the concessions he had won, which paralleled reforms being enacted simultaneously by the state legislature. These included the division of Texas into three political departments with government seats at San Antonio, San Felipe, and Nacogdoches, and a commensurate increase in representation in the state legislature; additional representatives to the federal congress (now three from Texas, nine from Coahuila); recognition of the English language for official purposes; a guarantee of religious toleration; and revision of the court system to give Texas appellate circuit courts, a superior court, and trial by jury. With a few swift strokes, the Mexican state and federal governments had removed virtually all the Texans' outstanding grievances. In light of these reforms, the cause of separate state government at the dawn of 1834 lost much of its force.

Austin would now suffer the consequences of his earlier impetuosity.

THE AWAKENING OF A TEXAN CONSCIOUSNESS, 1821-1836

On his way back to Texas in January, 1834, he unfortunately stopped at Saltillo, where his letter of the previous July had been returned. He was at once arrested and handcuffed, brought back to Mexico City, and thrown into prison. For the first three months, he was shut up in one of the dungeons of the inquisition — *"Incommunicado,"* he grieved, in a letter to Texas of August, 1834 — "that is, locked up day and night, with very little light except candles, and not allowed to speak, or communicate with anyone, nor to have books, pen, ink, or paper."[25] Later he was transferred to a city jail, but not until Christmas Day, 1834, was he released on bail. He was finally allowed to return to Texas in July, 1835, just in time to plunge himself into the revolutionary movement that was then brewing.

The cruel treatment of Austin, intensely resented by some Texans, while overlooked by others with political ambitions of their own, signaled the sudden apostasy of President Santa Anna. His liberal government under Farías, having met the solid opposition of powerful clerical and army personnel, as well as of the wealthy landed classes, faced a strong challenge from the centralist forces. In matters of power, Santa Anna (who fancied himself the Napoleon of the West) was no fool. Utterly unprincipled and capable of the most startling volte-face to preserve his authority, this Janus-faced creature, moving with the tides of conservative opinion, now donned the cloak of centralism. In April, 1834, he seized command from Farías and dismissed the cabinet; he dissolved Congress and began disbanding the state legislatures and even the local *ayuntamientos*. Amazingly, this usurpation brought barely a murmur from the civil officers of the country, much less from the Mexican masses long accustomed to authoritarian rule by church and state. The rigged election in the summer of 1834 of a new congress amenable to centralism and subservient to Santa Anna allowed the General to make a shambles of the federal system and the rights of individuals under the Constitution of 1824. "It is impossible that Mexico can long retain even the form of republican government," George W. Smyth brooded at the turn of the year. "She lacks the two great pillars upon which every edifice of that kind must rest — virtue and intelligence: her people are too ignorant and too visious [sic] for republicans — Texas is destined to change hands."[26]

The events of 1835 moved quickly and ineluctably toward revolution. As did their counterparts of the American Revolution, the Texan committees of safety and correspondence took the lead in alerting citizens to fast-breaking news and arousing them to organized resistance. The provocative rhetoric of these final months was reminiscent of the sloganeering against British rule in the colonies. "If the Federal system is lost in Texas," demanded Benjamin R. Milam, "what will be our situation? Worse than

24

that of the most degraded slaves."[27] Lawyers, merchants, militarists, and assorted speculators rode in the vanguard of the revolutionary movement. "There were a great many among them," a journalist later recorded, "who saw in the weak and distracted condition of Mexico a human certainty at least that Texas as poor as she was would be able to work out her emancipation," so that they might "add twofold to their possessions."[28]

The beginning of the year saw the reestablishment of garrisons at Anahuac and the mouth of the Brazos to enforce customs collections. This occasioned frequent altercations between merchants and troops as the agents demanded either bribes or exorbitant fees for their unwelcomed services. By June, news reached Texas that Santa Anna had dispatched reinforcements and rumors spread that Texans would soon be under a standing army. The lessons of the American Revolution were by no means lost on these expatriates and they fancied the unfolding events as almost a reenactment of that drama. Then a band of would-be Sons of Liberty took matters into their own hands. Led by William B. Travis and several other prominent citizens, they confronted the garrison at Anahuac and forced its surrender. When orders were issued from Mexico City to arrest the perpetrators, the excited Texans joined hands against their common enemy. In scores of public meetings and town councils throughout the country, the crisis exposed sharp contrasts in approach between the original colonists and the daring newcomers, but paradoxically, a true community spirit prevailed. They might argue among themselves and divide informally into war parties and peace parties, while self-seeking individuals jockeyed for advantage against their potential rivals, but they were united in thinking of themselves as Texans and linking their personal fortunes to the welfare of Texas. "I am determined for one," declared Travis, an avowed hawk, as he judged the strength of the peace party, "to go with my countrymen: right or wrong, sink or swim, live or die, survive or perish, I am with them."[29]

The Texan colonial experience had, willy-nilly, forged a keen sense of identity and generated a quickened instinct for community promotion. As these transplanted Americans began to assume the new nationality of "Texian" or (as some would have it) "Texonian," they exhibited a fierce pride and proprietary interest in Texas. It was *their* country! Already, the rallying cries were shouted — in slogans, oratory, and verse:

> Boys, rub your steels and pick your flints,
> Methinks I hear some friendly hints
> That we from Texas shall be driven —
> Our lands to Spanish soldiers given.
> To arms — to arms — to arms!

> Then Santa Anna soon shall know
> Where all his martial law shall go.
> It shall not in the Sabine flow,
> Nor line the banks of the Colorado.
> To arms — to arms — to arms!
>
> Instead of that he shall take his stand
> Beyond the banks of the Rio Grande;
> His martial law we will put down
> We'll live at home and live in town.
> Huzza — huzza — huzza![30]

"The rupture of the old British Empire," writes the historian Lawrence Henry Gipson, "had its source fundamentally in the fact that America now embodied a mature and powerful English-speaking community with a mind of its own and a future it considered peculiarly its own." A striking analogue to the coming of the American Revolution, in respect to the ripening of a society and the awakening of its consciousness, is the development of Texas within the Mexican Republic. "This nation," Stephen F. Austin had judged of Mexico in 1831, "has been in labor since 1810 and has not yet given birth to liberty, and must, I fear, undergo many years of the most agonizing throes before she will do it." Texas, he confidently predicted, would survive these vicissitudes:

> The natural & smooth current of events . . . will waft it into a safe harbor. The local situation of the country, the nature of its products and interests, and the character of its population, will form a bulwark around that harbor, which will be difficult to break down, if not impossible — I may not live to see it, but the destiny of that country cannot be otherwise, than prosperous & happy.[31]

Santa Anna administered the *coup de grace* to Texan-Mexican relations with his decree of October 3, 1835, which replaced the Constitution of 1824 with the *Siete Leyes,* converting the states into departments of a completely centralized government with the governors appointed by the president. The Mexican experiment in republicanism had ended. The federal constitution had declared the constituent Mexican states "Free, Sovereign, and Independent" in all that related to their internal affairs. Now the federal system itself was overturned. Already, Mexican troops were taking up their positions in Texas. On October 2, Colonel Domingo de Ugartechea ordered the seizure of the cannon at Gonzales, the seat of Green DeWitt's colony. The citizens arranged themselves quickly and fired at the approaching enemy force. This was the "shot" that triggered the Texas Revolution. A Mexican dragoon toppled dead from his horse and the government soldiers retreated in haste. "It was our Lexington, though a bloodless one," remarked Noah Smithwick. "But the fight was on."[32]

Santa Anna alone was not responsible for the Texas Revolution. The clergy, the military, and the Mexican people calmly acquiesced in the dictatorship, and in some circles the dashing despot was enthusiastically embraced. With the exception of a brief flurry of resistance in Zacatecas, not a single Mexican state raised a protest — much less an armed force — against the General. Only Texas prepared for war: "Fellow citizens, Your cause is a good one, none can be better," proclaimed the summons to arms in October, 1835, "it is republicanism in opposition to despotism; in a word it is liberty in opposition to slavery. You will be fighting for your wives and children, your homes and firesides, for your country, for liberty."[33] In the Texan view, the Mexicans, no matter who their leader, had shown themselves incapable of constitutional government. Over the years, the state and federal governments had arbitrarily prohibited immigration, invalidated land titles, levied customs duties, closed ports and trade routes, forbade coastal commerce between Texas and the southern ports, circumscribed the right to bear arms, and imprisoned persons without cause or trial. In Mexican politics, elections had no sanctity, succession no legitimacy, and revolution seemed a way of life.

What especially disturbed the Texans about their connection with Mexico was not rubbing elbows with those whom they considered their racial and cultural inferiors, but the destructive impact of centralist government on their local institutions and the devastating effect of Santa Anna's abrogation of civil liberties on future immigration. Revolutionary rhetoric, sloganeering, and talk of abstract rights and principles was cant. Immigration and home rule, on the other hand, made survival possible. Even as war loomed on the horizon, Texan colonizers were stepping up their campaigns to bring men and families into the country. "We [expect] a great emigration of good families this fall and winter. They will benefit themselves, and the country by coming, but there is no time to loose [sic] ," appealed Stephen F. Austin, the indefatigable land salesman. "The door for emigration is still open and men of influence all over the U.S. ought to exert themselves to send out families to Texas . . . but in a prudent manner."[34] Earlier in 1835 an American tourist had concluded that the Texans "confidently look forward to a time, when they will be enabled to throw off the Mexican yoke and establish a government of their own." But as long as Texas was ruled by a dictator and threatened with troops, he advised, the American emigrant, and above all the family man, should "reflect seriously before he leaves the U. States to go to Texas. There are plenty of good lands in our western States."[35] The discouragements to Texas immigration were now many. With the "tyrant" Santa Anna in the driver's seat, the flow of migrants to Texas would reduce to a trickle. This was the grim prospect facing the Texan people in 1835 as they made their decision to fight.[36]

"Ours is no rebellious or revolutionary warfare," William H. Wharton asserted. "It has been forced upon us."[37] We should not take Wharton's disclaimer at face value, even though Texan leaders at first refused to declare for independence. The Consultation of All Texas meeting at San Felipe issued on November 7, 1835 a "declaration of causes" for taking up arms against the Mexican government, but pledged its continuing support for the defunct Constitution of 1824. The resolution for an immediate break from Mexico was defeated 33 to 15. When the Provisional Government of Texas was created a week after the declaration, government officials took an oath swearing allegiance to the Mexican Constitution. Governor Henry Smith, in his first message to the General Council, referred to the "free and sovereign state of Texas," thereby acknowledging that Texas was still politically a part of Mexico.[38]

The professed loyalty of Texans to the Mexican Constitution was but a tactic to buy precious time. If they could forestall the wrath of Santa Anna's army by making some kind of conciliatory gesture, they might better prepare financially as well as militarily for the contest. It was also a feint to persuade Mexican federalists that the Texans were fighting *their* fight and not seeking dismemberment of the Republic. Finally, it promised to give greater justification to the Texan cause in the eyes of other governments and peoples. Their opposition to the dictatorship should be interpreted as a struggle for republicanism. Texans knew they could get little aid or sympathy if their traducers could brand them as mere filibusters and land-grabbers. "Let us give evidence," exhorted Branch T. Archer in his presidential address to the Consultation, "that we are the true descendants of that band of heroes, who sustained an eight years' war against tyranny and oppression and gave liberty to a new world."[39]

It was no secret that many Texans believed their salvation lay in a political amalgamation with the land of their birth. As early as 1833, Sam Houston informed President Jackson that "the vast majority of Texans wanted annexation to the United States. . . . "[40] Not surprisingly, the Consultation followed up its show of fealty to Mexico by appointing three of its leading men — Wharton, Archer, and Austin — as commissioners to the United States to sound out Washington on recognition of an independent Texas and admission to the Union. They also hoped to attract men and money to the revolutionary cause; for that, the American government must give its seal of approval. As if to convince the Americans and themselves of the correctness of their resistance to Santa Anna, Texan spokesmen conveniently slipped into the rhetoric of the American Revolution, proclaiming the cause of liberty and likening themselves to their revolutionary forebears. "The history of the revolution of the United States furnishes abundant lessons, worthy of the attention of the people of Texas," proclaimed the *Telegraph and Texas Register* as the Texan siege on the Mexican stronghold at San Antonio commenced. "The present situation of Texas is, in many respects, analogous to that in which the American colonists were placed. . . . " Heroes of the American Revolution, the citizens were reminded, had achieved immortality. "Texas now presents to her patriotic citizens the same opportunities of acquiring fame, the same opportunities of serving their country."[41]

In the first month following the November declaration of causes, one could detect a widespread sentiment for abandoning all pretenses and striking decisively for independence. William H. Wharton urged the immediate ordering of a constitutional convention elected by the people to set up an independent government. The choice for Texans, it appeared, should no longer be Mexican citizenship under a republican constitution, but American citizenship with Texas a state of the Union, or else independent nationhood. In mid-December the General Council accepted Wharton's recommendation and issued a call for a convention to meet in March with plenary powers to form a "permanent" government. Increasingly, rank-and-file Texans climbed aboard the revolutionary bandwagon. As a barometer of grass-roots feeling, the citizens of Goliad on December 20 signed a formal declaration of independence from Mexican rule, urging their countrymen to follow suit: "Men of Texas! nothing short of independence can place us on solid ground."[42]

There could be little doubt at this point that the Texans were playing for keeps. Edward Warren told his brother in Maine that the people were determined to have their independence and join the United States. In New Orleans, William Fairfax Gray encountered a member of the provisional government who also held the post of quartermaster general in the Texas army. The colonel, he recorded, "thinks a very large majority of the people wish to come into the Union with Uncle Sam." Apparently no one wanted Mexican statehood, and those who preferred a Texas nation were mainly "fugitives from the laws of the States, and a few ambitious men who desire to be leaders." From Nashville in February, 1836, Stephen F. Austin, busy recruiting volunteers and raising funds for his country's war, finally acknowledged the sham of Mexican citizenship, now arguing that Texans had a duty as well as a right to resort to arms and separate from Mexico. "Ours therefore is a *war of independence* – our object is to form a new republic, a new nation, or to become a part of the U.S. under such guarantees as we are justly entitled to."[43]

It was but a short step from here to the historic convocation at Washington-on-the-Brazos which convened, as scheduled, on March 1, 1836. Preparations had been underway for some time. The following day, March 2, George Childress presented to the members for their signatures the Texas Declaration of Independence, modeled after its famous namesake of 1776. It contained a statement on the nature of civil government, a long list of grievances which the delegates by this time could have recited by heart, and finally, a momentous pronouncement of Texan nationhood. "The convention," a young secretary wrote to his father in Connecticut two days after the signing, "has declared Texas *a free and Independent Republic.* If we succeed in maintaining it, of which I have no doubt, I would not leave Texas for any country on earth." Texas citizens made an easy adjustment to their new status: "If you write to me," Asa Brigham instructed a friend in the States on March 12, "direct to me, at Brazoria, Republic of Texas...."[44]

Republic of Texas! It sounded like something worth fighting for. What Texas now needed, to make independence a reality, was military victory. The inchoate nation passed through a baptism of fire with the Alamo and Goliad episodes, which took the lives of nearly every Texan combatant engaged, and the desperate Runaway Scrape, in which civilians plunged headlong for safety toward the Texas borders to escape Santa Anna's advancing troops. The General's intentions were bloody and ruthless and his army swept over the Texas plains like a blind reaper, cutting down everything in its path. For Texans, there could be no turning back and no surrender. "The fall of San Antonio [the Alamo] has created a great Alarm," Henry Austin reported, "but painful as the event is in itself, to me it came as the harbinger of Salvation to Texas." Only calamity, he believed, could jolt Texans into a realization of their imminent peril, unite them into one body, and galvanize them with an irresistible determination to beat back and destroy their despised foe. "The people have now taken the defence of the country into their own hands, & marched almost en mass with their rifles to shoot down every Mexican they can find – I have no fear for the issue."[45]

On March 17, 1836, the Texas Convention completed its work on the constitution of the new Republic, which would later be ratified by popular referendum, and handed the reins of the interim government to David G. Burnet, the first president of Texas.

On April 21, General Sam Houston with some nine hundred men delivered a swift and sudden blow to Santa Anna's force encamped at San Jacinto, just as the Napoleon of the West had settled down for his siesta. The impassioned fury of the Texans, amid roars of "Remember the Alamo," "Remember Goliad," erupted upon the astonished Mexicans and in eighteen minutes the fight was over. More than six hundred Mexicans were killed and more than seven hundred taken prisoner, including Santa Anna himself. With the capture of the Mexican general and dictator, and the decimation of his counterrevolutionary army (some six thousand Mexican soldiers remained in the country), Texan independence was all but assured. Over the next six months, Mexican resistance in Texas crumbled. Lacking a dynamic leader, the demoralized Mexican army retreated dispiritedly beyond the Rio Grande, while the triumphant Texans raised the flag of the Lone Star Republic.

CHAPTER TWO

The Promotion of Texas:
From Revolution to Civil War

I think that it would not be uninteresting to you to hear something about the State that I come from, Its inhabitants society etc. . . . The broad prairies (which can be compared to nothing except the ocean with any degree of justness to them,) is in one continual state of freshness flowers bloom all the year without the aid of any shelter except the broad canopy of heaven.[1]

There is hardly a state in the Union but what I have been in, and of all of those I have been in, give me Texas to live in with ease and have a home. The very poorest man may have a house and live well if he has any industry about him. What country is there that you can say that for?[2]

The dramatic victory at San Jacinto in April, 1836, allowed Texas to emerge as a new nation but by no means assured its continued survival. Less than a month after the decisive battle, General Thomas J. Rusk presciently cautioned his countrymen against any hasty assumption of their independence: "We are [at] war with a Nation weak & inefficient is true, but numbering several Milions of inhabitants. They are proud haughty & vain & who lives to see it will see, that defeating Santana at the head of fifteen hundred men does not terminate this War." Indeed, the Mexican government refused to concede the *fait accompli* of Texan nationhood, and for the next ten years plotted invasions of the infant republic by land and sea. Texans were never free from apprehensions of the enemy, 20,000 strong, marching across the Rio Grande. Even as Rusk spoke, General José Urrea was about to declare his intention of waging a war of extermination that would put to death every Texan man, woman, and child.[3]

The country had already been laid waste. General Houston's stratagem of retreat following the Alamo debacle had given Santa Anna the opening to advance across Texas from San Antonio to San Jacinto. His gleeful mercenaries set fire to everything in sight and did not hesitate to abuse civilians along the way. With the approach of the dreaded Mexicans, the panic-stricken people seized whatever possessions they could carry and ran pell-mell from their homes without turning to look back. A frontier woman recalled her fright when informed

that the Mexican Armey were ready to cross the Brasos river next morning and that we could not remain aney longer at our home . . . every one was now in utmost confusion, the negroes were told they could only take one change of cloaths with them, my self the same, the enemy where [sic] only seven miles from us, and it would not do to take aney thing that would retard our progress . . . every one as busy as a bee, I had no time for reflection which was at this time, perhaps, for the best.

William Fairfax Gray watched a constant stream of women and children with wagons, carts, and pack mules rushing across the Brazos by day and night. In Washington, where the Constitutional Convention had just adjourned, family men and shopkeepers were seen packing and moving in such haste that one could find pots, pans, crockeryware, and bedding strewn everywhere. As Gray galloped eastward with the rushing tide, he saw numbers of people "on the road flying from the invasion." At the ferry on the Trinity were "large crowds, all seeking a passage across for the same purpose, with their wives, children, negroes, horses, carts, wagons, and droves of cattle."[4]

These were the refugees of war, homeless but still not without their country. "The war has entirely broken up every kind of business in Texas. Thousands have been ruined in all but their lands," wrote a recent immigrant to his family in Connecticut. "In fact you can scarcely conceive of the suffering that this War has occasioned. All of the country west of the Brazos has been deserted and overrun and pillaged by the enemy."[5] These disastrous reverses only heightened the people's will to resist. The cruel conduct of the Mexicans, William Hale related to his brother in the States on the eve of San Jacinto, "has aroused a spirit of indignation throughout the Texian Army which nothing short of the destruction of the enemy or Ruin to themselves can check." The rage of the Texans at the Battle was understandable: "The majority of the people of Texas have been left without a home, some have lost every thing they possessed," another victim subsequently told his brother. "Such men will fight with desperation & a dreadful fate awates the enemy who may fall into their hands."[6]

The Texas Revolution retarded the immigration of families from the United States until it was clear that independence had been won, but it galvanized young, single men eager for the adventures of war. Some American volunteers fancied themselves liberators charging to the rescue of their beleaguered brethren in Texas. Still others, by no means a minority, envisioned the opportunities a new nation might offer them, most tangibly in the large parcels of free land which the revolutionary government dangled like bait to lure volunteers to its cause. "Some of our brethren of the United States of the north, hearing of our difficulties, have generously come to our aid, many more ere long will be with us," Branch T. Archer had announced in his presidential address to the Consultation of All Texas in November, 1835. "It will be proper for this convention to secure to them the rights and privileges of citizens, to secure to them their land . . . and in all other respects to place them on an equal footing with our most favored citizens."[7] Many who offered their services did earn land and remained to become Texans.

Archer had keynoted the land and immigration policies that would serve Texas in its formative years. What better way to secure loyalty to the country than to give men an actual stake in it? The *ad interim* government of Texas, created in March, 1836, made land (which was yet to become its property) the recompense for military service. Land was the government's only potential asset. The First Class Headright, established by ordinance, guaranteed a league and a labor of land (4,605 acres) to heads of families (Negroes and Indians excluded) living in Texas prior to the Declaration of Independence on March 2, 1836, but all who joined the Texas Army before August 1, 1836 were similarly entitled to a headright. Single men over seventeen qualified for one-third of a square league. This last provision was a frank enticement to American volunteers, for there was no certainty in the dark days of March that Texas, unaided, could win her independence.

The land bounties proved highly enticing. Of the 780 veterans of San Jacinto who obtained land grants, 775 got titles *after* the fight. Of these, only 166 had acquired land before the battle, clearly indicating that the majority of grantees were newcomers who came to take part in the revolution.[8] Why did men fight for Texas? Some aid may have been given unselfishly but a very great deal seems to have been rendered with an eye to profit. "If we can gain this country I shall be entitled to 5000 acres of land which will be a fortune to me some day," a volunteer from Mississippi exclaimed. Benjamin J. Holland of New York wrote home to tell of his acquisition of land worth (in his estimation) fifty thousand dollars. "After the close of the war, my dear sister, my trouble in seeking a fortune will be at rest . . . I fight for Texas and in fighting for Texas win a fortune. . . ." Even Davy Crockett, just weeks before his martyrdom at the Alamo, announced that "the best land and the best prospects for health that I ever saw is here, and I do believe it is a fortune to any man to come here," adding his hopes of making one too, "bad as has been my prospects."[9]

From the start of American settlement in Texas, the consuming hope of the landowners was to realize an independence or possibly a fortune in their own lifetimes. They did not self-consciously cast themselves in the role of heroic pioneers breaking the soil of an open country for the benefit of posterity. Such altruism would have been to them preposterous. They acknowledged their pioneering efforts in building towns and making farms but they fully intended to harvest the fruits of their labors (or speculations). As Ira Ingram, a Matagorda businessman, put it:

> I did not, for one, invade the wilderness of Texas, to speculate in cents, piccons, shillings, nor yet in dollars. I came here for a fortune expecting. This was the course of policy which I prescribed to myself when I first landed, and which I have steadily pursued with unvarying, and unaltered resolution. We shall now, soon begin to realize an income. . . . Whether I have misjudged in making my locations, in my investments in town property of a considerable amount, and concerning the importance and steady growth of this place, as a great commercial emporium, time alone will decide. . . . If I am sustained by future events . . . all my privations, all my sufferings, will . . . be amply, nay munificently rewarded. . . .[10]

Speculative activity was perhaps the easiest, if not the surest, way to wealth. As one scholar has documented, the "animating pursuits of speculation" infected most of the leading men of Texas. Stephen F. Austin was preeminent in this respect, but closely following were such notables as Sam Houston, Ashbel Smith, Benjamin Milam, Jim Bowie, John Wharton, Green DeWitt, Thomas J. Chambers, Samuel M. Williams, and Branch T. Archer. There were many others. "The makers of Texas," he claims, "both as a nation and as a state in the American Union — went out to Texas as adventurers in land in one way or another." A typical landshark was one John Felloseby, who busily surveyed the country even while the revolution was going on. Just three weeks after the fall of the Alamo, he conveyed his thoughts from the safe retreat of Natchitoches, Louisiana. Friends returning from Texas, he told his daughter, "all give a most enthusiastic description of the country," but many were wary of the unsettled political situation and would wait before buying land. His strategy was different. "I am clearly of the opinion now is the time to invest money & make large fortunes: the present crisis has alarmed the timid and will throw some of the finest land in the Country in the market for little or nothing."[11] If Americans from the beginning of their history as a people had betrayed an insatiable hunger for land, now that same impulse gave a quickened heartbeat when bold men cast their vision to the broad savannas of Texas.

The emigration, as we have seen, had been generated by stagnant economic conditions in the States, particularly in the western country. The bottom was reached in 1822, but from 1823 to 1834 Americans muddled through a slow business recovery with minor setbacks from 1825 to 1826 and again in 1833 to early 1834. "You may ask why we leave the United States of America, for that of the United States of Mexico," wrote a New Englander landing at Brazoria in 1832. "I can only say that it was through choice, with a view of bettering my fortune. . . . "[12] The recession of 1833 stemmed from the contraction of credit by the United States Bank after the removal of government deposits to Andrew Jackson's "pet" banks. A business upsurge between 1834 and 1836 was fed by brisk activity in land sales, but not all parts of the country were touched by the brief flurry: "Business in our town is at a very low ebb at this time," wrote William McAlister of Moulton, Alabama, to a Texas friend in 1835. "The citizens of this country are unsettled they are leaving here day by [sic]; some for Choctaw, some for the Chickasaw Nation some for Mississippi and a great many for Texas." Among the laboring element was one Vincent Hamilton of Georgia, who arrived in San Augustine in 1836. He at once contacted a fellow-Georgian in Nacogdoches, Thomas J. Rusk, to ask what his chances for employment would be in that town. "I am a good mecanic I must git to doing something to make my Expenses til times alter," he pleaded. "I can make a first rate wagon or any thing of kind. . . . "[13]

Business reverses in the southwestern states and elsewhere redounded heavily to the benefit of Texas. In the first two months of 1835, some two thousand emigrants landed at the mouth of the Brazos. "The emigration that has come in this last season is astonishing," testified Asa Brigham, a townsman of Brazoria. Prior to the onset of hostilities late in 1835, "Texas Fever" was sweeping the Mississippi Valley. "Our country is rapidly improving [in population]," declared George W. Smyth in May 1835. "The tide of Emigration has been great beyond any former Season. Men are moving in from all parts of the U. S." His observations were confirmed by a Nacogdoches paper at the year's end: "Emigration is very great into this country from the States."[14]

Many associated with Texas in these revolutionary times were anxious to attract others in order to increase settlement and boost land values. Whatever the salubrity of the climate, the agricultural and mineral treasures of the soil and rock, without fresh population Texas would revert to a barren wasteland. Thus Texans figuratively mounted the soapbox to orate before a world-wide audience on the magnificent features of their country, often employing the familiar selling technique of the personal testimonial. Even as the boom of cannon at Gonzales signaled the outbreak of war in October, 1835, a young San Felipe editor, Gail Borden, indignantly retorted to an article in the New Orleans *Bee* that warned all emigrants against Texas: "Ask the thousands of happy and contented families who compose the population of this delightful region, if they would exchange their present homes for those they have left. They would invariably tell you, no." As proof, he cited "the almost unparalleled rapidity with which this country has settled, the great number of wealthy persons who have established themselves here, [and] . . . the great increase in the value of lands. . . . " The personal testimonials, once independence was declared, descended everywhere. "Texas is no doubt the finest part of North America," Asa Brigham wrote to a friend in Massachusetts, and James P. McKinney proclaimed to a Missourian that "Texas is certainly the best country in the almost known world." "We have here the climate of Italy and the fertility of the Valley of the Mississippi," James Tarleton informed readers of the Louisville *Journal*. "Texas will soon become densely populated with industry, wealth, and honest talents, and be able to compete with any country in our western hemisphere."[15]

While those already settled put up a brave front, intimations of loneliness crept into their private letters. George W. Smyth was quick to praise the opportunities for farming and stock raising. "But to counterbalance this," he added in 1833, "the country is very thinly settled, society badly organized, and the education of children difficult." Sam and Mary Maverick of San Antonio occasionally lamented "the distance which separates us from so many near and dear friends," and the exchange of "civilization etc for Texian misry [sic]." Young Jennie Leeper assured her uncle in Arkansas that "we are all very well satisfied with our new home," while admitting that her family "would be perfectly contented were we not so widely sepperated from all the friends we love so dearly."[16] Thus, Texans regarded every visitor as a potential settler and neighbor. In their zeal to win converts, they earned a high reputation for hospitality, despite the impediments of frontier living. "Every body's house is open, and table spread to accommodate the traveller; the best of every thing is presented freely," Mary Austin Holley declared, "not indeed with the refinement and courtesy of a polished European community, but with the honest, blunt, but hearty welcome of a Texas backwoodsman." Many others reported like experiences of kindness and welcome, and a Northerner found Texans living in the isolated interior of the country generous to the point of sharing with a stranger "the last of everything."[17] The Texans, of course, were not entirely disinterested, and when travelers arrived they paid for their supper with bent ears. A folksy dissertation on the virtues of Texas could somehow preempt every conversation, and it was "looked upon as a species of treason for a man who visits Texas not to be pleased with it," as Alexander MacRae attested after a tour of the country. "If you wish to get along through Texas to the best advantage," he urged, "praise Texas, if you abuse it, you are certain of being treated with coldness."[18]

The booster spirit of "Texians" knew no bounds. The Republic was just two years old when a Texan congressman informed a Philadelphian that the swift rise of the Lone Star nation was without precedent in history. "Cities and towns are springing up like magic and we are rapidly concentrating in our borders, all the elements of National wealth and greatness." In common with boosters everywhere, Texans could not resist exaggerating their numbers. James Hamilton, a leading promoter and financial agent who tried without success to secure a foreign loan for the Republic, told the British minister in Mexico City in January, 1840, that during the last quarter of 1839, "upwards of 100,000 Emigrants have gone into the country . . . and 5000 waggons have crossed the Sabine this winter. . . . "[19] Such extravagant claims puzzled those foreigners who came to see for themselves, since the total population of Texas by 1840 did not exceed 75,000. "What I would impress upon any persons intending to visit Texas," a Britisher cautioned, "is to believe as little of the accounts given of it, as his credulity will permit. The great demand for Emigrants has instilled such a spirit of exaggeration into all the writings of those interested in the Country, that one w[oul]d suppose Texas was a perfect paradise."[20]

Early in her career as a nation, Texas again benefited from untoward economic developments in the United States. The Specie Circular of 1836, issued to curb inflation fed by land speculation through the expanded use of paper money as legal tender, required that U. S. public lands be henceforth purchased with hard coin. The subsequent decline in real estate prices late in 1836 kicked off a banking crisis that was followed in 1837 by a sudden collapse of stock and commodity prices. With the Panic of 1837 the nation plunged into its second major depression within a generation. For the next six years, Americans labored through the worst economic crisis ever known to the country up to that time. By 1841 public land sales had dropped to a fifteen-year low.[21] As a novelist several years later jocularly recalled:

In the years of '38 and '39, when the commercial horizon was dark and lowering, the sun of prosperity almost obscured by the dust from the overthrown Bank . . . it became very unsafe indeed, for the tradesman to doze too long of a morning, for if he did, it was at least an equal chance that upon arriving at his [client's] shop or store, the three ominous letters G. T. T. done in white chalk . . . would stare him in the face. . . . [22]

For the people who vanished to Texas, as for their creditors, it was no laughing matter. Alexander Jones of Natchez, Mississippi, addressed a plaintive note to President-elect Mirabeau B. Lamar in 1838 explaining that he was nearly ruined in business and hopelessly in debt. He was now "once more very poor, and cast again upon the world and my own resources. I have become much discouraged in my unlucky pursuits in the U. S. . . . Can I," he implored, "do any thing in Texas?" Another Mississippi merchant, successful in business until the 1837 depression, found himself penniless by 1840 and, bravely uprooting himself at the age of fifty, embarked for Texas with his wife and three children:

THE PROMOTION OF TEXAS: FROM REVOLUTION TO CIVIL WAR

Times were Getting very Hard in Mississippi as to Pecunary Matters—Bank Failures etc. . . . The Year 1838 passed off and we still thought we would Have Quite a Little fortune Left us — But in 1839 Times Got Much Worse — People all about the country Began to Fail. . . . In this year we found that we would have but Little Left If any thing at all after paying off our Debts — Every Person almost Engaged in Trade had Failed and Many Farmers also. . . . After this . . . Myself and Family made Preparations to Move to Texas. . . . All of us had then Become Insolvent.[23]

An endless tale of woe, somehow terminating in Texas, was the monotonous refrain of hundreds of debtors and destitutes fleeing the country in the late 1830s. "My exertions in the Southern Country have been considerable yet with poor success," a New Yorker confessed in 1839. He had gone broke in the saddling business by borrowing money for inventory and allowing his customers credit. "I will not do any more business on credit," he resolved, "and for this reason I have come to Texas." Many bankrupt citizens sought a refuge from the law, as imprisonment for debt was still practiced in several of the states. T. G. Gordon of Columbus, Georgia, reported many of the oldest and wealthiest citizens of the town in debt beyond redemption and their property advertised by the sheriff. "The situation of the people is truly appaling [sic] and ruin stares every man in the face," he wrote to President Lamar in 1839. "I think that the emigration to Texas [will be] immense this fall . . . *hundreds of thousands* will flee from the distress *here,* to find an asylum from *trouble and the sheriff* amidst the flowery lawns and rich lands of Texas."[24]

Historians are hard put to render a rigorous social or economic profile of the Texas population for lack of reliable census data before 1850, nor can they demonstrate statistically the proportion of "undesirables" in the total number. But impressions lead us to believe that the debtor-fugitive element of Texas was substantially higher than that of mature American communities. That the Lone Star acted as a lodestar for scores of bankrupts seeking asylum was pointed to by eastern newspapers and visitors to Texas alike: "Mr. Geddes, who mysteriously disappeared from Philadelphia last week," the New York *Evening Post* announced in 1840, "is on his way to Texas, owing to domestic and pecuniary difficulties." "J. B. Norris, late President of the State Bank at Mobile," reported the New York *Tribune* in 1841, "recently left that city for Texas, apparently poor and in embarrassed circumstances." "The fact is," a traveler to Houston averred, "these people are not happy, and perhaps are more to be pitied than blamed. Many of them have been unsuccessful in business elsewhere, and have been drawn to Texas by the protection their laws promise from the collection of foreign debts. . . . " "The inhabitants of this county [Red River] are generally people of broken fortunes," explained a sojourner at

Clarksville in 1852, "and they have emigrated here to build up their losses." As one refugee, whose family had lost their Alabama plantation in the late thirties, conceded, "If you have been unfortunate and met with reverses . . . here you will find many who will exchange sympathies with you and unite in fellow feelings having had similar difficulties to encounter."[25]

The establishment of a new republic in 1836 kindled a strong interest among people everywhere in Texas lands. Aware of flagging land sales in the United States, the Texas government quickly seized the initiative. Not only would immigrants be defended against the claims of foreign creditors, but in December, 1836, the First Congress established a Second Class Headright for those entering the country before October 1, 1837. This was a grant of 1,280 acres to heads of families and 640 acres to single men, with the right to preempt additional land at 50 cents an acre. A Third Class Headright was introduced in January, 1838, as depression became widespread in the States. For immigrants coming to Texas between October 1, 1837 and January 1, 1842, heads of families would obtain 640 acres and single individuals 320 acres. All who received land under the Second and Third Class Headrights were required to reside in Texas for three years and make improvements ("a log hut and cut down a dozen trees they call it here," one immigrant quipped) before their titles were complete. This was a clear effort to encourage true settlers while keeping mere land speculators at arm's length. Squatters were given preemption rights: they could purchase at 50 cents an acre land on which they were living, not to exceed 320 acres. This by far surpassed the U.S. preemption legislation of 1830, which permitted squatters to purchase up to 160 acres at $1.25 per acre. Additional legislation granted land to all citizens and new immigrants who would serve the Republic as soldiers. In lieu of pay, they could earn 320 acres for each three-month tour, not to exceed 1,280 for a full year's duty.[26]

These policies, in the face of the prevailing U.S. land laws and the Specie Circular, not to mention the ensuing economic depression from 1837 to 1843, could not but turn many eyes toward the Lone Star. There was Joseph Nail of Arkansas, who in 1837 got "it into his head, to leave an excellent country & try his fortune in Texas – A mighty common notion, in many of the western States at this time," as Mr. Nail's liaison reported to a Texan contact. "I therefore infer that, the news from your country must be favorable." William A. Force came to Texas in 1837 to work as a surveyor and was well-versed in the land law of the Republic, reciting the terms of the Second Class Headright to friends back home. "As to myself and prospects," he declared, "land is what I came after, land I will have (life and health permitting)." A new arrival from England acquired land under the Third Class Headright in 1839, just twenty miles from the site of the new capital, Austin, which he calculated would become the largest city in Texas. Still pinching himself, he wrote to his wife in New York that when she joined him, they would be entitled to another 320 acres. Such a piece of land could not be bought in New York State for $30,000! "We can grow every thing on it we need to make us comfortable," he promised. "In a short time after we live at Austin I will get a man to cultivate it and in a few years we shall sit in our own grove eat our own fig peaches and oranges and from our own wine press drink the nectarian [sic] juice."[27]

The well-publicized soil and climate of Texas in these years gave the country a misleading name as a land of mañana, where men not overly eager for hard work might bask contentedly. As Noah Smithwick recalled, when he left his Kentucky home for Texas at the age of nineteen, his ambition was "to seek my fortune in this lazy man's paradise." Those who entertained such notions were in for a rude shock. There was no way life on a crude frontier could be anything but strenuous. If Texas was "the country for young men," as one enthusiast stated, it was theirs only on the condition that they work for it and be willing to forego life's amenities. Not for many years would the country begin to approach the standard of civilization set by the older communities in the East. "Well, we are at last in Texas – in the sunny south – in this land of sunshine and flowers," a sharp-eyed Virginia lady arriving at Houston mocked, "in this glorious land of Texas this El Dorado of the South."[28]

Many prospectors believed that "this El Dorado" offered limitless opportunities for wealth. "As for making money," commented one, "I know of no country that presents such advantages as Texas." Another advised his father to leave New York State to join him in the quest. Texas "will prolong your life, add to your purse and I hope happiness. . . . You can make more here in one week than you can there in one month and easier." Dr. S. D. Mullowny of Missouri was told by a Texan that within a year he could be "one thousand dollars, or more in pocket better off than in Mo – from the practice of your profession. . . . Oh! My friend, had I your faculty as a man, & qualifications as a physician . . . t'would be but a little while till I should launch my bark Texas-ward." Even a Texan schoolgirl, writing a composition on her nation and its people in 1840, could not resist propagandizing: "Probably there is not another country in all the continent of America like that of Texas. It is both delightful and pleasant; with all the luxuries of life that any person can desire. . . . " While education had not received much attention, she admitted, "the chief study of the inhabitants is that of making [money] and to become a rich farmer."[29]

But for all the attractions of Texas land and the liberality of the government's immigration policies, life and property remained in jeopardy with aggressive enemies poised at the borders. The settlers themselves had to defend their homesteads, and Texan citizens, in correspondence with their relatives and friends in the States, spoke candidly on this point. The main drawback to settlement, they acknowledged, was the imminent threat of Indians or Mexicans descending upon the exposed frontier. "We now have an Indian war upon our hands," wrote Henry Austin to his sister, Mary Austin Holley in 1838. "You must not think of coming here this winter." Robert Sanders, in 1841, told his son John in Tennessee that the family property in Nacogdoches County was "no doubt very fine Land and will be in a few years the most desirable part of Texas;" however, he warned, "there is some danger in living there at present, on account of the Indians." In the wake of the shocking Mexican invasions of 1842, in which San Antonio fell twice to the enemy, John R. Jones confided to an Illinois friend that "the unsettled condition with Mexico, which prevents many from emigrating that would," had seriously disrupted the country. "I would not recommend Your removal, with an intention of making it a place of residence at present, etc."[30]

All through the Indian and Mexican wars of the Republic, Texas officials solemnly propagandized their nation's virtues, but realizing that some assurances for safety must be given those seeking free lands, emphasized the efforts of the government to secure the frontiers. "The malitia [sic] are now organized and are prepared and anxious to march at the shortest notice should a mexican army again cross the Rio Grande," affirmed the secretary of state in 1838. President Lamar predicted in 1839 that his aggressive Indian policy would inspire confidence in the energy of the government and give "a new impulse to emigration," while the Senate Committee on Finance promised that "the expeditions now on foot, to dislodge the savage & Mexican marauders on our borders will . . . give speedy & effectual protection to the watchful herdsman & industrious cultivator of the soil." At times they offered more than they could deliver. Secretary of War Albert Sidney Johnston's plan for a line of forts running from Red River to the Rio Grande was still no more than an idea when the Texas Indian commissioner unveiled the contemplated project to the American migrant: "The chain of block houses which is shortly to be thrown across our northern and western frontier," he grandly announced, "will be an effectual barrier against any depredations which are to be apprehended from Indian difficulties, and the emigrant may assure himself of as much safety, in any of the settled portions of this Republic, as he could in the Atlantic states."[31] The forts, as it happened, were never constructed.

The nation's press was quick to recognize that Texas could not attract worthy citizens – men with families who intended permanent settlement – unless something was done to purge the country of its predatory foes. The *Telegraph and Texas Register* in 1839 attributed the retardation of immigration to a single cause: Indian depredations. Following the 1842 invasions from the Rio Grande border, the paper added the Mexicans to the indictment, and admonished Texans not to expect heads of families "to expose themselves with their wives and children to the dangers arising from, not only the savages on the frontier, but from the Mexican enemy also."[32]

So concerned was the Texan government over the Indian and Mexican threat to immigration that Congress weighed the feasibility of planting a *human* cordon along the western frontier. Two French nationals, Jean Basterreche and Pierre Hassauex, offered to introduce 8,000 European families if Texas would provide them with three million acres for settlement. The colonizers promised to erect and maintain at their own expense twenty forts along the frontier west of Austin for twenty years, on the condition that their settler families be exempt from all taxes and tariffs over that period. A screen would thus be created between Anglo-Texans and their enemies. The ensuing debate over the quixotic Franco-Texienne Bill of 1840-41 showed how far the Republic might be prepared to go to secure its borders.

At first the plan was greeted with enthusiasm but as its implications became apparent, particularly that it might alienate sovereignty, Texans began to back away. "And in this grand scheme of conquest where would Texas be found?" protested the *Telegraph and Texas Register.* "The puny fraction of a French colony!" Others disagreed: "I have heard it objected to this project, that it would be admitting 8000 Frenchmen into Texas, who might take advantage of their situation, and ultimately usurp her government!!" Samuel Swartwout of New York City, a speculator in Texas lands, wrote to President Sam Houston. "But this notion is too shallow and can have no place in your imagination."[33] President Houston endorsed the measure after the bill was approved by the House of Representatives in January, 1841. Meanwhile, Count Alphonse de Saligny, the French chargé in Texas, went about Austin buttonholing the senators to urge their acceptance. But with growing uneasiness among the people – for many Texans feared an intrusion by thousands of Frenchmen more than they did an invasion by Mexicans – the bill was finally allowed to die in the Senate without reaching the floor.

The Texan government still actively pursued prospective settlers and colonizers. Not content merely to publish the laws, it circularized them in the American and foreign press. Through resident agents and land companies the government endeavored to advertise the many advantages of Texas homes. "It is the decided policy of the government," the State Department declared in 1838, "to encourage and invite the emigration of industrious and good citizens of all Countries." The secretary replied to hundreds of inquiries about the possibilities of settlement — for example, in a letter to a Mr. Bullman of New York City, who considered locating a party of colonists in a group project:

> The Constitution of the Government requires a residence of six months only, and the usual oath of allegiance to entitle the emigrant to all the rights and privileges of citizenship.
> It guarantees protection of his person, property and religion and the laws exempt from charge or duties all the implements and utensils . . . and all such provisions and stores as the Emigrant may bring with him for his own or his families use. . . .
> It is believed this Country offers stronger inducements to the enterprising and industrious emigrant, than any other open for settlement.[34]

Notwithstanding repeated solicitations, the government was less than successful in attracting families. Instead, a large contingent of foot-loose individuals and drifters found their way to Texas, and by 1840 the population appeared to contain an appalling number of adventurers, desperados, and bankrupts ready to take advantage of the land grant policy. The transient character of this population persuaded Congress that year to postpone a national census for fear that the results would hurt both the nation's image and its pride. The immigration, "from which much had been expected," President Mirabeau B. Lamar admitted to Congress in 1841, "proved generally not to be of that industrious and laboring class, which give wealth and vigor to a nation. . . ." Instead, the country had drawn in large measure a rowdy collection of castoffs who "rather destroyed, than strengthened the hopes, that our fertile plains would be shortly subjected to the plowshare."[35] Lacking population stability and its quota of sturdy yeomanry, the young Republic appeared to be stumbling.

The Fifth Congress in 1840-41 undertook reconsideration of the Headright system, which embodied the nation's immigration laws. Adjudged a failure by a majority of the members, the land grant program, scheduled to expire in 1842, was abandoned by Congress in favor of group colonization projects. The hope was to place a large number of settlers within a relatively short period of time along the northern and western frontiers. Contracts would be made with immigration agents to plant whole communities in certain designated areas to be known as "colonies." Within such bounds, all unappropriated land would be closed to entry by outsiders until the agent had fulfilled his obligations or the government declared the contract forfeited by default.[36] The Franco-Texienne Bill would have satisfied this objective if only the French promoters had not insisted on maintaining a separate enclave under their control. Congress had no intention of compromising the public domain or relinquishing jurisdiction over the population. All settlers, furthermore, were expected to become Texan citizens. The colonization legislation, admittedly a throwback to the old *empresario* system under Mexico, remained in effect until 1848. During the 1840s, it helped to sustain the flow of immigration from the United States and Europe and made a significant contribution to the diversified character of the Texas population. (See map 1, p. 46)

The Peters Colony, established in 1841 on the northern frontier, was the most successful, bringing some 10,000 to 12,000 people to Texas within ten years. Hailing mainly from the Ohio Valley, New York, and New England, these immigrants bore a Yankee stamp. They expressed northern sympathies and an antipathy to slavery during the sectional crisis of the 1850s, tended to congregate in towns as was customary in the Old Northwest, founded Dallas as the nucleus of settlement, and counted among their numbers many skilled artisans and professional men. They gave Dallas and the surrounding villages a distinctly Northern flavor. One sojourner on the eve of the Civil War noted the brisk free labor market of North Texas, where the staple was wheat, and concluded that there was "consequently more energy displayed in that section than in other portions of the State."[37]

The Texas Republic hoped to draw in not only Americans but European emigrants as well. "With open arms and generous hearts we welcome the stranger to our shores," an Independence Day (March 2) orator proclaimed in 1841. "Here the exiled and the oppressed, of every clime, may come, and beneath our proud banner carve out a home, where industry will reward itself." The *Telegraph and Texas Register,* following the passage of the colonization legislation, declared that the term "foreigner" did not apply to anyone who wished to settle in Texas and become a citizen. The Republic welcomed men of every country and language; all would contribute to the national glory, and all should meet on equal ground. "They are to us all alike, and we would stand shoulder to shoulder beneath the standard of our country, or co-operate with them without one feeling of distrust or prejudice. . . ."[38] Texas made a bold effort to realize these sentiments. Consular agents were appointed not only in major United States cities — New Orleans, Philadelphia, New York, Boston, Baltimore, and Charleston, as well as at such outposts as Key West, Bangor, and Detroit — but also in the British Isles and on the European continent. Texas consuls opened offices in London, Liverpool, Plymouth, Glasgow, Dublin, and a half-dozen smaller English towns; in Paris, Bordeaux, Cette,

Rouen, Bayonne, Antwerp, Bremen, Amsterdam, and Rotterdam. Spreading the gospel of Texas to the world, the consuls served as liaison between prospective colonizers, immigrants, and the home government. They drew no salary but earned fees and commissions on the sale of Texas land scrip or bonds and on the notarization of legal documents for use in Texas.[39] With fewer than 100,000 people, the upstart Republic of Texas was acting in a manner befitting a major power.

Ashbel Smith, the Texan minister to Great Britain, reported home in 1843 that "emigration to Texas is exciting an immensely increased attention, especially in this country and Germany."[40] Indeed, the Texan initiative bore fruit. Over the next two decades, small colonies of Irish, French, English, Scottish, Canadian, Swiss, Scandinavian, Czech, and Polish emigrées established themselves in Texas. A sizeable French-speaking community was founded under the colonization law by Henri Castro of Alsace. Between 1843 and 1847 he settled, largely at his own expense, 2,134 French and French-Swiss colonists in an area southwest of San Antonio. Castro, who had been a Texan consul, made maps of his colony grant, which he circulated throughout the Rhine districts of France to induce emigrants to join his settlements. These maps did much to advertise Texas to Europe.[41]

The greatest impact on Texan culture from foreign immigration was made by the German communities founded in the 1840s. An organization called The Adelsverein (Society of Noblemen) acquired a contract to settle 6,000 Europeans in a 3,000,000-acre tract southwest and west of Austin. Under the leadership of Prince Carl von Solms-Braunfels (author of a book called *Texas, 1844–1845)*, the first immigrants landed in Galveston in 1844 and a year later founded the town of New Braunfels. The Prince was succeeded in the directorship in 1846 by Baron Ottfried von Meusebach. Calling himself John O. Meusebach upon acquiring Texas citizenship, he was instrumental in founding Fredericksburg, a brave community on the edge of the Comanche country. During its five years of operation, The Adelsverein brought to Texas more than 7,000 German-speaking colonists. The flood tide of German immigrants swelled from 8,000 in 1850 to more than 20,000 by 1860. Thousands of Germans departed for the New World to the tune of Hoffman von Fallersleben's refrain:

> On to Texas, on to Texas
> Where the Lone Star in its glory
> Prophecies to a world of freedom,
> Beckons to each heart resounding
> To the call for truth and justice —
> There alone my heart would be.[42]

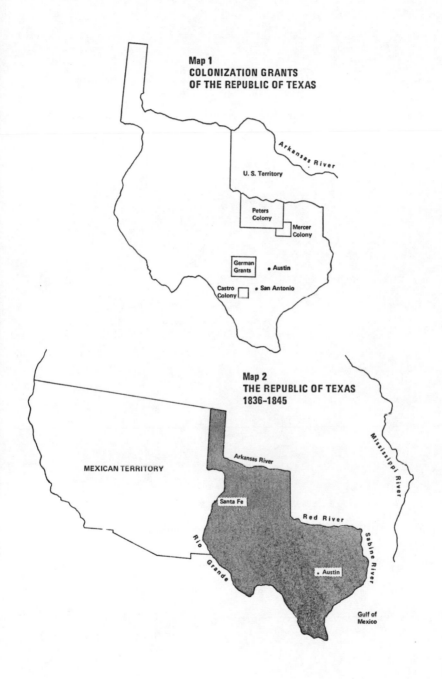

Map 1
COLONIZATION GRANTS
OF THE REPUBLIC OF TEXAS

Arkansas River

U. S. Territory

Peters
Colony

Mercer
Colony

German
Grants

• Austin

Castro
Colony

• San Antonio

Map 2
THE REPUBLIC OF TEXAS
1836–1845

MEXICAN TERRITORY

Arkansas River

Mississippi River

Santa Fe

Red River

Rio Grande

Sabine River

• Austin

Gulf of
Mexico

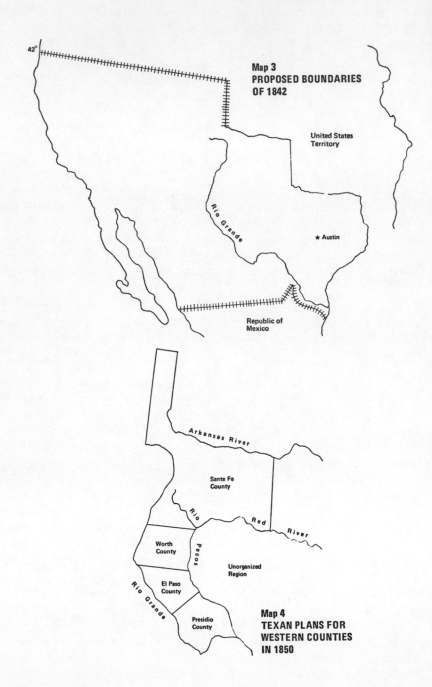

Map 3
PROPOSED BOUNDARIES
OF 1842

United States
Territory

Rio Grande

★ Austin

Republic of
Mexico

Arkansas River

Sante Fe
County

Rio

Red

River

Worth
County

Pecos

Unorganized
Region

Rio Grande

El Paso
County

Presidio
County

Map 4
TEXAN PLANS FOR
WESTERN COUNTIES
IN 1850

THE PROMOTION OF TEXAS: FROM REVOLUTION TO CIVIL WAR

Texas statehood, beginning in 1846, gave an added stimulus to the influx of immigrants from America and abroad. The prospect of the U. S. Army standing guard over the Indian frontier and the Mexican border now comforted many who earlier had been tempted by cheap lands but intimidated by a perilous environment. Even though federal troops were to prove a disappointment in combating the plains Indians, the movement of emigrants to Texas steadily accelerated.

The annexation agreement actually strengthened the ties of the people to their state government by allowing Texas continued jurisdiction over its public domain. Since federal land offices were not to be found, the eyes of Texans remained focused almost exclusively on Austin rather than on the nation's capital. The citizens could properly feel that the whole of Texas was theirs. The nourishment thus given to a ripening nationalism can hardly be overstated. As William C. Holden has emphasized, every settler who became a land owner did business with the Texas government.

When he purchased a piece of land, his negotiations were with the state instead of with the central government. When he made his annual payments on his land he paid the state. When he paid interest, he remitted to the state. When he "proved-up" on his wilderness homestead, he did so to the state. When a dispute arose . . . he carried on his litigation in a state court. When he felt the need of a law . . . he petitioned the state legislature.[43]

In all other states, the public lands were held by the federal government and Congress determined through its land laws the terms of sale. By retaining her public lands, Texas could formulate her own land policy and might sell acreage at prices lower than the federal government's. Up to the Civil War, the state offered choice land for as little as 50 cents an acre compared to the federal rate of $1.25. The Texas preemption act of 1854 granted 160 acres to homesteaders; comparable federal legislation was not enacted until 1862. Texas stayed one step ahead of Uncle Sam, and according to Texas historians, the lure of its cheap land was "second only to that of gold in Califonia."[44]

In 1850, the population of Texas stood at 212,591, including 58,161 black slaves. While the figure amounted to less than one percent of the total United States population, it represented a sixfold increase in the fifteen years since the Texas Revolution. The 1850s witnessed an even greater surge of immigration. As Paul Gates has shown, many public lands in the Middle West were by this time beyond the reach of the average settler. Land speculators had gobbled up nearly all of the desirable farming country and were waiting for their holdings to appreciate. The chances for the westering migrant were generally reduced to tenancy, "unless he was willing to go far beyond the railroad into areas lacking social facilities and market opportunities."[45] He could still go to Texas — as many did — where the shortage of white labor was attributable to the fact that "any man of temperate and industrious habits can obtain lands and go to farming on his own account."[46] By the end of the decade, the native Texan-American white population climbed to almost 400,000, nearly a threefold increase over the 1850 figure. The total population, including slaves and foreign-born, had reached 604,215, or about two percent of the total for American states and territories.

From all quarters of the state, delighted residents observed the stream of migrants. "The emigration to Texas is very great and the price of land advancing daily," J. Locke Smith reported in 1850. "The Emigration to Texas is immense," marveled Fred Oberthier in East Texas after his journey from Virginia in 1852. "Nearly 7000 families crossed the Mississippi before us at Memphis, a great many were behind us, and a great many crossed at other places, all wending their way to Texas." Another new arrival related the news from North Texas: "The emigration this fall is immense," he wrote his mother in 1852. "No day passes without wagon after wagon passing through town [Paris] and sometimes as high as a hundred wagons pass by the same day. They . . . are going to Grayson County, the Trinity (River) and the Colorado River." The Nacogdoches *Chronicle* in 1854 reported the city's streets crowded each day with the horses and wagons of new arrivals and watched the progression of people westward deep into the heart of Texas. "Our ideas of the State, her prosperity, wealth, and greatness, grow daily as from our office window we contemplate the moving scene before us. With such an influx of population . . . Texas must soon become the leading State of the South."[47]

From the beginning of American migration to Texas in the 1820s, the majority of emigrants were non-slaveholding backwoodsmen and farmers from the hill country of the trans-Appalachian West. A considerable portion had spent their early life on an Indian frontier and were accustomed to hunting and fighting for survival. A tough stock of men and families made Texas their new home in the antebellum years. They were, by all demographic indices, frontiersmen to the core. The 1830 census of Stephen F. Austin's colony reveals Texan settlers to be mostly young, male, and unattached: men outnumbered women 4 to 3 and single persons (over age sixteen) outnumbered married couples 1,403 to 466. Only six percent of the population was older than forty. The 1834–36 census of the San Augustine district shows a continuing predominance of young, single men, and the trend is closely maintained through the 1850 federal census. Only by 1860 does Texas begin to show signs of maturation as the distaff side makes its presence felt (at least numerically) and the number of males of military age (18 to 45) falls more into line with the national average.[48]

The total population of 604,000 in 1860 consisted of 153,000 Texas-born (25.3 percent), 201,000 Southern-born whites (33.3 percent), 24,000 Northern-born whites (4 percent), 43,000 foreign-born (7.2 percent), and 182,000 black slaves (30.2 percent). Only 4.6 percent of the South's total slave population was by then located in Texas. As in other frontier states, the free "colored" population of Texas was practically nonexistent, never numbering as much as five hundred. Consequently, as a result of black laws dating to the inception of the Republic, the Lone Star State in 1860 accounted for a mere tenth of one percent of the free "colored" population of the slave states. Only five of the fifteen — Arkansas, Delaware, Florida, Maryland, and Missouri — had fewer slaves than Texas, and none of these approached Texas in the extent of its cotton culture. Compared to the other heavy cotton-producing states of the South, Texas had an unimposing slave population. Texas also differed markedly from the Southern states in its substantial Northern and foreign-born element, which together accounted for about twenty-five percent of the white population born outside the state.[49]

As a state, Texas continued to mount an energetic campaign to bring in foreign and domestic emigrants. The press, the politicians, the speculators, and the hometown boosters trumpeted to a hearkening world the splendors of their country. "We have the brightest waters, the broadest ranges, the tallest grass, the fattest cattle, the fastest men, the prettiest women to be found within the realm of 'Uncle Sam'," declared a Texan in New Orleans, and the Houston *Telegraph* unabashedly proclaimed: "We are indeed a wonderful people." Could anyone take more pride in his state identification than this citizen: "I have stated facts to the best of my Texian knowledge," he told a British audience in 1858, "and drawn conclusions to the best of my Texian ability."[50] Frederick Law Olmsted, journeying through Texas in the 1850s, was struck by the "hard-sell" tactics of the people he met. "So anxious is every one in Texas to give all strangers a favorable impression, that all statements . . . must be taken with a grain of allowance. We found it very difficult . . . to obtain any unfavorable facts." Unfavorable facts indeed! as old Jesse Burnam revealed in a cautionary note to his brother William in Austin:

You must not let it get abroad that you have any sickness up there, for health is all the inducement you have to make People move up there, & if they hear it is sickly up there you will not have many emigrants.[51]

The promotional efforts carried well beyond the Texas borders.

THE PROMOTION OF TEXAS: FROM REVOLUTION TO CIVIL WAR

Jacob De Cordova, Texas's multilingual "Publicity Agent for an Empire," traveled extensively through the Atlantic states, and to London, Paris, and other European capitals, lecturing large audiences on the opportunities in the Lone Star State. His widely disseminated immigrant guide books, published in 1856 and 1858, offered all manner of information to prospective settlers. In London in 1858 he preached the advantages of free labor for cotton production. In the North he addressed himself not to men of wealth who would establish themselves on plantations but to "the poor man and the man of moderate means, who wishes to become a FARMER and STOCK-RAISER." De Cordova's tours highlighted the fact that even with an impending sectional clash, Texas desired Europeans, Yankees, and Cavaliers alike. "Let but the stimulus of the enterprise, industry and genius . . . of New England," he orated before a Boston gathering, "be felt upon the natural resources of the great State of Texas, and the time will not be far distant when her splendid cities, her commerce, her agricultural productions, her railroads, her telegraphs, her schools, her social relations and her people might challenge the world without fear of finding a successful competitor."[52]

The Texans made no particular appeal to any section or nation and took equal delight in each group that arrived. "From every land emigrants are flocking, in welcome crowds, to partake of our prosperity," Governor Peter H. Bell exulted in 1851. "From the vine-clad hills of France and Germany, from Ireland's green shores and England's smiling fields, and from our own sister States, they swell the living tide — until the solitary plains have been made to rejoice and the wilderness to blossom as the rose." The southern editor, J. D. B. DeBow, also recognized in the 1850s the diversity of the Texan population and how it differed from the other slave states: "The active and enterprising New Englander, the bold and hearty western hunter, the chivalrous and high-spirited southern planter, meet here upon common ground, divested of all sectional influence, and lend their combined energies to the improvement of this infant but delightful and prosperous country."[53]

Stephen F. Austin had set the tone of Texan impartiality as early as the 1820s, when he observed that Mexico's policy against slavery was checking the emigration from the southern states and looked to other parts of the country. "I have had an idea of endeavoring to procure emigrants from Pennsylvania and other non Slave holding States," he informed Thomas Leaming of Philadelphia, "and . . . [am] asking your opinion whether any emigrants could probably be obtained from the Eastern or Middle States." Austin's unrelenting efforts brought a significant number of Northerners to Texas during the colonial era.[54] Years later in 1853, the Committee on Public Lands urged the passage of homestead legislation, contrary to the position of the other slave states, "to induce the laboring classes of other communities to immigrate hither, and become permanent citizens among us." No special overtures were made to slave-holders or to Southerners in general. "Again, we want population — we want more tillers of the soil — we want more of our rich lands in cultivation," a committee member declared five years later, "and every inducement, however slight it may be, ought to be held out to emigrants. Let the policy of Texas be to offer cheap homes to those in the Old States who are laboring upon worn out soils, and she will reap her reward in increased wealth and population."[55]

Thus, Texas gathered under its banner within twenty-five years a diverse population in a recruitment calculated to attract people even at the cost of giving away the public domain. For ten years land policy was generously set by the government of the Republic; from 1846 on, the state government, by virtue of the annexation agreement, maintained authority over the public lands and continued to offer advantageous terms. The promotion of the Lone Star featured, in addition to liberal land and immigration laws, inspired public relations work and ceaseless testimony by citizens and government spokesmen alike to the glorious future of their country, Texas. James Pike of Ohio recalled an overland journey he made in 1859 with a Colonel Johnston of Dallas. "If you want fun, just go to Texas," Johnston advised him, "that is the place to find it; plenty of all sorts of game, fine horses, and clever people. It's just the spot for a young man. If you ever go there, you will like the country so well, that you will never leave it." As Pike soon discovered, his friend believed every word of it. "We crossed the Red river at Colbert's ferry, when the Colonel gave a shout of delight as he once more landed in Texas."[56]

The attachment of the people to the soil of Texas had a unique dimension. Boosterism, of course, took many of the same forms here as elsewhere on the American continent, and land speculation had much to do with it. But the Texans evinced a proprietary interest in their land that went something beyond mere titles and profit. Having struggled for it against both human and natural enemies, they now identified with it intimately.

CHAPTER THREE

Aspects of the Texian Character

To reckless spirits journeying from afar,
'Tis Texas yet presents a Polar Star;
By misfortune, crime and oppression driven,
From every State and Kingdom under heaven.[1]

It was once the fashion at the north, to name Texas as the inevitable terminus of every moonlight flitting, whether occasioned by that innate modesty which impels a reserved man to save his creditors from interviews, unpleasant and unprofitable upon both sides; by a too warm admiration of a neighbor's wife; the desire to sever one's own matrimonial fetters, by "cutting" one's self; or, in fine, any of the thousand and one reasons which so suddenly at times impart to men a fondness for travel, or desire for the society of strangers. . . .[2]

Economic considerations figured importantly in the movement of men to Texas. But there was more to it than that. Beyond the pale of the law, the country provided a haven not only for bankrupts and debtors, but also for criminals, malcontents, and adventurers of every description. From the very first, the individuals who surrendered nationality to locate in a no-man's land under the Mexican aegis stirred suspicions: "Thare is a number of people coming in to the Country & settleing between this place & the river Sabean . . . without any kind of leave or permission whatever," James Dill of Nacogdoches informed Governor Antonio María Martínez in 1822, "& I cannot tell who they are from Character, nor what their intentions may be, as they do not so much as come forward to report themselves nor make any inquiries . . . in respect of settleing the Country." The Mexican government soon would learn who those interlopers were; many more would follow seeking a second chance in life across the borders of the United States. Benjamin Milam, himself an American adventurer in Texas, observed this phenomenon as early as 1825:

As Texas forms a protection at all times . . . all frontiers bordering on the U. S. are apt and posibly Inosently to admit not only Slaves but Every class of depridators and refugees. It father appears that maney parts of this Country rather Encourag and harbour Such delenquents or refugees and outlaws as obscond from our Country to this, not beeing able to live under one of the best goverments Existing.[3]

As to why so many of the early Texans should have found it difficult to "live under one of the best gover[n]ments Existing," the answer was given: they were men on the run. "Texas has had so many crooks and outlaws," testified one witness in the 1840s, "those who were charged with murder, theft, fraud, bankruptcy, and other crimes, fled from the United States and took up their abode in Texas and here, considering themselves safe, mocked the laws of their country." George W. Smyth agreed that the country served as a hideout for desperadoes. Coming to Texas in 1830 as a surveyor, he discovered his fellow citizens to be largely fugitives from justice seeking "a more convenient sanctuary" beyond the jurisdiction of the United States. As a reporter for the Alexandria (Louisiana) *Gazette* found upon entering several Texas villages during a visit in 1830,

he was invariably surrounded and accosted sans ceremonie, by numbers of the citizens, enquiring *what he had done* in the United States, that made it necessary for him to seek refuge among them? On expressing astonishment at their mode of saluting a stranger, he was assured that it was *their constant* rule to enquire thus of all who came, and that no incivility was intended. He was moreover informed, that when a new-commer averred that he had *ran away from his creditors* ONLY, he was regarded as a gentleman of the *first water*, and welcomed on all hands. But if he had been guilty of *murder*, or any high misdemeanor, he could only be assured of their *protection....*[4]

There were logical reasons why Texas should have become a haven for fugitives. As early as 1806, the Neutral Ground Agreement between the United States and Spain created a lawless territory between Louisiana and Texas that served as an asylum for outlaws from both countries. From this time onward, Texas acquired a deserved notoriety as a place where men could do as they pleased without annoyance from the law. As one American jailbird, arrested for manslaughter in the States, self-righteously announced:

Now-a-days you can't put an inch or so of knife into a fellow, or lam him over the head with a stick of wood, but every little lackey must poke his nose in, and law, law, law is the word. ... I tell you I wont stay in no such country. I mean to go to Texas, where a man can have some peace and not be interfered with in his private concerns.[5]

During the tumultuous period of revolutionary activity in Mexico from 1810 to 1821, American expansionists conducted filibustering campaigns to wrest Texas away from Spain as her New World empire was crumbling. The founding of the Mexican Republic in 1821 and the subsequent instability of the Mexican governments added fresh ingredients to the cauldron of turmoil, including the unwelcomed participation of more daring spirits from the United States. In the 1830s and 40s, the Texas Revolution and the new Republic's continuing difficulties with Mexico attracted legions of action-seeking young men. Since no extradition treaties existed between the United States and the Mexican or Texan republics, the Sabine River represented "the magic line between freedom and prison for refugees."[6] The Murrell Conspiracy of the early 1830s, for example, which plotted to turn the southwestern states over to a mob of freed slaves and hoodlums, was nipped in the bud when Murrell himself was arrested in Arkansas and sent to prison in 1834. But his organization had been quite extensive, and by 1835 the gang had scattered to Texas as a place of refuge — "Where else," asks C. L. Sonnichsen, "could they go?" The result was a gathering of feuders who brought the saying "Hell in Texas."[7]

The Indian wars of the Texas Republic and the Mexican War of 1846–48 drew many more to the Lone Star, as adventurers and delinquents continued to enjoy anonymity in the Rio Grande Valley. Fugitives hid out in wilderness areas where "no-man laws" operated as late as the Civil War. If the trail got too hot, they could easily slip into Mexico. "The Americans of the Texian frontiers are, for the most part, the very scum of society — bankrupts, escaped criminals, old volunteers," a sojourner on the borderlands concluded in 1858, "who after the treaty of Guadalupe Hidalgo, came into a country protected by nothing that could be called a judicial authority, to seek adventure and illicit gains."[8]

While a goodly portion of the men of Texas had come for adventure's sake, many more, whatever their age or station, looked to Texas as a *last* resort. One William B. Aldridge, late of Virginia, confided to his sister back East in 1837 that sorrow and misery had plagued him all his life. "Here in Texas therefore must be my only & last home." Another, Ira M. Freeman of Camillus, New York, had journeyed to Texas for land: "I am as [sic] determined to make property," he vowed to his father, "or lose my life in the attempt."[9] Still other Texans were heard making similar declarations. What must be the feelings of men who could think of a howling wilderness as their last stop in life?

Curiously, a clue may be found in their style of humor. Humor enabled Texans to inflate themselves and to expand their already ample territory. Some ranked with the very best of the Old Southwest storytellers and every Texas village had its "loafer's log" where the yarn-spinners held sway. A laconic drawl, a professed ignorance of book learning, and a quiet wisdom in the ways of prairie life marked these raconteurs as an eccentric bunch. Like other frontier regions, Texas germinated a crop of tall tales and more than a few live characters to go with them. Men such as Strap Buckner, Deaf Smith, Old Paint Caldwell, and Bigfoot Wallace allowed considerable play to the imagination. While the exaggerated humor of Texas grew out of the southern tall tale, the protagonist was no longer the riverboatman or lumberjack of the Mississippi Valley, but the ranger and desperado of the dusty plains. Texans took immense pride in these types — so capable of explosive violence — and border lawlessness somehow became the focus of a number of Texas jokes. Above all, the Texan humorist enjoyed raising himself to gigantic proportions and could employ a ready wit (as well as boasts and bluffs) to achieve this effect. Even one such as Sam Houston, who required few embellishments, rarely could resist an opening. "I have come to this city," the Hero coyly purred before a New Orleans crowd in 1848, "the companion of men far more distinguished in the history of my country than myself." When the citizens protested with loud cries of "No!" "No!" "No!" Houston rejoined in his accustomed fashion with a story about a boy who was scolded by his mother for coming home drunk. When the young fellow insisted that friends had *forced* him to drink, his mother retorted, "Pshaw! I don't believe it" "Well, mother," said he, "they were *going* to force it down me, and so, seeing that, I took it freely." "Now, gentlemen" the famed Texan roared, "seeing that you *will* force this distinction down me, *I'll take it freely!*"[10]

A hunger for distinction seems to have afflicted many Texans, big and small, and the proliferation of titles and degrees among them was remarkable. The most popular were military titles, but for those who could claim no martial experience — and there must have been few indeed who never had tented for a night in the open prairie — such honorifics as "Judge," "Doctor," or even "Squire" served just as well. Visitors to Texas, especially Europeans, were surprised to find in a democratic nation more individuals graced with dignities than one was likely to see among the aristocracy of the Old World. At least, as Tocqueville might have argued, the practice in Texas was democratic enough, for such badges were borne by the high and the low alike. True, people all over the western states of America were susceptible to this indulgence, but in Texas it was carried to an extravagance — well beyond even those immodest proportions. "Every body is judge this or General that or Col. or Major," commented a disdainful Britisher.[11]

When Ferdinand Roemer of Germany landed at Galveston, Christmastide, 1846, he joined a party at the Tremont Hotel for holiday festivities. There he mixed in with a large and boisterous company imbibing a

Yuletide punch but was soon puzzled to find among them "several generals, colonels, majors and a number of captains." "A stranger just arrived from Europe," he remarked, "would conclude that Texas possessed a large standing army upon hearing these high military titles." He then learned that Texas boasted of no less than forty persons who carried the title of general. American guests, taking things less literally than the uninitiated European, poked fun at the Texans. Henry Thompson, author of a Texas guide for emigrants, wrote from Philadelphia to President Lamar (himself a "General") saying that he had discovered Houston to be a famous place "for *phantom fame* – and if there were more misters and less titles, it would not be so ludicrous. A lady asked me," he related, "'if the Gentm of Texas were not Generals generally?' I told her the *Major* part of them were quite Captains in their own way." But all this may be understandable in a society of the displaced and the uprooted. As another German visitor observed of the men of Houston,"It was everyone's wish to be somebody in the general company, and therefore everyone threw a veil of oblivion over past deeds."[12] Why should they not, in their remnants of self-esteem, be vulnerable to a title that tells the world at last that they are "somebody"? Would not "Texian" eventually satisfy the same craving?

What might be other expressions or displays of a people wishing to escape ignominy and groping for worthiness, recognition, and even fame? What might be the manifestations of grandeur and despair – a crusading fury on the one hand, perhaps, and a wish for martyrdom on the other? We may wonder at the readiness of the Texan revolutionaries to *die* for the cause of a country that was not yet theirs.

Many Texans, in their capacity as citizen soldiers, fancied themselves knights-errant, the ornament of a romantic age, and looked upon their country's wars against Mexicans and Indians throughout the antebellum era as an opportunity to win glory, renown, and even immortality. The Texas Revolution, with the world watching, presented an exceptional opportunity for heroism and honor. One revolutionary stalwart, James Butler Bonham from South Carolina, was known to be "imbued with patriotic impulses, with chivalric ideas of knights in shining armor, with Sir Walter Scott's medieval England." Bonham, on a volunteer mission, dashed with reckless courage through the startled Mexican troops encircling the Alamo to locate reinforcements for the beleaguered fortress. He returned empty-handed, but in time to take his place beside his comrades on death row. Another champion of losing causes, Jim Bowie, refused to be moved though confined to a sick bed and barely able to rise in his own defense. Nothing better betrays the Byronic mystique of some of these heroes than the famous lines of Commander William B. Travis as the Alamo's walls were about to be stormed: "The enemy has demanded a surrender," he declaimed. "I have answered the demand with a canon shot, & our flag still waves proudly from the walls — I *shall never surrender or retreat.*"[13]

Ordinary soldiers who volunteered for the war likewise revealed a romantic vision blended, one cannot help believing, with suicidal impulses. What one scholar writes of Travis, that his egocentricity and lofty self-dramatization suggest "a spirit determined not to die in ignominy" (he was all of twenty-seven years old) might be said of all 188 men at the Alamo.[14] Given the choice to leave the fortress or stay to meet a certain death, all remained. Daniel W. Cloud, one of the less renowned defenders, had announced his readiness to die for Texas before he even got there. In a letter to his brother in December, 1835, he said: "Death in the cause of Liberty and humanity is not cause for shuddering. Our rifles are by our sides and choice guns they are, we know what awaits us and we are prepared to meet it." Travis calmly noted that his boys were determined to hold the Alamo "as long as there is a man left," because they preferred death to disgrace. "Their threats have no influence on me, or my men," he proclaimed, in his last appeal for aid, "but to make all fight with the desperation, and that high souled courage which characterizes the patriot, who is willing to die in defence of his country's liberty and his own honor ... *God and Texas — Victory or Death!*"[15]

A week after the bastion fell, March 6, 1836, another Texan officer promised a like performance: "I will never give up the ship whilst there is a pea in the ditch," stated Colonel James W. Fannin, whose force of more than four hundred was destined to be massacred within a fortnight. "If I am whipped," he predicted, "it will be well done, and you may never expect to see me."[16] (Actually, it was not so well done: Fannin and his followers were methodically executed by order of Santa Anna after surrendering on the assurance that they would be treated as prisoners of war.) Contemporaries apotheosized the Alamo heroes (and Fannin's "Men of Goliad") in song, oratory, and poetry. The recurrent theme in these eulogies was the nobility of death in a worthy cause:

> Welcome the Spartan's death
> Tis no despairing strife
> We fall — we die — but our expiring breath
> Is freedom's breath of life.[17]

As the Revolution proceeded, other Texans seemed prepared to make a similar offering. Elisha M. Pease, a future governor of Texas, related to his father the dramatics of the Alamo episode, concluding, "While we mourn their fall we rejoice that their end was so glorious."

Private G. H. A. Giddings, an American volunteer, wrote to his parents after the Alamo that "Rather than be driven out of the country, or submit to be a slave, I will leave my bones to blanch on the plains of Texas." James W. Robinson resigned his position as provisional governor in March, 1836, to enlist as a private in the revolutionary army. "In this her hour of peril and danger," he orated, "Texas shall not find me wanting in devotion to her interest and honor, and this pledge I am ready to redeem with my life." Mirabeau B. Lamar, the most incurable Texan visionary, addressed his charges at the battle of San Jacinto in rhythmic words that bespoke the sentiment of all: "Nor life, nor death, be deemed the happier state, But life that's glorious, or a death that's great!"[18]

The vainglorious ceremony of Texans may have been much in keeping with the pomp of a romantic era. And yet there seems to have been a special predisposition among these particular revolutionaries. Texans "would prefer Death itself," insisted the Brazoria *Texas Republican*, to submission "to the despotism of Santa Ana." Even youngsters were seized with the unnatural notion of the ultimate sacrifice, hearing so much from their elders about the fallen men of the Alamo. Thirteen-year-old John H. Jenkins felt a wound to his pride as a soldier when a veteran of the war peered down at him before the battle of San Jacinto and told him to stay in camp to look after the baggage. "No, sir, I am here to fight," he replied indignantly, "and would sooner die than leave my place in the ranks." Guy M. Bryan, who would survive this and many Texas wars to become a U. S. congressman in the 1850s, had one of his proudest moments when, at the age of fifteen, he skirted danger and carried Travis's "Victory or Death" letter to the towns of Brazoria and Velasco.[19]

In the years following the Revolution, Texans were seldom without opportunities to give their lives in defense of the country. Up to the Civil War they volunteered for military service whenever duty called, and as the land was frequently disturbed by Indian or Mexican aggressions, they found numerous occasions for a hero's death.[20] They remained captives of the Alamo example throughout. The *Telegraph and Texas Register's* eulogy of March 24, 1836 was as much a challenge to their successors as it was a tribute to the Alamo defenders:

Spirits of the mighty, though fallen! Honors and rest are with ye: the spark of immortality which animated your forms, shall brighten into a flame, and Texas, the whole world, shall hail ye like the demi-Gods of old, as founders of new actions, and as patterns of imitation.

The spirit was typically expressed a year after the event by Colonel John N. Seguin of the Texas Army, who bade his men in memory of that "iron-hearted band" to emulate "their mighty deeds, to secure like them a mighty place upon the scroll of immortality." Even President Sam Houston, who normally had a stronger instinct for survival than most men, indulged in the same exhortations: "Our soil is consecrated by the blood of martyrs," he reminded his countrymen, "and we will defend it or perish." This fixation, and the acts of valor which sustained it, prompted the American minister to Texas in 1842 to speculate, following the first of three Mexican invasions that year, that Santa Anna "might possibly exterminate the Texans but never can conquer them . . . and 5000 Texans would at any time give 20000 Mexicans a battle."[21]

Travis, indeed, was not the only Texan stalwart to take his men down suicide road in exchange for a touch of immortality. Nicholas Moseby Dawson, of "Dawson Massacre" fame, did not even offer his boys the choice of meeting death with gallantry or clinging to life with shame. After a Mexican army under General Adrian Woll captured San Antonio in September, 1842, Dawson rounded up fifty-three cohorts to pursue the invader. His contingent was intercepted by a detachment of Mexican cavalry near Salado Creek. The outnumbered Texans took cover in a mesquite grove as the enemy rolled its artillery into position. At this point, before the barrage began, Dawson ought to have surrendered, since he and his men were hopelessly exposed to the deadly cannon fire. "But that *dare me devil dont care* which is characteristic of *Texians*, led these brave spirits on to the slaughter," Harvey A. Adams related. "Some of his men spoke of retreating . . . Dawson raised his rifle & said that he would shoot the first man who said retreat or surrender." Perhaps at that desperate moment the hallucinated Dawson heard echoes of the "Texan Hymn" (1838):

> Arise, arise brave Texians, awake to liberty:
> To Mexican oppressors, no longer bend the knee;
> But hasten to the combat, with freedom's flag unfurled,
> That the glorious deeds of Texas may echo through the world.
> For we are determined to die or to be free,
> And Texas triumphant our watchword shall be.[22]

Tragically, thirty-five Texans, including Dawson, were killed; fifteen were captured, five were wounded, and three escaped. Such was the fate of the "Dawson Men."

It is hard to calculate just how lightly life sat on the Texas frontier, just how eager men were to surrender their lives for a transcendent purpose, or the extent to which the common citizens of Texas were drawn by the urge to self-destruction. But one does wonder at their relish for extreme peril, and at their zeal in after years to recall the "Spirit of '36." There is surely something here of what Emile Durkheim calls "altruistic suicide."[23]

59

We cannot know how many Texans died by their own hand, nor, since no state or federal statistics on suicide were kept in these years, how Texas compared in this respect with other states, regions, or countries. But the casual researcher in Texas history is struck by the incidence of suicide among the leaders of the community.[24]

In the presidential election of 1838, the Houston party nominated Peter W. Grayson to run against Mirabeau B. Lamar. Grayson's Texas career had been a busy and notable one. Unmarried, he came to Texas from Kentucky in 1830 at age forty-two. He became good friends with Stephen F. Austin when he journeyed to Mexico City in 1834 to argue for the *empresario's* release from prison. A lawyer by training, he was appointed attorney-general by interim-president David G. Burnet in 1836, and in that capacity signed the Treaty of Velasco with Santa Anna, which acknowledged the dictator's recognition of Texas as a self-governing republic. In the new administration of Sam Houston, Grayson was chosen attorney-general in 1837. Later that year he was sent to Washington, D.C. as the President's confidential agent, perhaps to feel out the American government on the subject of annexation. In December, 1837, Houston authorized him to purchase ships in the United States for the Texas Navy.

Here was a man reaching the pinnacle of his career as the 1838 presidential campaign commenced. Inexplicably, two months before the balloting, Grayson ran off to Tennessee (some said because of a disappointing love affair). At Bean's Station on July 9, he blew his brains out with a pistol. His pathetic death-note to the innkeeper revealed a man still unconvinced, at the age of fifty, that he deserved to live:

Mr. Mayse

I pray you pardon the frightful scene I have made in your house. You will ere long learn that I have not been wholly an unworthy man.... I beseech you to pardon the trouble I give you.[25]

The Houston forces back in Texas hastily recovered from the shock of their candidate's untimely demise and selected James Collinsworth to run in Grayson's place. Collinsworth, who at the age of thirty-two was actually too young to qualify for president under the 1836 Constitution, had likewise enjoyed an illustrious career in his brief association with Texas. Coming to the country in 1835 after abruptly leaving his post as U. S. district attorney for the Western District of Tennessee, he quickly established his credentials as a lawyer and was elected a delegate to the Constitutional Convention of March, 1836. He nominated Sam Houston for commander-in-chief of the Texas Army, and later served Houston as aide-de-camp. In May, 1836, he was appointed along with the same Peter W. Grayson as a commissioner to the United States. The two traveled to Washington together to seek recognition of Texas as an independent government. Collinsworth was President Houston's first choice for attorney-general in October, 1836, but he declined the office because of "personal circumstances." So highly was he esteemed that in December, 1836, he was elected almost simultaneously a senator to the First Congress and first chief justice of the Texas Supreme Court. He accepted the latter position. Collinsworth was also instrumental in founding the town of Richmond in 1837 and became a charter member of the Philosophical Society of Texas, organized that same year. His reputation was so exceptional that if he had won the presidential vote the country might have awarded him the office despite his age. But shortly after his nomination, in July, 1838, Collinsworth, without warning, jumped from a steamboat in Galveston Bay and disappeared under the waves.[26]

George C. Childress, author of the Texas Declaration of Independence, came to Texas early in 1836 after the death of his young wife. Thirty-two years old, he was a college graduate from Nashville where he had been a member of the Tennessee bar and editor of a local newspaper. In the latter capacity, he was active in raising volunteers and money for the Texan revolutionary army. A few weeks after his arrival in Robertson's colony, he was elected a delegate to the Constitutional Convention of March, 1836. As chairman of the committee to compose the Texan Declaration of Independence, Childress penned the historic document himself, being one of the few men at the Convention whose schooling and vocation prepared him for such a role.

At the conclusion of the Convention, Childress was sent to Washington, D. C., along with Robert Hamilton, as a diplomatic agent to open negotiations with the United States government for the recognition of Texan independence. After two months of futile effort, he was replaced by James Collinsworth and Peter W. Grayson. Depressed over his failure, Childress did not return to Texas but went back to Nashville, whereupon he met the woman who would shortly become his second wife. They were married in December, 1836. Now a man without a position but with a wife to support, he attempted to establish a law practice, at first in Nashville, then in Houston. Three trips to Texas between the depression years of 1837 and 1841 failed to get him started. Business was so dull and his financial situation so bleak that he was reduced to asking President Lamar in 1841 for a position as a private secretary. Meanwhile, his family had remained for most of four years without him in Tennessee. According to his biographer, his sensitive nature and tendency toward melancholy could not bear the stress of material need and the embarrassment of forced dependence on friends. Four months after his overture to Lamar, in October, 1841, Childress ended his agony in a boarding house in Galveston, slashing his abdomen with a bowie knife.[27]

No introduction or case history needs to be made for Anson Jones or Thomas Jefferson Rusk, as their names show up again and again when the story of the Texas nation is told. Jones, the last president of the Republic, was an intensely brooding soul who never recovered his brief eminence after lowering his nation's flag as Texas entered statehood in 1846. Jones's biographer reveals that after he disabled his arm in an accident and failed to win election to the United States Senate in 1849, "he became increasingly moody and introspective," and his distaste for his former political ally, Sam Houston, turned to hatred. Jones's autobiography, published posthumously in 1859, is a morbidly self-righteous account justifying a career no longer of interest to anyone but the historian. When Jones failed to receive a single legislative vote in his bid for the Senate in 1857, he had suffered the final humiliation. He ended his days in a Houston hotel, shooting himself in January, 1858, at the age of sixty.[28]

Thomas J. Rusk, on the other hand, hardly seemed the brooding type. His papers reveal on the whole little introspection and deal only occasionally with personal matters. One senses in them, however, the rectitude characteristic of a man firm in principle.[29] His career as a soldier-statesman is one of the least controversial of all Texan leaders, a remarkable feat given Rusk's constant presence at the center of action. Dedicated and hardworking, Rusk was described by a contemporary as "one of the strongest men in the nation, with the people."[30] Affable and inoffensive, outwardly unambitious, he repeatedly turned away suggestions by his friends that he run for the presidency. Nearly everyone judged that he could have beaten any candidate, Sam Houston included. He was that rare kind for whom the office does seek the man, and was perhaps the only Texan politico who could have been embraced by partisans of both Houston and Lamar. Remaining for his entire career in the giant shadow of Sam Houston, Rusk dutifully served Texas in many capacities from his arrival in 1835, including general-in-chief of the army, secretary of war, major-general of the militia, chief justice of the Supreme Court, president of the Annexation Convention, and United States senator (three times elected) from 1846 to 1857.

So highly regarded was Rusk in the councils of the national Democratic party that his name was frequently mentioned for the presidency in 1852 and again in 1856. So popular was he among his colleagues in Washington that he was chosen president pro-tempore of the Senate in March, 1857. But the death of his consumptive wife nearly a year earlier had apparently thrown him into profound grief. In the summer of 1857, reportedly overcome by loneliness and depression, Senator Rusk stunned the nation by putting a bullet through his head. He was fifty-four.[31]

Since we cannot equate a horse culture with an automobile culture, it is impossible to erect a standard by which to measure death by accident in the nineteenth century against the twentieth century. It is still worth observing that of the 359 members of the Texas conventions and congresses from 1832 to 1845 whose deaths are registered, forty-four, or about one in eight, did not die of natural causes. Violence or mishap cut short their lives in one way or another: drowning, assassination, street fighting, soldiering, accident, or suicide. A psychic proneness may have contributed to this. Nearly ninety percent, 321 of the 359, left their bones to be buried in Texas, notwithstanding the transient nature of frontier populations. A fair number of this generation had indeed predicted that Texas would be their last stop in life.

If it is reasonable to assume that the public men in a democratic nation will reflect the attitudes and even the life style of the electorate, perhaps we can delineate the "Texian" character by taking a closer look at the lives of the leaders. Are they actually representative? One curious fact relating to the total conventional and congressional membership of 482 from 1832 to 1845 is that fewer than ten percent had held a public office before coming to Texas. This figure seems low in view of the fact that most had emigrated directly from the frontier states of the trans-Appalachian West where a high degree of political participation might have been expected.[32] Even though nearly twenty percent had some training in law, the U. S. chargé in Austin noted that members of the Texas Congress had "but little experience in the science of legislation."[33] Political power was widely diffused, the consensus being that a man must not be disqualified for his past failings or misdeeds. The absence of any entrenched leadership or social hierarchy in Texas enabled those who served at the national level between 1832 and 1845 to achieve their first public office, on an average, within two years of residence. By no means the patriarchs of their communities, these were relatively young men to be running a country, averaging 36.5 years upon their first election. While only a handful were laboring men, nearly as few were wealthy planters or merchants. Statistics on the economic status of state legislators in the 1850s reveal an overwhelming number of "middling" sorts.[34] Rotation in office was the rule. Only 21 of the 482, or less than five percent, were able to make a career of public service. The rapid turnover (nearly eighty percent) in the annual congressional and legislative elections from 1836 to 1861 indicates that these politicos were selected on a rather trial and error basis. In training, experience, and background, Texas leaders were "typical" Texans, as portrayed by a visitor to the country in 1852:

> You meet a man in the road, he is dressed in coarse cotton pants; cowskin boots, a heavy rifle on his shoulder, his waist encircled with a leather belt, a large Bowie Knife dangling from it. You speak to him; ask who he is, he is a member of the legislature from somewhere.[35]

Let us examine briefly a number of the leading personages with a view to the circumstances that impelled them to burn their bridges and seek rebirth. We will discover that they too encountered difficulties in their former homes and looked to Texas as a place to shake off past embarrassments. Adventurous, opportunistic, and unready to accept defeat, they display remarkable persistence. And yet their determination and daring seem almost that of the desperate gambler willing to risk all on a last throw.

Mr. Texas himself, Sam Houston, forty years old when he settled in Nacogdoches in 1833, had actually been the governor of Tennessee four years earlier when the bottom suddenly fell out of his life. His marriage in 1829 to the daughter of a prominent Nashville man lasted only a few weeks. Houston never divulged the cause of his separation but the mysterious circumstances were so painful to him that he abruptly resigned his position, throwing a promising career in national politics to the winds, and ran off to Arkansas to live with a band of Cherokees. For the next three years he slept in wigwams, hunted and traded with his red brethren, and took an Indian squaw for his wife. Houston emerged from his eclipse in 1832, apparently restored to full vigor. He made his first trip to Texas in December, 1832, from which time his life was linked to the fate of the Lone Star.

Three other men served as president of the Texas Republic. David G. Burnet, born of a prominent New Jersey family, was buffeted by a life of ups and downs. Reared by an older brother after the untimely death of both parents, he took a job with a New York counting house at the age of seventeen, only to lose his inheritance of $1,400 in a futile attempt to save the company from bankruptcy. From 1806 to 1808, he tried his hand at filibustering in the Caribbean and took part in the Venezuelan revolution at Caracas. Nine years later, at twenty-eight, he tried to establish a trading post in Louisiana but developed tuberculosis and was forced to abandon the venture. Sick and depressed, he rode westward into the Texas wilderness and finally toppled from his horse at the Colorado River into the hands of a band of Comanches. The Indians befriended him and for the next two years nursed him back to health. He moved to Cincinnati in 1819 to study law but could not get his mind off Texas. Over the next seven years he alternated his location between the two countries. Finally, in 1826, he returned to Texas for good and acquired the following year an *empresario's* contract from the Mexican Republic. Soon known as a promoter of settlement, Burnet rose quickly to prominence in pre-revolutionary politics, beginning with the 1833 convention, and was chosen in 1836 to head the *ad interim* government of the newly created Republic of Texas. For the next thirty years, Burnet remained active in Texas politics, most notably as vice-president from 1838 to 1841. As a lifelong foe of Sam Houston, however, he rarely achieved public office again.

Mirabeau B. Lamar started his political career as a private secretary to Governor George M. Troup of Georgia in the 1820s, playing an active role in his program to drive the Creek and Cherokee Indians from the state. Elected a state senator in 1829, he was a candidate for reelection in 1830 when his wife of four years succumbed to tuberculosis, leaving him with an infant daughter. He withdrew from the race but bounced back two years later to enter a contest for U. S. congressman. Defeated in the 1832 election, Lamar returned again in 1834, standing for Congress on a platform of nullification. When beaten for a second time in the 1834 campaign, Lamar was of a mind to sever his American ties altogether and the groundswell of the Texas Revolution presented a timely alternative.

He arrived in Texas in 1835, thinking himself at age thirty-seven a failure, but as the revolutionary events unfolded, his "health and spirits began to mend," according to his biographer, and he eagerly awaited the impending clash. "I am resolved, in the event of a revolutionary struggle," he declared, "to make *her* destiny *mine* for good or ill." The war gave Lamar a chance to display his chivalry and win some prominence as a military hero. In the new government, he pursued his political ambitions by defecting from Houston's administration (he was vice-president) and forming an opposition faction. "I do not feel at liberty," he proclaimed, in accepting his party's nomination for president in 1838, "to decline the duties of any station, however high and honorable, to which the voice of my fellow-citizens may call me."[36] Lamar, like other Texas leaders, was not one to underrate his own importance.

The fourth and last president of Texas was Anson Jones. A sullen, querulous person, he seldom found favor with associates. Before coming to Texas, Jones's life had been one of unmitigated failure. Licensed to practice medicine in New York State, he was unable to launch himself as a doctor in Bainbridge in 1820 and subsequently went out of business as an apothecary in Norwich, New York. Twenty-six years old in 1824, he decided to seek his fortune in the West but was arrested en route to Harper's Ferry by a creditor who caught up with him in Philadelphia. For the next eight years in the Quaker City, Jones struggled again to establish a physician's practice but could barely make his bread and remained mired in debt. (One can guess that he did not have much of a bedside manner.) Finally giving vent to his frustrations, he renounced medicine in 1832 and embarked for New Orleans to set himself up as a commission merchant. Failure dogged him once more. Lasting just a year in the Crescent City, Jones managed to survive the cholera and yellow fever epidemics of 1833, but could not survive in business. At the age of thirty-five, without money or friends, his plight was desperate. Now shriveled to a mere 120 pounds (on a 5' 9" frame), he drifted on to Texas, following what his biographer calls "the path of least resistance." He landed at Brazoria, saw at a glance that the town was bereft of medics; and shrewdly assumed the title "Dr. Jones" once again. "In Texas," Jones recorded for his memoirs, "I commenced the world anew." He achieved rapid financial success in his trade and even served briefly as the Texan minister to the United States in 1838. In the 1840s he gained political prominence clinging to the coattails of Sam Houston. All the while Jones smouldered with concealed ill-will toward all three of his fellow Texas presidents.[37]

Other leading Texas politicians had ample reason to escape their former abodes. Branch T. Archer, descended from the F. F. V., was trained as a physician in Philadelphia and tutored as a politician in the House of Burgesses. Suddenly, in 1831, he headed for Texas, after "domestic afflictions had disposed him to quit the scenes and associations of his earlier life," and abandon a promising career in Virginia. Forty-one years old upon his arrival, Archer immediately assumed a commanding role in Texas affairs. A member of the Convention of 1833, he also served as president of the Consultation of All Texas in 1835 and as commissioner to the United States in 1836. Archer rounded out his notable Texas career as speaker of the house in the First Congress and as secretary of war under President Lamar.[38]

Thomas J. Rusk, whose career we have outlined, was, as a young lawyer in Georgia, swindled out of his money by corrupt mining and land speculators in whose stock he had invested. Rusk made the mistake of putting all his eggs in one basket, and when the managers absconded with the funds in 1835, they left him in poverty and debt. He followed the crooks westward, hoping to recover some portion of his lost funds; when he finally overtook them across the Sabine, he learned that they had squandered and gambled away all of their ill-gotten gains.[39] Coincidentally, Rusk arrived in Texas in time for a revolution and was at once recognized for his leadership qualities. With the eager townsmen tugging at his sleeve, Rusk made a brief survey of the land around Nacogdoches, pronounced it satisfactory, and called for his wife in Georgia to join him in starting a new life.

Robert Potter came to Nacogdoches in July, 1835 after a tempestuous public career in North Carolina. Three-times elected to the state House of Commons and twice to the U. S. House of Representatives, Potter had a way with the people. But a violent temper was his undoing. In 1831, in a fit of extreme jealousy, he attacked his wife's cousin, maiming both him and another man who had come to the relative's defense. Potter was fined $1,000 and jailed for two years. In January, 1835 (after being re-elected), Potter again struck and crippled a rival — this time over a card game. Expelled from the North Carolina legislature he made his way to Texas. The good citizens of Nacogdoches found him enough to their liking to elect him a delegate to both the Consultation of 1835 and the Constitutional Convention of 1836. He was a signatory to the Declaration of Independence and was chosen by his convention colleagues as ad interim secretary of the Texas navy. (Potter was not without qualification. He had served as a midshipman in the American navy from 1815 to 1821.) In the years following the Revolution he was elected from Fannin and Red River counties to the Fifth and Sixth Congresses of the Republic. But old habits persisted and he engaged in the Regulator-Moderator War (1839-1844), a raging feud involving several hundred East Texas ruffians. "Welcome the Spartan's death," he had poeticized in his Hymn of the Alamo (1836), and his end was predictably bloody. His enemies found him at home from Congress on March 2, 1842, the sixth anniversary of Texas independence, and riddled him with bullets as he tried to dive into the lake behind his house. Potter's body was never recovered.

Other Texans destined to be elected to the Congress of the United States had comparable experiences prior to their rendezvous with the Lone Star. Louis T. Wigfall, U. S. senator from 1859 to secession in 1861, had killed one man in a duel and wounded Preston Brooks before slaying a second man by the code. Hot-tempered and frequently embroiled in bitter political feuds, Wigfall departed his native South Carolina in 1846 to escape his financial obligations as well as the animosity of the community over the death of his most recent victim, one Tom Bird. "Wigfall loved South Carolina," a biographer comments, "but he fell into two categories of migrants to Texas — those who owed debts or had killed someone."[40] Volney E. Howard, a member of the 31st and 32nd Congresses (1849-1853), was editor of a Mississippi newspaper before coming to Texas, and his vitriolic opinions on local issues created such heat that he ended up fighting duels against two former state governors and a rival editor. He was seriously injured in a match against ex-Governor Hiram G. Runnels (who himself later went to Texas and served in the Annexation Convention). After practicing law for a short period in New Orleans, Howard headed for

Texas in 1844, where his career in politics was immediately launched by his election as a delegate to the 1845 convention. Congressman John H. Reagan, one of the few Texans whose political career was not eclipsed by a Confederate role in the Civil War, had as a youth drifted through an assortment of odd jobs, sometimes finding no work at all, until he reached Texas in 1839. He was lured by "prospects of adventure and success" in this "new land of opportunity."[41] No sooner did Reagan arrive than he took part in the Cherokee War, and for the next few years remained active in campaigns against both Indians and Mexicans. Another member of Congress, George M. Smyth (1853-55), likewise had known little success before coming to Texas. A self-educated man of the southern frontier, Smyth was "determined to try my fortune in Texas," as he related to a friend upon his arrival in 1830, "and . . . like Columbus, I set out on my voyage into the great unknown ocean of adventure."[42]

A number of leading men were attracted mainly by the chance to fight in the Revolution and win for themselves a new country, even though "it was bidding adieu to the rest of the world," as one patriot admitted.[43] Among these were future state Governors J. Pinckney Henderson (1846-48), Peter H. Bell (1849-1853), Elisha M. Pease (1853-57), and Francis R. Lubbock (1861-63). Others drawn to Texas by the promise of war were Ben McCulloch, the famous Texan ranger, who was elected to the Fourth Congress of the Republic; Richardson A. Scurry, Supreme Court justice (1840-41), speaker of the House of Representatives (1843-44), and U. S. congressman from 1851 to 1853; John S. "Rip" Ford, whose divorce coincided with the flashing of guns in 1836, whereupon he went on to distinguish himself during a long Texas career as legislator, editor, physician, and ranger; Albert Sidney Johnston, "soldier of three republics," who resigned his commission with the U. S. Army just prior to his wife's death in 1835, and "at a moment when his career was in shambles and his life without meaning,"[44] decided to volunteer for the Texas Revolution; George C. Childress, who like Johnston had suffered the loss of his spouse; and Francis C. Moore, Jr., three-time mayor of Houston, senator from Harris County (1839-1842), delegate to the Annexation Convention of 1845, and editor for seventeen years of the *Telegraph and Texas Register*, who, notwithstanding the loss of one arm in an accident as a youth, came to Texas with the "Buckeye Rangers" of Ohio in 1836.

Still others driven to Texas by domestic travail were William B. Travis, whose wife had been having a sexual liaison with another man; Julien S. Devereux, recently divorced and in debt: his "reasons for leaving home and moving to Texas to get a new start in life," notes his biographer, "were similar to situations faced by men like Sam Houston, Anson Jones, Mirabeau B. Lamar and others who had also experienced marital problems and political and financial reverses;"[45] and Judge Robert M. Williamson ("Three-legged Willie"), whose biographical sketch speaks for many in drawing a curtain of mystery over its subject: "An event of an unpleasant and unfortunate character occurred . . . that determined him to emigrate to Texas."[46]

CHAPTER FOUR

The Emergence of a Nation

The days of the Repùblic were 'the days of our glory' . . . deeds of devoted patriotism and daring chivalry were then performed which would have graced the heroic pages of Greece and Rome. . . .[1]

Texas is . . . more than twice as large as England, Scotland, and Ireland combined. Should the vicissitudes of human governments bring disruption upon ours . . . then Texas united, can stand alone and raise her head proudly among the nations of the earth.[2]

The decade of Texas nationhood impressed a stamp of identity upon all people then and thereafter who would call themselves Texans. The Republic of Texas was more than an embattled province waiting only to be embraced by its parent nation, the United States. The Republic was itself a nation. The Lone Star flag took its place with the banners of the world, vying for prestige, trade, credit, population, and respect. A measure of the new nation's success was its recognition by the United States and by the leading commercial and military powers of Europe. As President Mirabeau B. Lamar proudly proclaimed in 1840, within four years, "Against such fearful odds, she has not only achieved, and secured her independence . . . but has maintained a well organized Government, established friendly relations abroad; more than quadrupled her population, and now exhibits to the world a Country teeming with all that is essential to the necessities or happiness of man."[3]

Texan nationalism was fostered both in the process of nation building and in the further struggle for survival against Indian enemies within the Republic and Mexican enemies without. The Texans took extravagant pride in their embryonic country, their heroes, and their achievements; from the winning of their independence, they thought of themselves first and foremost as "Texians." "They came to regard themselves as a breed apart," writes William W. Newcomb, and possessed an *esprit de corps* unmatched by their enemies. This was of great importance in winning and keeping the country.[4] At the same time, they never wholly lost sight of their native land, and of the benefits a union with the United States might provide. Unlike most new nations, Texas could entertain a real alternative

to the vexations of an independent national existence.
Meanwhile Texas, like the United States, began its national career
with a military hero as president, who served — if only briefly — as a
symbol of the nation's unity and purpose. Like the United States, Texas
was plagued from the start with problems of finances and national credit,
and like America, soon found its revolutionary leadership split asunder by
these weighty issues. And like many other new nations and their nationalist leaders, both Americans and Texans saw themselves as the special favor-
ites of a divine Providence, who watched over them and guided them
onward to national greatness. "While reflecting upon the dispensations of
an Almighty Being, who has conducted our country through scenes of
unparalleled privation, massacre and suffering," President Sam Houston
solemnly intoned in 1837, "it is but gratitude and sensibility to render to
him our most devout thanks, and invoke his kind benignity and future
providence, that he will preserve and govern us as a *chosen people.*"5

"Texas has assumed to herself a new and permanent *name* & character . . . hoping and believing that we will be received and recognized by all
civilized Nations on Earth," a citizen of the Republic wrote to relatives in
Massachusetts following the Declaration of Independence on March 2,
1836. "[There] will be adopted this day the *constitution* by which the
free & soverign [sic] people of the Republic of Texas will in future be
governed."6 The event of independence was indeed hopeful, but it is fair
to say that most Texans did not have quite so simple a view of their
nation's future. Rather, the weight of public opinion and expectation
growing out of the revolutionary war rested on the side of annexation to
the United States.7 Annexation promised financial solvency and economic
prosperity, a steady flow of American emigrants and rising land values, and
a strong bulwark against renewed Mexican or Indian aggression. Few
Texans looked forward to a separate national existence in 1836. The
country was ravaged and the people were destitute, their farmland and
ranches having been overrun by Santa Anna's armies. A spare harvest and a
grim winter lay ahead as the planting season was lost, and much of the live-
stock had strayed off to become wild. The country's borders remained vulnerable to attack by both Mexicans and Indians, and by the summer of
1836, the interim government was torn with dissension and a military
coup loomed as a possibility. Annexation enjoyed the nearly unanimous support of the leading
men of Texas, many of whom feared for the newly-liberated people's
liberty. Even General Mirabeau B. Lamar, already an ardent Texan nationalist, admitted that the country was "labouring under many serious and
alarming disadvantages — almost destitute of civil government — trembling,

as it were, upon the verge of anarchy, with too little credit abroad, and too much of the fiery elements of discord at home." With leaders vying for prominence in affairs of state, revolutionary Texas appeared to have too many ambitious men for its own good. "Corruption stalks abroad in this Land, the still small voice of reason and truth is suppressed," lamented General Thomas J. Rusk as the last of the Mexican army retired beyond the Rio Grande. "We have so many great men and such small space for them to move in I fear they will get mightily tangled in their machinery. Lord have mercy on us," he prayed, "save us from the enemy and from the mighty operations of our own Great men."[8]

At this point in the life of the infant nation, interim President David G. Burnet, clutching his Bible with one hand and his pistol with the other, took inspiration from the former and wisely decided to bow out before one of his decorated soldiers bumped him. He issued a call for a general election for national and local offices, for ratification of the Constitution, and a referendum on the question of annexation. The election, set for September, came off without disturbance. By a wide margin, General Sam Houston won the presidency and the Constitution was approved; an overwhelming vote of 3,277 to 91 was tendered in favor of a union with the United States.

The Hero of San Jacinto was the obvious choice for president. A liberal man of high intelligence, native shrewdness, and plain resourcefulness, Houston radiated strength and confidence. As an enraptured woman from the East once marveled, "He is decidedly the most splendid looking man I ever saw, one of Nature's noble men . . . a man born to govern."[9] His broad, commanding figure, shoulders draped with an Indian blanket and head crowned by a wide-brimmed hat, rose above any crowd of men. But Houston's affinity for whiskey was such that the Indians affectionately called him "Big Drunk" and historians have tended to consider him an alcoholic. No matter, he always seemed to be sober when it counted. A folksy drawl and a fondness for whittling gave him an air of republican simplicity that endeared him to most of his countrymen. Somehow, they could rely on "Old Sam."

The new administration of the Republic took office late in October, 1836. It might be euphemistic to call the government buildings at this date "offices." Burnet's office had consisted of one room "in a house little better than a shack." Houston's slovenly quarters were even worse. The wooden floor was so deeply covered with mud it could not be seen; papers and books were piled on two tables passing for desks, and a few chairs completed the furnishings. When he visited the presidential mansion, John James Audubon reacted with disbelief. He found Houston studying some papers and admitted his difficulty in understanding "how he could be so indifferent to his surroundings."[10] Perhaps Houston was inured; several years before he had slept with an Indian wife on the muddy floors of a wigwam.

For the sake of national unity, President Houston appointed to his cabinet the very men who had opposed him in the election — Henry Smith as secretary of the treasury and Stephen F. Austin as secretary of state. His other appointments, based on talent as well as expediency, included General Thomas J. Rusk as secretary of war, S. Rhoads Fisher as secretary of the navy, and J. Pinckney Henderson as attorney-general. Altogether, these were commendable selections. William H. Wharton was sent to Washington, D.C. with the critical task of seeking recognition and annexation. "Our public affairs have taken a favorable turn," Henry Austin related to the inquisitive Mrs. Holley. "All parties having . . . made advances for a general reconciliation which resulted in the formation of a cabinet of the leading men of all opinions. . . ." The government, he observed, "was formed on the spirit of compromise to save the country."[11]

The First Congress had convened early in October, nearly three weeks ahead of the President's inauguration, and taking to heart retiring President Burnet's valedictory plea that upon them rested "the high responsibility of giving political character, and moral reputation, to one just born into the family of nations,"[12] they went to work setting up the county governments and establishing the nation's court system. Before the year was out, the First Congress had generously fixed the boundaries of the Texas Republic, enacted the Second Class Headright system to attract new settlers, and authorized a military establishment of 3,587 troops, a battalion of 280 riflemen, and a chain of forts and trading posts on the frontier. Not waiting for the American government to come to them or expecting annexation to fall into their laps, the Republic's first legislators tackled their assignment with energy and foresight. It was a remarkable demonstration of how a transplanted American population could recreate, as by habit, the political institutions of their native land.

Rather astonished by the Congress's self-sufficiency and ability to work in unison, the Committee on Foreign Relations daringly speculated that if Texas were refused admission to the United States, "If we should continue as an independent nation, it will ultimately accelerate our advance in wealth and prosperity." But inasmuch as the people had spoken for annexation, the government should proceed in good faith toward that goal, at least until the expiration of Andrew Jackson's presidency on March 4, 1837.[13] Already, members of the Houston administration, notably Austin, were beginning to hedge on the question. "Notwithstanding the vote of the people at the September election, in favor of annexation," the Secretary wrote to Wharton in Washington, D.C., "you are aware that very many persons of influence who voted for that measure, merely yielded to the peculiar circumstances of the times, and incline strongly to the opinion, that Texas ought to remain a separate and independent Republic." Public opinion as well, in Austin's view, appeared to be shifting, and if the foreign relations of the Republic took a favorable turn – in the form of a peace treaty with Mexico and recognition by England and France – the people would probably prefer independence. "It should be borne in mind," he cautioned, "that Texas makes a great sacrifice by agreeing to the annexation at all."[14] The Father of Texas was speaking mainly for himself at this point, but he shrewdly recognized that the administration must not appear too anxious or seem too desperate if it was to have a strong bargaining position in negotiations with the American government.

By the end of 1836, miraculously, conditions had stabilized and the country showed marked signs of improvement. James F. Perry reported several noteworthy achievements of the Republic in a letter to Thomas F. Leaming of Philadelphia.

> With regard to our public affairs we are geting on verry smothly, Our Courts of Justice have been established, and all due respect is paid to our authorities, which I think speaks well of a people who have been so long from under the pale of civil authority, our little army is under good diciplin and well provided for, and every thing appears to be doing well from recent accounts. We feel no apprehension of an invasion from the Mexicans this season. Should they come we are prepared for them. Our planters are all preparing with much energy for a crop under the beleaf that we can never again be drove from our homes.[15]

No one could have predicted such a turnabout within the space of three months. The only sad note at the turn of the year was the not unexpected death of Stephen F. Austin, who had been mortally weakened by his experience in a Mexican prison two years before.

Despite the encouraging outlook, the sentiment for annexation remained strong. President Houston, an eminently practical man, entertained no grand illusions about the future of an independent Texas. "It is policy to hold out the idea (and few there are who Know the contrary) that we are very able to sustain ourselves against any power," he confided to President Jackson, "yet I am free to say *to you* that we cannot do it."[16] Houston relied on his good friend from Tennessee to use the powers of the presidency as well as his considerable personal influence to effect annexation without delay. But Jackson found himself in a delicate position. He did not wish to antagonize England and France any more than his administration already had, and he was not prepared to provoke a war with Mexico. Domestic political issues also weighed heavily on him, and not wanting to endanger the Democratic coalition formed under his aegis, he temporized. A sizeable portion of the American public wanted nothing to do with Texas, viewing the Revolution as a giant land grab on behalf of speculators and slaveholders. They also hesitated to incorporate a population bearing the shady reputation of this one. Even Southerners had their reservations, and a number of them in Washington urged Wharton to resist a connection with an oppressive federal government that would burden the new state with high tariffs and other Northern measures. For their part, Northerners objected vociferously to the addition of a slave state covering an area more than one-third the size of the existing states of the Union. All in all, annexation had a long road to travel.[17]

In March, 1837, the United States formally recognized the Republic of Texas and President Jackson, on his last day in office, appointed a minister to the new nation. The news lifted the people's spirits tremendously. "It infused new life into the bosom of every Texian," an American journalist reported from the scene, "when he was told that his country . . . had at last received the countenance of one of the independent nations of the earth." Texans suddenly displayed a burst of pride in their nationhood; whereas the anniversary of their independence on March 2 had passed almost unnoticed and unheralded, the occasion of San Jacinto Day, April 21, 1837, now gave much cause for cheering. "Texas — May her foes turn pale at her name, and may she flourish until time is no more," cried a toastmaster at the town of Liberty; "The Heroes of San Jacinto — Champions in the struggle for Liberty, they justly merit the gratitude of their Country," roared another. At Houston, the citizens displayed their patriotism with the erection of a "liberty pole" capped by a resplendent Lone Star.[18] From town to town, speakers orated before large crowds proudly waving the Texan tricolor.

But all was not joy and festivity. At Columbia, the outpost town serving temporarily as the nation's capital, President Houston and his cabinet soberly pondered the implications of recognition: what was the United States trying to tell them? Were they unwanted after all? Was recognition merely a calculated alternative to annexation? William Fairfax Gray found the administration in considerable perplexity. "Their hopes have been so highly raised of a speedy annexation to the United States," he recorded, "that they can't be at once reconciled to a new state of things presented by the recognition. Texas independent, and compelled to fight her own battles and pay her own debts, will necessarily have to impose heavy burthens on her citizens."[19]

While many citizens at first believed recognition to be the necessary stepping-stone to the still hoped-for annexation, they also marked it as a grand milestone in their long struggle for sovereignty. Ironically, this halfway measure proved a turning point in the meteoric rise of Texan nationalism. The government interpreted it not as a prelude to annexation but as a signpost of rejection. Given the strong feelings against Texas in the United States, the citizenry soon came to see it in the same light. Thus, by the summer of 1837, Texans were becoming, for the first time, psychologically prepared to carry on by themselves. "In another year we will have nothing to fear from Mexico and should the United States not think proper to annex us," wrote James F. Perry, "we will be able to go it alone."[20]

Talk of annexation did not cease at once, and some still zealously desired it, but Texans now spoke with scarcely concealed excitement of the possibility of establishing contacts with Britain, France, and other powers. Upon word of American recognition, President Houston had dispatched J. Pinckney Henderson to Europe to seek diplomatic relations and commercial agreements with London and Paris. The Texas government continued to pursue annexation through its delegation in Washington, but with its growing prestige, it seemed to regard the application of August 4, 1837 more and more perfunctorily. Whereas Secretary of State Robert A. Irion had at one point derided the "visionary schemes of a glorious Republic" as detrimental to the true interests of Texas, which he thought could best be served by annexation, at the year's end he judged that the failure of annexation "only postpones our prosperity. . . . Fresh vigor will be imparted to every arm when it is distinctly and generally understood throughout the Republic that annexation is impracticable." Fairfax Catlett, the secretary of the Texas legation in Washington, may have been carried away in a moment of euphoria, but his pride in the home government accurately reflected the felicitous mood of the country:

[Texas is] collecting her strength, developing her resources, maturing her youthful prowess, and rapidly unfolding to the gaze of many an astonished civilian the anomalous spectacle of a wilderness converted as by the stroke of some magic wand into a glorious little Republic, already renowned for her heroism and magnanimity . . . and whose statesmen are gaining an enviable reputation for moderation and wisdom, for sagacity, patriotism and liberal and enlightened views of the true objects of government.[21]

Toward the end of the year 1837, a Methodist missionary named Martin Ruter came to Texas. As he toured the country making converts and attempting to organize churches, his keen eye recorded the vast panorama before him. A short while later, Ruter was ambushed and killed by the Indians, but we are fortunate that he found time to describe to his wife at home in Indiana something of the condition of Texas in its infancy. "It is only 18 or 20 months since the Mexican army of 8000 overran a great part of this country," he wrote in December, 1837, "burning houses, killing the people, destroying furniture and provisions. The accommodations are of course very poor." He continued:

Most of the houses are cabins, without glass windows, & half of them without doors, many of them without floors, and very little furniture even of a rough kind. The chief food is corn bread, sweet potatoes, & meat — such as beef, some pork, venison, squirrels, some fowls, etc. Neither butter nor cheese, nor milk, can be often seen — milk scarcely once in a week, & butter & cheese are out of the question. . . . Add to this, the emigrants are numerous, & render most articles of provision scarce and dear. . . . Tea, such as we use is not to be found here — or very rarely. The people have coffee, sometimes good, except the want of milk. Most of the beds are made of straw laid upon boards, with a sheet, blanket, & quilt. . . . In riding over the prairies it is often necessary to travel from morning till night without dinner, & without seeing a house. . . . On some of the prairies, when near the middle, it resembles being on the ocean, the scene appears boundless. . . . Notwithstanding what I have said of the want of comforts in Texas, yet there are many who are rich. The war has caused difficulties and wants that did not before exist to half their present extent.[22]

As Texas continued to rebuild and recover from the revolutionary war, the traveler could sense a heightened degree of self-sufficiency among the people and their leaders. The feeling was growing apace that if the United States did not act — and quickly — *its* chance for annexation would be lost forever. In London, J. Pinckney Henderson attempted to lay to rest the question of annexation as he discussed the prospects of Texas with Lord Palmerston. He told the cagey British statesman that Texans "were aware that they would possess many advantages as an independent Nation, which they could not enjoy as an integral part of the United States" — freedom from sectional jealousies between North and South and a wide range of commercial advantages in determining their own tariffs and in trading with every country. At the beginning of 1838, Irion instructed Henderson that his negotiations with the European governments should be conducted "with a view to a permanent and separate existence, as an independent power." The people of Texas, he said, had lost interest in annexation and unless the United States Congress at once offered Texas admission to the Union, "the subject will be abandoned by this Government; and I am confident it will never again be renewed by this, or any future administration."[23]

77

Meanwhile, in Washington, American partisans of Texas reintroduced the annexation measure along with a stream of memorials and petitions, pro and con, from citizen groups around the country. Texas was still a warm issue in the United States, but the Texans themselves had cooled considerably. "The people of the United States, old maids of Yankee land, Abolitionists et ceteri are bawling and crying aloud against our Annexation," commented a former Pennsylvanian, David S. Kaufman, in a letter to a friend in Philadelphia, "while the people here, care, talk and think nothing about it. Indeed I feel perfectly convinced that if the Portals of Your Union were now thrown open to us, that we would refuse to enter in — I myself am most religiously opposed to it." Dr. Ashbel Smith, late of Connecticut, conveyed the same point of view. "Nothing of interest in regard to our affairs occurs to me to mention at this time," he wrote to the Texan minister in Washington, D.C. By chance, he added: "Annexation is out of the question, I am more fully convinced than ever." On the Red River frontier, General Rusk, unmindful of the supposed necessity of American arms, exhorted the militia to protect the women and children and elevate their country "to that proud Station in the Scale of nations . . . [from] which, no dangers can deter or prevent us."[24] And so it went.

What the most casual observer could recognize in Texas in the spring of 1838, its gala second anniversary, was a people touchily proud of their independence and inseparably linked to the country and its fortunes. "Texas has already astonished the world with her civil, political and military achievements," the Matagorda *Bulletin* boasted in a typical statement. "Her prowess in arms, is altogether unparalleled in the history of nations; and her unprecedented progress in civil and political government, has burst like a blazing meteor upon thousands and millions of wondering admirers."[25] While intense local feeling was a strong sentiment among Americans everywhere, in Texas it became, within a remarkably short time, an exclusive national feeling. Precious little was left of their patriotic sentiments for the United States. They were Texans. As a Britisher discovered in 1839, "the Texians are at present Americans but more in customs, manners, habits, than in feeling."[26]

Six months' residence in the Republic conferred citizenship under the Constitution of 1836, and men were quick to embrace their new status. A visitor from Germany, having arrived at Houston in 1837, stayed on four more years and found himself acquiring Texan citizenship in the process. As with so many others, the Lone Star had mysteriously magnetized him and while he traveled about the United States he continually sang the praises of Texas, much to the annoyance of the Americans he encountered. "After crossing the Rubicon [the Sabine river]," he recalled merrily of his return, "when I stood again on Texas soil, I raised a loud 'Hurrah for Texas!' . . . As an echo, the ferryman thundered over from the Louisiana bank a 'Damn your God-damned Texas! Go to hell with your lone star!' So jealous at that time were the neighbors of the fertile vergin Republic." Those from the United States generally effected a smooth transition in their change of national loyalties. Within a year of establishing residence in Texas, Elisha M. Pease could no longer return "home," as he put it, to Connecticut. "My feelings, interest, all are identified with Texas," he told his father as the new government was about to be inaugurated in 1836. "I feel that Texas is my home," he explained a few months later, "and that here I shall spend the balance of my life, with the exception of an occasional visit to the north." Another veteran of the Revolution, William B. Aldridge, likewise resolved never to leave Texas. "I feel that I am . . . living on a Soil that I have assisted in defending, reclaiming and liberating," he wrote to his sister in Virginia. "If ever we enjoy the happiness of each others Company it must be here. here alone can I pledge to befriend & Protect you if necessary." The youthful Guy M. Bryan went off to Kenyon College in Ohio in 1837 and wrote home two years later to say that although he was willing to stay "in a foreign country" to obtain his education, "still my country is uppermost in my thought – the fine undulating and level prairies, sweeping out before our extended view for miles and miles over rivers, and along the briny deep . . . [are] enough to make every true Texan heart thrill with pleasure and be anxious to add to the comfort of that country."[27]

Texans could not always easily forget that they had once been Americans, but whenever they journeyed to the United States, they knew it their duty not to compromise their Texan citizenship. Secretary of State Abner Lipscomb in 1840 reminded his minister in Washington, Barnard Bee, late of South Carolina, not to evince any interest in the heated presidential election of that year. "I know how very difficult it is for a native of the United States to separate himself entirely from their party contests, and be a mere looker on," the former Alabaman instructed, "yet it is very proper that you, as the Representative of an Independent Government, should occupy precisely that position. This is important to our maintaining that elevated rank with other nations . . . we must show them, that we cherish, an independent Texan feeling, to whatever country we may owe our birth." Indeed, Texan leaders at home and abroad preached a fervent patriotism for their adopted country, and whatever their party differences, they were united "in their strong love for Texas," as the *Democratic Review* reported, "in a devout faith in the glories of her future." As Mirabeau B. Lamar put it, "The land of my adoption must claim my highest allegiance and affection; her glory and happiness must be my paramount consideration."[28] His countrymen, from all appearances, wholeheartedly agreed.

With sentiments such as these, it is not difficult to understand why the Texan interest in annexation waned during the flushed years of nationhood. By 1838, the Texans were seeking a future of their own. They had cut the ties of emotional bondage to the United States, and in the absence of domestic turmoil had no compelling reason to seek a political attachment. "Our Congress is now in sesion arringing such Matters as are necessary for the prosperaty of the Country," Charles Chamberlain informed a friend in New York. "As yet we have no politicle partys and all Meashures are taken up for the generall wellfare of the republic." So buoyant were Texans in their expectations of national greatness that the chairman of the Foreign Relations Committee in May, 1838 could find no advantages whatsoever in annexation: neither an increase in land prices, nor protection against foreign invasion, nor defense against the Indians. Whatever the United States might possibly do for Texas, he calculated, Texas could do better for herself. Even a Texan visitor to Washington, D.C. refused to be impressed and concluded that there was "nothing extraordinary in the appearance of any of the great men of this nation. . . . I have not seen one among the whole Congress that will compare with Sam Houston and there are but few, I believe, that can make a better speech than he can, on many subjects."[29]

Among the speechmakers in Congress during this period was the venerable American statesman, John Quincy Adams. Adams probably spent much of his breath haranguing the House of Representatives in opposition to annexation during the morning hours of each day's session from June 16, 1838 to July 7. Had Congress enacted the measure before its adjournment in July, it is quite possible that the American government would have been rebuffed by Texas. But no action was taken, and without regrets, President Houston instructed his minister in Washington, Anson Jones, to withdraw the offer formally. Immediately, the word went out to Europe, where J. Pinckney Henderson was ambitiously carrying on negotiations with Britain and France. "I now have the pleasure to announce to you," Secretary Irion prefaced his remarks on the fate of annexation. "You know well the considerations which prompted the measure. Those causes operate no longer. Texas is prospering to an extent that no one could have reasonably anticipated when you left us."[30]

The presidential election of 1838 confirmed overwhelmingly the satisfaction of the people of Texas in their government's independent course. The Constitution forbade President Houston to succeed himself, but Vice-President Lamar easily won on a platform unalterably opposed to annexation. The Texas Congress also expressed the consensus of the people by casting, in October, 1838, a near unanimous vote against any further consideration of the subject. Upon contemplating the high destiny awaiting Texas, Lamar declared in his inaugural address, "I cannot regard the annexation of Texas to the American Union in any other light than as the grave of all her hopes of happiness and greatness; and if . . . the amalgamation shall ever hereafter take place, I shall feel that the blood of our matyred [sic] heroes had been shed in vain."[31]

Once the United States balked at having Texas join the Union, a perceptive Frenchman commented in 1839, "No longer were Americans to be found on the land extending from the Sabine to the Rio Grande:

people began to refer to themselves only as Texians. A nationalistic sentiment issuing from wounded pride grew with the help of continuing success. Now that it has firmly taken root in this soil, it would be difficult to eradicate.[32]

During Sam Houston's presidency, the leaders of Texas found themselves weaned away from annexation and nurturing the idea of nationhood. Now President Lamar, a dedicated nationalist, set out enthusiastically to make nationhood a reality. A man of intellectual bent and urbanity, Mirabeau Buonaparte Lamar was a romantic as flowery in style as his name would suggest. Eloquence on paper perhaps compensated for a short and stocky figure that rendered Lamar unprepossessing in person and markedly shy in his public appearances. (He had his secretary read his inaugural address, although hundreds had waited several hours through the ceremonies to hear him.) A native Georgian, Lamar had arrived in Texas in 1835 in time to take part in the Revolution. He distinguished himself in battle, rose to the rank of general, and emerged a hero at San Jacinto. Like so many others who had cast their lot with Texas, he was determined to have nothing more to do with the United States. "Let us love our country," he proclaimed from the presidential pulpit, "with a single eye to her glory and greatness."[33]

This sentiment was voiced repeatedly by other leaders during the Lamar years (1838-1841). The speaker of the house, David S. Kaufman, typically called upon his colleagues in 1839 to impart "a fresh impetus to our national energies, and elevate us in the scale of nations," and his successor in 1841, K. L. Anderson, likewise urged Congress to meet its responsibilities and "our beloved country . . . will at once stand forth, the pride and admiration of all the lovers of civil liberty."[34] The people themselves expressed a reverence for their nationhood that even amused some foreigners. "To hear a Texian talk of his country you would suppose that he lived in as civilized a place as there is on the face of the globe," the

Englishman Francis C. Sheridan remarked. "What appears so very strange is that the Texian people should labour under the delusion that they have as yet become a distinct people & one of the nations of the earth, when after all they form but a little Nucleus & a very indifferent one from wh[ich] an independent power can be formed."[35]

Doubters there were, but domestic developments, despite mounting financial difficulties, augured well for the future. The international setting also showed promise; no one doubted that Texas could defend herself against Mexico, and with annexation a dead letter by 1839, diplomatic relations with the European nations were imminent. Already, a trade agreement had been signed with Great Britain, and others were in the making. The "young empire," predicted a visitor from the United States in 1840, "is destined to become a power to be respected among the mighty ones of the earth." Other foreign observers concurred in what appeared to be a common opinion.

Since the battle of San Jacinto, Texas has organized a complete and practical system of laws and government, together with all the elements of agricultural and commercial prosperity; her population has increased with a rapidity which is unexampled; and she stands conspicuous, not only as the smallest community ever formally recognized by the great powers, but as presenting, in her internal progress, the most remarkable monument of human energy and industry perhaps ever raised in the same short period.[36]

Nevertheless the Texan people remained prisoners of their unhappy reputation. It was mainly in the political sphere that their spokesmen thought the country might still redeem itself in the eyes of its detractors. Editors and concerned citizens warned repeatedly against the election of individuals who, by their sullied characters or manifest incompetence, would discredit the nation. Texas, too, they insisted, had its aristocracy of talent, and the election of such men to office would help erase the black marks of the past.[37] Foreign visitors often attended a session of Congress, where the groundwork of their impressions was laid. Some, of course, saw the members as nothing other than "adventurers, sharpers, and . . . black-legs," but the more open-minded were willing to concede their virtues: "Although they have no Clays, Websters, Crittendens, or Calhouns," the American minister to Austin attested, "yet take them as a body and I believe for their number they are equal to any legislative body in the United States. . . ."[38]

The country's press took the lead in exhorting the electorate to choose men of demonstrated integrity and ability for public office. "If we are at home but true to ourselves, and elect to our public offices men worthy of commanding respect abroad," sermonized the *Telegraph and*

Texas Register, "we may rest assured that a high and glorious destiny awaits us." The paper acknowledged that apathy had already permitted the election of "the most worthless, drunken vagrants; even horse-thieves and marauders" to positions of responsibility and honor. The indifferent voters responsible for this were themselves "little better than criminals. . . . " Similarly, at the outset of the congressional races in 1840, the *Brazos Courier* regretted that "the reputation of our public servants, has not always been such as to do honor to our national character." The denouement this time was more pleasing. At the conclusion of the canvass three months later, the paper applauded the absence of violence and the respectable manner in which the election was conducted. This performance gave "evidence of the intelligence of our electors, and a signal rebuke to those slanderers, who delight to hold up our country to the eyes of foreigners, as the scene of anarchy and corruption."[39]

Texans understandably resented the prevailing assumption that "the inhabitants of this country [are] a set of semi-savages, unmannered, illiterate and entirely unacquainted with the ways of the more civilized."[40] Their successes in nation-building had already refuted the more damning popular notions. But they were forced to labor under a sentence of moral and intellectual inferiority to Europe and to the settled portions of America. They could not help feeling suspicious toward outlanders and holding to a belief that much of the world was in league against them to disparage their reputation and retard their progress. Spokesmen for good government, it must be admitted, seemed more concerned about the image Texas projected than about the object itself. Let us "proclaim to the world," urged an orator on the fifth anniversary of Texas independence, "the justice of our cause . . . and may the rude points of our national character gradually and forever disappear, and truth, intelligence and order . . . preside over our deliberations."[41] Texans were sensitized to the subject of "national character," and for good reason. They could not escape it — nor did they wish to.

The makers of Texas had a fertile ground in which to plant the seeds of nationalism. There was a revolutionary tradition to call upon, replete with heroics, and a period of independence marked by almost uninterrupted progress. One hallmark of nationalism is said to be a collective celebration of national symbols. Such was the reverence with which Texans treated their Lone Star. Beginning in March, 1836, when the Washington-on-Brazos Convention adopted George Childress's resolution that "a single star of five points . . . [be] the peculiar emblem of this republic: & that every officer & soldier of the army and members of this convention, and all friends of Texas, be requested to wear it on their hats or bosoms,"[42] the nation of Texas bore a symbol that her people would forever venerate. The Lone Star became the theme of practically every patriotic utterance; never could Texans speak of their country's destiny without allusion to the gleaming single star pointing the way. In a typical instance, when Santa Anna in 1843 presumptuously offered Texas a return to the Mexican Republic with guarantees of statehood and internal autonomy, the Clarksville *Northern Standard* all but wrapped itself in the folds of the Lone Star banner and issued a stinging rebuke:

> The white, red and green flag, of 1824, has floated over our head, but we could not consent to withdraw the single star from the galaxy of nations, or in any degree dim her effulgence by the protective embrace, and allegiance of any other emblem . . . No! Our banner is reared upon the field of many a hot little fight, it has cheered on the spirits of men who do not exchange their fealty lightly and frequently; and so long as one ray of its light gleams upon the eyes and warms the heart of the patriot, it must float upon the breeze as our banner, for which we will have no other.[43]

Texans also gloried in the very name – "Texian" – their nationality conferred upon them. "Texian" was the appellation attached to the first settlers of the 1820s and it was steadfastly maintained during the Revolution to reinforce the people's identity with Texas. President Lamar fastidiously used the term "Texian" to engender a feeling of national character, and it was retained for the remainder of the Republic's existence.[44] Thus, when William Kennedy, a British chargé in Texas, published his highly touted two-volume *History of Texas* in 1841, employing the term "Texan" throughout, Texian reviewers objected strenuously. As one explained:

> It is an indubitable fact that the inhabitants of Texas, literate and illiterate, have almost universally adopted the term *Texian* to define their political individuality, and we are not apprised of any rule of language that is violated in doing so. . . . We believe every man has originally the right to determine the orthography, and, if you please, the *rhythm* of his own proper name; and certainly communities are equally privileged. We fancy that *Texian* . . . has more of euphony, and is better adapted to the convenience of poets who shall hereafter celebrate our deeds in sonorous strains, than the harsh, abrupt, ungainly appellation, *Texan* – impossible in rhyme to anything but the merest doggerel.[45]

One scholar of nationalism comments that nationalist leaders can be expected to "contrive a synthetic culture" for their country, and thus the historian must take great care in distinguishing between a genuine and a "trumped-up nationalism generating the pretense or illusion of a culture."[46] It is true that Texan leaders hammered away at the theme of national greatness. They took pains to touch the springs of nationalist sentiment and they assiduously encouraged the inculcation of values and ideas founded in "Texan culture." But this conscious endeavor does not gainsay or render artificial that nationalism. The very effort to promote nationalism is itself an expression of nationalism. To view nationalism properly, we must see it as a process, not a final product answering a checklist of criteria.

Take, for example, two expressions of Texan educational policy. In one, the Philosophical Society of Texas, founded in 1837, states in its preamble the obligation of all patriotic citizens to indoctrinate their children in the principles of "Texian liberty" and instruct them in a "respect for their country's laws, love of her soil, and veneration for her institutions." In another, President Lamar envisions the Spartan spirit of the young Republic ripening into "Roman firmness, and Athenian gracefulness and wisdom," if Congress would provide for a public school system and a national university. The failure to establish public education, he admonishes, could force young Texans to seek a foreign education that might prejudice them against the institutions of their own country. They should all be educated at home, he advises, and "their education should be a *national one.*"[47] Texan culture, at this early period of the nation's history, did require some nourishing, but such sentiments were heartfelt and should be recognized as true manifestations of nationalism.[48] In no other light can we consider the gesture of a Texan official, Washington D. Miller, in sending to Senator Robert J. Walker of Mississippi a specimen chip from the walls of the Alamo — "that sacred Altar of Texian Freedom," as he stated in his accompanying note. "You will, therefore, please accept it from the hand of a citizen of Texas, whose heart . . . has always recognized in you a warm and efficient friend of his country."[49]

Nationalism is also expressed in a shared pride in the recollection of national experiences, as when the people turned out in great, exuberant throngs for the annual celebrations of their Independence Day and San Jacinto Day. No compulsions were needed to make them listen to the countless orations of those occasions. "With this day will thousands congregate with joyful emotions, to celebrate the birth-day of liberty, in liberty's new home," proclaimed a speaker at Houston on March 2, 1841. "Fellow-citizens," he exhorted, "may this day on each returning year find us in gratitude and thanksgiving. . . . May our daughters desire no other land, our sons no other home."[50] The sons and daughters in their jubilation seem to have needed little prompting. "There is incessant talk of the single-starred banner — the glorious 2nd of March & banquets are given to distinguished citizens, who in return make distinguished speeches," a British visitor observed. *"March 2nd, 1842,"* chronicled another Englishman. "This is one of the great days in Texas — the anniversary of its Independence — the 4th of July of these parts."[51] Everywhere in the land, it was the time for rejoicing.

Heavy *preparations* are being made to *keep fast* on the Second of March! [an Austinite reported]. Eggs are in demand!! It is said that they are to be *drunk — not* eaten!!! It seems also . . . that the fast is to continue *only* during the day and not the night!!!! Hence the *night* is to be appropriated to *feasting* as the day was to fasting. So you perceive the good people hereabouts are determined to have Thanksgiving as well as fast day.[52]

San Jacinto Day offered yet another occasion for fireworks, cannon fire, speeches, parades, barbecues, banquets, and balls. Frederic Gaillardet, visiting Texas in 1839, climbed aboard a steamboat leaving Houston on April 21 for the nearby San Jacinto battlefield. He wanted to see the excitement for himself:

It was midnight when the steamboat reached the plain known to the Texians as the Battleground. . . . No sooner had we arrived at this scene of recent glory and importance for Texians than the passengers, who filled the steamer to capacity, broke forth into frenzied shouting, mingled with artillery fire and military band music. It was a curious spectacle to witness, this really terrifying explosion of patriotic enthusiasm! . . . Soon we went ashore, and the patriotic throng, armed with resin torches, formed a fiery frame around the field. There the famous patriotic song "Yankee Doodle" was sung, and the ceremony concluded with three cheers, shouted in not inharmonious chorus by the exultant crowd, who, with this triple adieu, honored the memory of their heroes who had died for their country.[53]

The heroics of the Revolution offered an expansive theme for patriotic outpourings. In a flourishing tribute to the men who had fought at San Jacinto, David G. Burnet characterized the battle as "a triumph not only of arms, but of soul: not of mere animal power, but of intellectual and moral impulse." Gathering up his own powers, the orator outdid himself. "It was feeling, determination, and indomitable resolution to conquer, that achieved the conquest. Such feelings are the highest possible exemplification of patriotism." And what full-blooded Texian, what citizen of the Republic, could enter the sacred tomb of the Alamo and not stand in silent awe or shed a reverential tear? So believed Colonel Edward Burleson, another indomitable hero of the Revolution as he spoke before that edifice in 1842:

Citizens, the feeling inspired by events, within these consecrated walls, of so recent date, fills my bosom with emotions that it would be in vain to attempt utterance. This sacred spot, and these crumbling remains — the desecrated temple of Texian liberty, will teach a lesson which freeman [sic] can never forget; and while we mourn the unhappy fate of Travis, Crockett, Bowie, and their brave compatriots, let it be the boast of Texians, that though Thermopylae had her messenger of defeat, the Alamo had none.[54]

Thus, the lore accumulated and Texans learned to recite endlessly the interminable verses composed to immortalize those deeds. Contemporaneously, the development of nationalism proceeded in the United States, and Henry Steele Commager has noted "the speed and the lavishness with which Americans provided themselves with a usable past: history, legends, symbols, paintings, sculpture, monuments, shrines, holy days, ballads, patriotic songs, heroes, and — with some difficulty — villains." Indeed, the very same could already be said for the Texans. "Huzza! nevermore will our Lone Star surrender," they chorused triumphantly in the "Texan Song of Liberty," "While a true Texan heart is left to defend her."[55] Such is the stuff of nationalism, and in such a spirit the Republic of Texas entered the ranks of nations.

CHAPTER FIVE

Nationalist Strivings of the Texas Republic

"If the internal experience of a community generates its characteristic ideas and culture," posits Max Savelle in *Seeds of Liberty*, "it is its external experience that develops its self-consciousness."[1] Nothing contributed more to Texan self-consciousness than the foreign relations of the Republic. An ambitious and bumptious new country, Texas engaged in a quest for glory (almost acting out a chivalrous role) and unleashed its aggressive impulses against both Mexico and the United States. The attention lavished upon the young nation by its neighbors and by European powers understandably amplified its sense of self-importance. Rejected but later wooed by the United States, cursed by Mexico, flirted with by France, embraced by Great Britain, Texas cut a dashing figure in international society. Although inherent weaknesses eventually brought its downfall as an independent state, the pride of its people was not diminished. Texas nationalism would long survive the days of the Republic.

Following the battle of San Jacinto in 1836, the Mexican chieftain, Santa Anna, bargained for his release as a prisoner of war by signing the Treaty of Velasco, providing for the cessation of hostilities and the withdrawal of all Mexican forces beyond the Rio Grande. The dictator promised that he would never again take up arms against Texas and would secure from the Mexican Congress acknowledgment of Texas independence. Within days of the May, 1836 signing, the government in Mexico City repudiated Santa Anna's treaty and refused to recognize Texas as a sovereign state. Peace would never prevail, the Mexicans vowed, until rebel Texas returned volitionally to the fold; otherwise, the government would undertake a war of reconquest. Thus, the stage was set, at the commencement of Texan nationhood, for an era of hostilities that would not be officially terminated until the Treaty of Guadalupe Hidalgo in 1848.

Perhaps as an act of defiance, the First Congress in December, 1836, established by fiat the limits of Texas to include the territory of neighboring Mexican states north and east of the Rio Grande. As a province of Mexico, Texas had always been bounded to the south by the Nueces River and to the west by the Pecos. By claiming as the new boundary the Rio Grande from its mouth at the Gulf to its source in the Rockies, and thence northward to the 42nd parallel, the founders of the Republic obliterated Mexican territorial rights and brought into their jurisdiction more than 240,000,000 acres (or 379,054 square miles) — land extending to portions of the present-day states of New Mexico, Colorado, Kansas, and Wyoming. Such extravagant claims outraged the Mexicans, made diplomatic recognition unthinkable, then and forever, and precipitated a war with the United States following the annexation of Texas in 1845. (See map 2, p. 46)

The Texans, far from reconsidering their unilateral act, swelled with pride in their new-found size, and henceforth looked upon their spacious country with imperial delight. The very vastness of Texas — the seemingly limitless space — animated the Texan people, informed their humor, and gave them an inflated sense of power. "From the Sabine river on the east to the mountains around El Paso," writes John Q. Anderson, "there was a type of terrain to please every taste: hardwood-covered bottom land, small prairies ringed with oak, blackland prairies embracing thousands of acres, cedar brakes along the upper reaches of the rivers, vast tablelands of the High Plains, rocky waterless semi-deserts, and vast purple-shadowed mesas." Although the appropriated area was largely devoid of settlement and quite beyond the resources of the nation even to explore, much less retain in its entirety, "Such pretensions," comments Donald W. Meinig, "gave an important impetus to the persistent Texan dream of empire." By 1840, a Britisher could cite the limits of Texas, not supposing there might be another version of them, with the description: "On the Texian side of the Rio Grande are numerous towns and villages, the most important of which are Santa Fe, Taos, Albuquerque, and Laredo."[2]

Except towards Mexico, the Texans upon their entrance into the international community followed strict protocol in their relations with other countries. Diplomatic recognition and, concomitantly, most-favored-nation status in commercial intercourse, were the paramount objectives. These goals were accompanied by a persistent desire to establish the good reputation or "national character" of Texas in the family of nations. "It is proper for our diplomatic representatives," Secretary of State Robert A.

Irion instructed in 1837, "to observe a modest, prudent, yet firm course; being always careful not to afford grounds of offence to the Governments to which they are accredited." Texas must earn the respect and confidence of other governments and her diplomats should "be always ready to cooperate with the known friends of our cause, and act cordially with them in the promotion of measures calculated to advance our interest."[3] The sense of nationhood was present almost from the beginning and the outlook of the Republic's "foreign ministry" pointed to a long career as a nation.

Ever mindful of international opinion (the Texans fancied the whole world was watching them), Texan leaders sought to portray the nation as benevolent and peace-loving, yet never afraid to resort to the sword when challenged. President Houston's decision to ship Santa Anna out of the country alive and allow him to return to Mexico was in part geared to American and world opinion, and indeed, the move "redounded greatly to our character," as William H. Wharton reported from Washington, D.C. late in 1836. "Texas stands mountain high here for heroism and magnanimity and our enemies as low as can possibly be imagined."[4] Her spokesmen, however, would engage in no fawning or flattery (having bled too much), and would take an unswerving stand when the honor of Texas demanded it. Secretary of State Austin informed Senator Thomas Hart Benton in November, 1836, that Texas had won rights that would have to be recognized in any annexation settlement. "We took up arms against Mexico to secure the right of self Govt. We consider that we have secured that right, and consequently expect to retain it as a state when annexed to the U.S." In Washington, Wharton exploded with indignation when told by President Jackson that Santa Anna would accept a price for Texas paid by the United States and would relinquish all claims, thereby facilitating Texas annexation. Wharton replied that the United States government had no business discussing the sale of Texas with anyone, that the country belonged to the people of Texas, and that "It was truly humiliating to us to consent to be even nominally sold, after we had won the country by privations, sufferings, dangers and triumphs . . . unsurpassed in the history of man."[5]

As Texas steered away from annexation to the United States, her confident posture vis-a-vis Mexico and persistent diplomacy in the leading courts of Europe won for her diplomatic recognition from France in 1839, Britain and the Netherlands in 1840, and Belgium in 1841. The United States had been the first to confer recognition in 1837. Commercial treaties were also concluded with England, France, and the Netherlands. But diplomatic success with Europe and the United States was always tempered by the omnipresent Mexican menace. Mexico was determined to reclaim Texas and, if necessary, drive the Anglos into the sea. Constantly the two governments threatened each other with invasion; twice each actually made such an attempt. For both nations, a border enemy heightened the chauvinism often displayed by struggling young countries.

Rumors of invasion for most of the era of Texan nationhood kept the citizens in a state of perpetual tension. Between 1836 and 1842, repeated alarms were sounded of Mexican preparations for war or of actual marching columns approaching the Rio Grande. "War, in all the strength of the word, is still subsisting between Texas and Mexico," a Mexican leader declared, "just as it was at the time of the capture of . . . the Alamo."[6] Paramilitary agents from Mexico were discovered trying to stir the Indian tribes in Texas into rebellion. One such collaborative effort, the Cordova-Flores episode, had been afoot for two years before the polyglot force of Indians, Mexicans, and blacks was splintered and punished by General Rusk's militia brigade in 1838. A year later the Mexican minister of war submitted a plan for the reconquest of Texas. Mexican troops were to encroach upon the western settlements of Texas in small detachments and rendezvous on the Brazos until their combined forces numbered 8,000 or more. Their assignment, according to John M. Nance, was to conduct "a war of extermination, giving no quarter, destroying all houses, and pursuing a policy of universal pillage." The Texans waited expectantly but nothing happened. Again, in 1840, Texan Secretary of War Branch T. Archer learned that General Mariano Arista had crossed the Rio Grande and was fast approaching San Patricio. This intelligence, which proved false, prompted Archer to call for volunteers to defend the homeland. "It is the duty of every good citizen to aid in driving the insolent intruder back to his own domain." Talk of an invasion continued to build. At the close of 1840, Colonel John N. Seguin informed President Lamar of a contemplated naval and land war involving some 15,000 men. "The campaign against Texas is most certain and I am sure we shall be attacked very soon," he warned after his return from Mier. "I have never witnessed such enthusiasm as that which exists amongst all classes of Mexicans against Texas." Identical information was conveyed to the government by a source in Matamoros. Early in 1841, urgent word was again heard from an informant near the border. "Genl. Arista is on this side of the Rio Grande, with four or five thousand men, and contemplates an attack immediately. I hope to see the Govt. act without delay, and not suffer the whole frontier to fall a victim to the Mexican Guillotine. . . ."[7]

The war of nerves intensified the Texan animus against the Espano-Indian race. Expressions of contempt reached a crescendo during the years of the Republic. That the Mexican could not be trusted was the common presumption. He had no sense of honor; he was lowly and mean; he despised you (so the Texans thought) and would plunge a knife into your back. So would the Mexican government subvert or despoil Texas by any means at hand, without regard for the lives of helpless women and children. Had this not been demonstrated by Santa Anna's army in the Runaway Scrape? Former president David G. Burnet knew (at least in retrospect) as he signed the abortive Treaty of Velasco with Santa Anna "that the general faithlessness of the Mexican character would present some formidable obstacles to the completion of the treaty." Deceit was a distinguishing trait in the Mexican, agreed an American visitor; thus, "It creates no surprise when he forfeits his honor or violates his pledges." Memories of Mexico's bloody treachery in the Revolution were regularly revived with the likes of J. M. Parmenter's "Texas Hymn" (1838):

> Our foe the lonely covert seeks, unseen to strike the blow,
> He loves defenseless murder, and tears of grief and woe;
> He burns our homes and temples for his infernal glee,
> But o'er their smoking ruins we'll fight for liberty.

> We'll never trust his honor, assassin he is bred.
> Brave Fannin and his warriors thus found a gory bed.
> And Travis with his heroes on San Antonio height,
> Before the foeman legions fell in unequal fight.[8]

When the Mexican government on several occasions invited Texas to return to the protective embrace of the mother country, Texans recoiled from the idea with elaborate horror: "Water and fire would sooner amalgamate than the two nations join hands," one newspaper scoffed. "No — if Mexico ever is united to this country, it will be as the conquered province of a mighty empire." As another paper put it, "A union with Mexico, would be a union between freemen and slaves . . . the union of intelligence and ignorance . . . of vigorous youth with decrepitude and disease . . . There could be no unity; no similarity; no fellow feeling. All would be jarring, opposing, and disgusting."[9] Mexico, rather, should bow to Texan superiority — or be annihilated. "Are there not freemen enough in Texas, to rise and at once crush the abject race," demanded the *Telegraph and Texas Register*, "whom, like the musquetoe, it is easier to kill, than to endure its annoying buzz?" Friends of General Sam Houston, the conquering hero, prodded him to fulfill the destiny of the Anglo-Saxon race and bring enlightenment, liberty, and true religion to the benighted inhabitants of Mexico. Such a crusade for civilization was, in their view, the historic mission of Texas.[10]

The infant Republic, like many an emerging nation, fixed upon a neighbor enemy to insure solidarity and patriotism at home. The people must be ready to defend their land and maintain independence. This objective was often interpreted to require *offensive* operations (preemptive strikes) meant to humble the Mexicans and whip them into an acknowledgment of Texan nationhood. As early as January, 1836, before Texas independence was even in sight, Stephen F. Austin spoke of the possibility of taking the revolutionary war into the heart of Mexico. By summer, with independence then a reality, the commander of the Texas Army, Thomas J. Rusk, predicted that the war would carry the Republic's boundaries far beyond the Rio Grande. The splendid territory thus conquered, he said, "will be a great acquisition to the Country and will make Texas capable of sustaining such a population as to ensure at no very distant day an efficient & good Government & make her one of the richest Countrys on earth." Hardly was the First Congress seated before more voices were heard advocating offensive war, and from Washington, D.C., William H. Wharton urged an immediate invasion to punish civilians as well as mercenaries, "and make them in turn experience the ravages and calamities which they once so cruelly inflicted upon us."[11]

The imperial ambitions of Texas were not easily disguised. Early in 1837, plans for an invasion of Mexico by way of Matamoros emerged in the nation's military councils. Although President Houston opposed provocative acts, believing that independence could best be insured by an alert defense, his general-in-chief, Felix Huston, had other notions. General Huston dreamed of marching a conquering army to the Halls of Montezuma. A tall, blond, blue-eyed cavalier, hot-headed and impetuous, Huston aroused the passions of his troops by vividly picturing the tropical delights of the land beyond the Rio Grande. Restlessly he paced and demanded to know why brave men should be kept in idleness. Huston's menacing flourishes, toward not only Mexico but also the Texan government sitting in Columbia, prompted President Houston to remove him from command. But his successor, General Albert Sidney Johnston, also wanted to launch offensive war, as did other militarists, such as Hugh McLeod and William Fisher. The rank and file were similarly disposed, and the citizenry, according to the New Orleans *True American,* strongly favored a bold stroke such as the capture of Matamoros: "Nothing would be more popular than to carry the war into the enemy's lines."[12]

Hyperbolic dreams of empire emanated from all levels of the society.[13] The nation's press led the charge, bellowing with unseemly bellicosity. "Texas will be prepared for them whenever they may wish to show their cowardly faces on the east bank [of the Rio Grande]," the *Telegraph and Texas Register* exclaimed. Should Mexico refuse to make peace with Texas, the army of the Republic will plant its banner west of the Rio Grande and march onward and onward "till the roar of the Texian rifles, shall mingle in unison with the thunders of the Pacific."[14] The irresolvable problem of securing the declared borders and wresting recognition from Mexico led government officials to consider even greater accessions of territory. If Texas was to enjoy sovereignty, Secretary of State Irion asserted, her limits should inevitably "embrace the shores of the Pacific as well as those of the Gulf of Mexico." His minister to the United States, Memecun Hunt, was asked by Secretary of State John Forsyth in 1838 how far west Texas contemplated running its boundary. "I unhesitatingly replied," Hunt wrote, "as far as the Pacific Ocean." The American government appeared anxious to procure the Bay of San Francisco, he reported, and would attempt to make Texas relinquish any claims to the Californias. Texas must guard against this: "As a separated Power, the splendid harbours on the South Sea or Pacific Ocean, will be indispensable for us; and apart from the great increase of territory by an extension of the line, the possession of the harbour of St. [sic] Francisco alone, is amply sufficient."[15]

Texas now appeared as a rival to the United States in the quest for possession of the American continent. Both countries talked about the disposal of Mexico's territory as though it had already been alienated. In addition to establishing a "window on the Pacific," American spokesmen were already unfolding designs on the Oregon Country and even the whole of Canada. "This bravado," remarked a disdainful British agent in Texas, "is quite in the Anglo-Saxon-American style." Little wonder that Edward Everett Hale, looking over his shoulder at the oncoming Lone Star, urged New Englanders to "Conquer Texas before it Conquers Us."[16]

The accession of Mirabeau B. Lamar to the presidency in December, 1838, gave Texas a chief executive in full sympathy with the expansionist mood of the country. Running on a platform of national independence and aggrandizement, Lamar promised to pursue an aggressive policy toward Mexico and make Texas an imperial power. On this issue he parted company with Sam Houston and opened the way for intense factionalism in Texas politics. As with the first new nation under George Washington, foreign policy put enormous strains on national unity. Partisans of Houston and Lamar were to become as bitterly antagonistic as the followers of Hamilton and Jefferson in the 1790s. Each faction saw itself responsible for laying the foundations of what would someday be a great nation. Where a fathering role was at stake, emotions soared. Houston believed in strict economy, a merciful policy toward the Indians, and forebearance in foreign affairs. Lamar took no account of treasury receipts, insisted on evicting or exterminating the tribes, and relished the prospect of competition with the United States. Houston was not permitted by law to succeed himself and the Houston candidates (two of whom removed themselves by suicide) could not withstand the popular urge for expansion. "The people should elect a chief whose heart beats for the national glory, whose mind foresees the high renown to which Texas can attain," a Brazoria paper trumpeted in announcing for Lamar, "whose arm is ready to second the decree of Destiny, that the name of Mexico shall be blotted out from the nations of the earth." Elisha M. Pease, an aspiring young lawyer, optimistically predicted that with the election of Lamar, the war of words would cease and active operations against Mexico might begin. "If peace can be obtained only by the sword," Lamar promptly proclaimed to Congress upon taking office, "let the sword do its work."[17] This would be the keynote of his administration.

Among Lamar's first official acts, conceived to enhance national power and prestige, was the appointment of commissioners to locate a new capital site on the edge of the western Indian frontier. If Texas was to make good its claim to New Mexico, much less lay claim to California, her capital city should be clearly identified with the West. (Perhaps Lamar seethed inwardly at the thought of Sam Houston's namesake town serving as the base of empire.) The commissioners surveyed the country north of San Antonio and settled upon a location on the Colorado river nestled in undulating hills. Known as "Waterloo," the site was renamed in honor of the late Father of Texas, Stephen F. Austin. The large mound or capitol hill at the north end of what would be called Congress Avenue afforded a splendid panorama that gave one a sense of the Lone Star Republic's vastness. "The citizens bosom must swell with honest pride when standing in the Portico of the capitol of his Country he looks upon a region worthy only of being the home of the brave and the free," the commissioners declared. "Can a feeling of Nationality fail to arise in his bosom or could the fire of patriotism lie dormant under such circumstances?"[18]

Indeed, Austin offered impressive possibilities as the hub of a future empire, but for the present, the selection only displayed the remarkable daring of the makers of Texas. The were willing to create from the ground up a new government city situated in an utter wilderness infested with hostile Comanches. All the functionaries of government would be brought some two hundred miles by wagonloads from Houston; the government archives would be hauled by muletrain to be rehoused in a freshly-boarded shack; members of Congress would travel great distances on horseback to attend the annual sessions; and the President and his cabinet would establish permanent residence in a crude frontier community. All for a greater Texas! Congress was almost unanimous in its approval of Austin, and one speaker, John W. Harris of Brazoria, called the location "highly important in a national point of view." If the government itself stood in the vanguard of the western movement, the settlers soon would follow. Austin would require a strong defense against the Indians, but that could simultaneously give protection to the scattered frontier families. Most important, the time would not be distant when the Lone Star flag would "wave in security, and triumph over the utmost borders of Texas."[19]

Foreigners were impressed. Some marveled at the boldness of the Texans in exposing the government seat to both Indian and Mexican intruders while mustering their forces in an attempt to drive their enemies entirely away from the settled portions of the country. "This policy smacks of the ancient Romans," thought one Frenchman. "It is undeniable that the government, to do this, possesses both wisdom and courage to a high degree."[20]

Meanwhile, the Mexicans, apart from a few feints and jabs at the Texas border, were battling among themselves during 1839 and 1840 in the "Federalist Wars." The Federalists were now fighting the cause that Texas had enlisted in four years before, and in Yucatan and the northern states bordering the Rio Grande, they sought to break away from Mexico City and set up an independent confederation. The Texans were understandably sympathetic to Federalist aims and hoped for the disintegration of the Mexican Republic. Several hundred militants volunteered their services on the Federalist side but the Texas government maintained an official neutrality.

Lamar's policy toward Mexico was surprisingly temperate, involving several diplomatic initiatives. As a means of settling the border issue short of bloody conflict, he considered purchasing from Mexico the disputed area between the Nueces and the Rio Grande. Richard G. Dunlap, the Texan minister to the United States, advised Lamar that Mexico, if offered a price, might consent to draw the boundary as far as the Pacific to include California. "This may seem too grasping," he admitted, "but if we can get it ought we not to take it and pay for it? Texas is *the* rising sun of the day."[21] Intrigued by such a possibility, Lamar sent Secretary of State Barnard Bee to Mexico in July, 1839 with the authority to offer the Mexican government as much as $5,000,000 (to be procured by a foreign loan) in exchange for Mexican recognition of Texan independence and the entire Rio Grande boundary. But representatives of the Lone Star were not yet being received in Mexico City, and Bee's ill-timed venture never got beyond his landing at Vera Cruz. The Centralists were trying to hold the country together and could not hope to remain in power by consenting to its dismemberment. They insisted on the fiction that Texas was still a part of the Mexican Republic.

The Mexican government consistently spurned Lamar's diplomatic overtures and the administration, in turn, became fired with resentment.

"Texas is sincerely desirous of peace, but that desire does not result from any apprehension of her ability to prosecute a vigorous and successful war," Vice-President Burnet told James Treat, a confidential agent sent to Mexico later in 1839. Burnet made no secret of his desire to unsheath the sword, believing that war would cost Texas less in treasure than diplomacy and that "the incidental expenditure of blood will be richly compensated in her acquisitions of glory." Nearly a year later, Secretary of State Abner Lipscomb reiterated his country's readiness to wage offensive war in the face of Mexican intransigence. "Our forbearance is nearly exhausted," he told James Treat, still assigned the improbable task of treating with Mexico, "and the patience of the people will not much longer submit to procrastination."[22] When Treat's tortuous negotiations for a settlement failed to produce anything, President Lamar finally recommended to Congress, in December, 1840, a declaration of war. Following this dramatic pronouncement, the product of months of exasperation, Lamar took to his sickbed and David G. Burnet took over as acting chief.

The pugnacious little judge was nobody's mouthpiece. He seized the opportunity to impress upon Congress his personal conviction that the country had slumbered too long and the time for decisive and manly action had come.

We have sought reconciliation through pacific overtures. . . . Our overtures have been rejected — our punctilious observance of all the rules of national faith and of humanity, have been condemned — and another invasion of our soil is threatened. Be it so — it is better now than here-after — for if the sword must decide the controversy, let the decision be prompt and final. . . . Texas proper, as defined by the sword, may comprehend the Sierra del Madre. Let the sword do its proper work.[23]

As one sober editor had earlier cautioned, in discussing the possibilities of an offensive, "we are too poor now to attempt it."[24] Lamar's expenditures for wars against the Cherokees in 1839 and the Comanches in 1840, added to huge appropriations for the army, had greatly exceeded the trickle of revenues from import duties and a foreign loan for any purpose did not seem to be in the offing. While Houston had carefully nursed the country's meager funds, Lamar indulged in a spending spree that was prostrating the national treasury. Extravagance came naturally to this impatient executive and his country was now paying (or trying to pay) the price. How could offensive war be prosecuted without money? Certainly Burnet should have known better. Even more surprisingly, a joint committee of Congress instantly returned an assenting report to the President's war message. Four years of cold war had depressed the people's spirits. "The injury to our interests which this state of things has produced is only surpassed by the indignity which it offers to our national honor." In January, 1841, the joint committee and a select war committee, still panting with war fever and still somehow oblivious to the nation's finances, again urged that the saber be drawn. The present "temporising and conciliatory policy," they charged, had cost Texas the respect of other countries.[25] But the rapidly depreciating redbacks and the government's depleted treasury at last persuaded a majority of Congress that a call to arms was folly. In fact, the debts of the Republic had by this time mounted so high that the House, as an economy measure, declined in the spring of 1841 to make its annual appropriation for the Army of the Republic. President Lamar sorrowfully followed the course then dictated by ordering total disbandment of the regulars. Henceforth, the Executive would have to rely entirely upon patriotic appeals to the citizen soldiers.

The great misadventure of the Lamar years, a fitting capstone to his frustrated ambitions for Texas, was the Santa Fe Expedition of 1841. A paper claim to New Mexico was one thing, but effective control over the territory and its inhabitants was quite another, and as early as 1839, Lamar's covetous eye had fallen on the commerce of the Santa Fe traders:

From their proximity to some of the most valuable mines in Mexico, they are known to be rich in the precious metals; and heretofore that wealth has found its outlet principally through the United States of the North . . . That this commerce may, by adopting the necessary and proper measures, be changed into its legitimate channels, and brought to our own doors and seaports there can be no doubt.[26]

In the spring of 1840 he warmly addressed his westernmost subjects, the people of New Mexico.

The great River of the North [Rio Grande] which you inhabit, is the natural and convenient boundary of our territory, and we shall take great pleasure in hailing you as fellow-citizens, members of our young Republic, and co-aspirants with us for all the glory of establishing a new, and happy, and free nation.[27]

A year later, disappointed in his Mexican policy and frustrated by monetary constraints, Lamar noticeably hardened in his attitude toward the New Mexicans. Like so many of his American contemporaries in this age of Manifest Destiny, he made a mockery of the principles of 1776 as well as those of 1836.

Although residing within our established limits, you are at present paying tribute to our enemies, professing allegiance to them, and receiving laws from their hands — a state of things utterly incompatible with our right of sovereignty. Constituting, as you do, a portion of the civilized population of this Republic, you cannot . . . be allowed to exist as a separate and independent people, but must be finally compelled to unite with us under the same Constitution and laws, and share our destiny as an undivided nation.[28]

Always an important consideration was national prestige, and Santa Fe should be made indisputably a part of Texas. Particularly attractive at this time, when the government faced financial collapse, was the trade between Missouri and New Mexico along the famed Santa Fe Trail. If Texas could possess the New Mexico territory, the slow-paced caravans laden with precious metals and furs would have to pass through Texan custom houses. Control of that traffic would yield Texas some sorely needed specie and bolster its sagging economy; it would give Texas a commanding position in the interior of the American continent and prepare the way for its anticipated leap to the Pacific. Subjugation of California, the consummation of Lamar's imperial designs, would give Texas the incomparable commercial advantage of a frontage on two oceans.

Lamar wanted to send a large expeditionary force into New Mexico to carry out this scheme, but Congress frowned upon what many considered a quixotic venture in view of the country's distressed economy. Not to be thwarted again, the President proceeded to recruit volunteers on his own responsibility. His assembled party of more than three hundred armed men consisted of adventurers, health seekers, merchants, and teamsters (it was common for Westerners to double as soldiers) under the command of a former Texan army officer, Colonel Hugh McLeod. Four commissioners represented the government with instructions to establish its jurisdiction over New Mexico and persuade the inhabitants of the incomparable benefits of Texan citizenship. If opposed by Mexican troops, they should not resort to force unless it appeared that the populace welcomed their arrival. Without popular support and with no means of retreat, they were counseled, theirs would be a desperate fight.[29]

The ill-fated expeditionaries never came close to their objective. Crossing the Texan plains from Austin in the broiling summer months, they wound northward and then westward over unknown terrain, at times overcome with thirst and hunger. By September, after a tortuous journey of some 1,300 miles, they had come within one hundred miles of their destination; all were exhausted and for days had subsisted on the flesh of their horses, the cactus of the desert, and such reptiles and rodents as they could catch. They were met by an army of fresh dragoons sent by the New Mexican governor to crush the "invaders." The enfeebled Texans surrendered without firing a shot. They were bound and marched to Santa Fe and then onward to Mexico City — walking at rifle point a route of 2,000 miles — where the survivors were clapped into the dungeons of Perote Castle.

The hideous Santa Fe affair (the Sage of the Hermitage called it "a wild goose campaign")[30] was Lamar's last hurrah. When news of the outcome of the mission reached Austin, Congress voted the President a public censure for violating his constitutional prerogatives and might have impeached him on the spot had not his term of office been nearly over. "The farce which we have been playing, of attempting to sustain a government on the scale of an empire, can no longer amuse the world or profit ourselves," a special congressional Committee on Retrenchment admonished. "We have arrived at a period in our career, at which visionary schemes of national grandeur are entertained only by weak heads or selfish hearts."[31] But even now, the imperial ambitions of many members of Congress were not entirely subdued. Carried away by a rage for avenging the sufferings of the Texan prisoners, the Sixth Congress in a burst of madness passed an act in January, 1842, extending the boundaries of Texas to include the Mexican states of Chihuahua, Sonora, New Mexico, the two Californias, and portions of Tamaulipas, Coahuila, Durango, and Sinaloa — more than half the entire territory of the Mexican Republic.[32] (See map 3, p. 47)

Lamar's successor in the presidency, Sam Houston, wanted none of it. When he took office in December, 1841, he found the nation's treasury in ruins. Lamar's expenditures during his three years in office had reached nearly $5 million, while revenues from imposts and taxes over that period amounted to little more than $1 million. This heavy deficit now called for a policy of retrenchment at home and circumspection in foreign relations. In his veto message to Congress, Houston bluntly pointed out that Texas had neither the money nor the population to warrant or sustain such preposterous boundaries, which embraced (including Texas proper as defined in 1836) a territory larger than the states of the American union. From the standpoint of national prestige, other countries "would regard the measure as visionary — or as a legislative jest — inasmuch as it would assume a right which it is utterly impossible to exercise."[33]

Now in his second term, President Houston had no intention of restoring the Army of the Republic. His economy measures meant a drastic reduction in government offices and payroll. He hoped to inaugurate an era of peaceful relations with the Indians and to achieve a *modus vivendi* with Mexico through the good offices of a major power. If necessary, he would reopen the annexation issue with the United States. He would urge upon his people the wisdom of a purely defensive posture vis-a-vis Mexico.

NATIONALIST STRIVINGS OF THE TEXAS REPUBLIC

The events of 1842, however, forced Houston's hand in unexpected ways. Mexico, again under the rule of Santa Anna, prepared to invade Texas, and the Texans for their part were in no mood to turn the other cheek. Late in February, Mexican troops under General Rafael Vásquez crossed into Texas unopposed, spreading terror on their way northward and capturing San Antonio on March 5, 1842. After raising the Mexican flag, Vasquez returned to the Rio Grande. The long-anticipated invasion, breaking six years of suspense, was in a way actually welcomed in Texas; and when Santa Anna added insult to injury by inviting Texas "to cover herself anew with the Mexican flag," President Houston shot back in a style reminiscent of his predecessor:

You certainly intend this as a mockery. . . . You have threatened to plant your banner on the banks of the Sabine. . . . You threaten to conquer Texas; we will war with Mexico, and believe me, Sir, ere the banner of Mexico shall triumphantly float upon the banks of the Sabine, the Texian standard of the single star, borne by the Anglo-Saxon race, shall display its bright folds in Liberty's triumph, on the isthmus of Darien.[34]

But Houston's words could not mask the weakness of the Republic. Without massive American aid in both manpower and money (and the performance of 1836 was not likely to be repeated), Texas could not begin to mount a counteroffensive. Houston knew this full well, and his experience as a military man disinclined him to entrust the nation's fortunes to military chieftains. A large expeditionary army on the soil of Texas could prove as dangerous to the liberties of the people as the enemy himself. Consequently, in the months following the Vásquez incursion, Houston tried valiantly to hold the dikes against powerful currents of public opinion that demanded vengeance. The President's old nemesis, Felix Huston, now practicing law in New Orleans, received word from private sources that 2,000 men were already in the field and waiting for such a leader as himself to take command. "The conquest of Mexico," he was told, "is the richest and easiest prise offered to the enterprize of this age." Even Houston's vice-president, the brave soldier Edward Burleson, was ready to abandon him. "I am free to admit," he cried, "that seven years' patient endurance of insult and injury — of outrage and oppression, from our Mexican enemy, makes me exceedingly anxious to end this war." The irony of the situation could not but amaze the American minister to Texas, Joseph Eve:

It is a Phenominan in the history of man to see a young nation just emerging from its cradle with a population of less than 100000 souls without a dollar in its Treasury, nor a regular soldier belonging to it, without credit sufficient to borrow a dollar at home or abroad, constantly at war with numerous tribes of canibal Indians, and at the same time making offensive war upon a nation containing a population of eight millions, strange as it may seem such is the fact.[35]

Congress, meeting at Houston in June, issued a formal declaration of war and appropriated ten million acres of land to meet the expense. While waiting for the President's signature, the House Committee on Military Affairs reproached the administration for its indecisive and inactive course, charging that the defensive policy was having "a most blighting and baneful influence upon our institutions, and people throughout the whole country." Houston replied with a firm veto to the war measure. Texas, he repeated, could afford only to act on the defensive and must rely exclusively upon its volunteer militia.[36]

The second Mexican invasion of 1842, executed in September by General Adrian Woll at the head of more than a thousand troops, was the blow that not even Sam Houston could withstand. San Antonio was again captured and more than sixty of its citizens were taken as prisoners of war. Without waiting for word from their government, Texans everywhere leaped into their saddles to chase after the enemy. The President himself now appreciated that some kind of military exercise was in order. He authorized General Alexander Somervell to lead a volunteer army of seven hundred as far south as the Rio Grande and to invade Mexico if circumstances permitted. With the enemy in retreat, Somervell's men reached the river unmolested, capturing the border towns of Laredo and Guerro. The commander now called a halt to further pursuit, but three hundred members of the expedition disregarded his decision and splashed into Mexican territory to carry out a counter-invasion. For the second time in little more than a year, a Texan force was overwhelmed by a massive Mexican army, this time at the border town of Mier. After the surrender they were decimated by a firing squad (one in ten was shot by drawing a black bean), and like their compatriots of the Santa Fe escapade, the Mier prisoners were taken in chains to Mexico City and cast into the cells of Perote.[37]

Meanwhile, President Houston, considering what might be realistically done in the way of retaliation, found his mind drawn as Lamar's had been toward the Santa Fe Trail. An interruption of commerce might strike a blow at Mexico and bring Texas badly needed revenues. In August, 1842, in the aftermath of his war veto, Houston quietly commissioned Colonel Charles A. Warfield to recruit an army of several hundred men in the name of Texas and undertake a march to Santa Fe, capturing Mexican property and towns along the way and delivering to the government one-half of the spoils. The plan would cost the treasury nothing. A similar authorization was given to Major Jacob Snively early in 1843, except that Snively's sole function was to raid the traffic on the Santa Fe Trail; he too would divide the prizes with the Texas government. Snively's party of two hundred men headed northward, well armed and provisioned, but Warfield's assorted forces of Texans, Missourians, and western mountain men quickly ran into trouble. Lacking coordination and failing to rendezvous, separate elements struck out on their own. The mountain men attacked the village of Mora and were repulsed by a Mexican cavalry force that sent them scrambling back to their fastnesses; the Texans under a Captain McDaniel recklessly plundered a New Mexican caravan one hundred miles inside United States territory. Embarrassed, the Texan government disavowed the latter act and ordered Warfield to abandon his mission. The Snively operation, as things turned out, fared no better. Armed with his letters of "marque and reprisal," the rugged Snively beat back a small Mexican cavalry company in the Cimarron Desert and encamped to await the passage of the caravan from Independence. To his amazement, when the train appeared it was under a strong U.S. Army escort. The commander, Captain Philip St. George Cooke, peremptorily ordered the Texans to drop their guns and surrender. Snively and his band, having no wish to take on the superior United States force, handed over their weapons and meekly started the long trek back to their homes.

This time the Texan government reacted with indignation, claiming that Cooke had disarmed the men on Texas soil, an inhumane act and a violation of the Republic's sovereignty. Issac Van Zandt, the Texan minister to Washington, thought that the American government should apologize "for the indignity offered to our flag" by hoisting it nearest the point where Snively was arrested and saluting it with guns. U.S. Secretary of State Abel Upshur politely turned aside the Texan protests, adhering to his government's view that the incident had occurred within the United States. Texas would be reimbursed for the confiscated weapons, but that was all. A court of inquiry later vindicated Captain Cooke.[38]

In all, the events of 1842–43 dealt a staggering blow to Texas's presumptions of nationhood. Intelligence reports already indicated that when the Mexican government finally crushed the rebellion in Yucatan it would commence a full-scale invasion by land and sea. President Houston's pleas for national unity went unheeded; dissension was rife and morale very low. From Washington, Van Zandt bemoaned the press reports furnished by Texan editors, whose excoriations of their government gave foreign readers the impression that Texas could not stand: "Diplomatic success," he believed, was only possible if "our friends who wield the pen or speak aloud will but talk and write in our country's cause and

Texas present an undivided front. . . ." From France, the Texan minister Ashbel Smith lamented the "ill advised" Santa Fe and Mier expeditions, which, he said, "have done our national standing [in Europe] infinite harm. They have seriously impaired the high reputation we enjoyed for valor, and of course the confidence at one time universal here, in our ample ability to maintain our independence." The domestic front was the scene of bitter post-mortems, and only the very real danger of another Mexican invasion held Texas together at all. Congressman James S. Mayfield denounced Houston ("this great military captain and illustrious Cherokee Chieftan") and his Mexican policy as a source of shame to the Republic. Samuel A. Maverick, a former mayor of San Antonio who had spent several months in a Mexican prison after being seized by General Woll, likewise deplored the fallen state of his country. "Since we do not deserve it, I am ashamed of the miserable position in witch I think Texas now stands. With abundant native strength and resources and valor to boot, we have permitted the best opportunity of relieving ourselves to pass by, whilst we stand until we have almost become palzied in the cringing attitude of beggars."[39]

Houston himself was now showing the strain of the many pressures upon him, and while he might overlook his critics at home, he could hardly ignore the menace of Santa Anna. Nor could he be confident of his power to control the passions of his own people. "If another foray is made by Mexico," he confided to Secretary of State Anson Jones, "it will not be possible to restrain the people of Texas. And though I have heretofore sought a pacific policy, under the most annoying circumstances, if the war is necessarily begun again, I will use all my energies in sustaining it and ensuring success to our arms."[40] The President was putting up a brave front; what he really began to look to, as the only salvation for Texas, was annexation to the United States.

Annexation had never been completely out of the people's minds. It had always stood somewhere as a last recourse, a kind of psychological safety-valve. Whatever the pride of Texas as a nation, the spiritual satisfactions of independence were beginning to pale before the concrete economic and military advantages that American statehood might bring. The average Texan settler trying to make a home for his family in a country beset by economic hardship and physical insecurity was, by 1843, beginning to feel discouraged. The nation's financial condition looked especially dismal against the background of a stubborn economic recession stemming from the Panic of 1837. The contagion of the American depression had spread to Texas by about 1839 and for nearly four years the country had been in the grip of slow economic strangulation. President Houston kept an ear to the ground and could sense a sharp turn in public opinion following the Mier debacle; there was now many and many a doubt as to whether Texas could pull through. Not that she would ever be conquered by Santa Anna — but as long as the country remained a battleground, depopulation and economic collapse might well do the job for him. "The people of Texas," sighed Guy M. Bryan, "want a respite from their toils."[41] Union with the United States now seemed a panacea.

The reversal in Texan fortunes and the government's renewed interest in annexation coincided with the growing belief among Americans that the destiny of the United States was continental expansion. Texas could not be separated from the total design; an aggressive and independent Texas, possibly financed or otherwise supported by Great Britain, could stand in the way of that expansion. When the British and French ministers to Mexico helped to arrange a truce between Houston and Santa Anna in the summer of 1843, American fears were awakened to the possibility that the two European powers might gain a firm foothold on the continent. The United States was ready to take the initiative, and in October, Secretary of State Abel Upshur invited the Texas government to resume negotiations leading to annexation.

Houston immediately sent to Washington his most skillful diplomat, James Pinckney Henderson, the man who had opened the door to diplomatic relations with Britain and France. Yet the President betrayed some ambivalence on the subject of union. He was responding to the evident wishes of his countrymen, and while probably favoring annexation himself, he was also mindful of his country's other foreign relations and of the possible pitfalls of negotiations with the Americans.[42] The talks might break down, or a completed agreement might be rejected by the United States Congress. So Houston tried to keep his alternatives open and in balance. Contacts with the Mexican government were maintained, and in February, 1844, an informal armistice was concluded with the implicit understanding that Texas would seek no connection with the United States. At the same time, Houston openly dallied with Britain, encouraging speculation that Texas was ready to make binding commercial and political commitments to that power. His jaunty insouciance as to the outcome of annexation diplomacy produced considerable consternation in the United States. Opinion in Texas, however, was decidedly hostile to any alliance with a monarch; most Texans hoped fervently for favorable terms from the American government; while some still preferred to carry on as an independent nation.[43]

Negotiations in Washington were completed on April 11, 1844 with John C. Calhoun, who succeeded Upshur to the secretaryship when the Virginian was killed in a steamboat explosion. Calhoun drafted and submitted the annexation treaty to the Senate for ratification on April 22. In Texas, the treaty got a warm reception even though it provided only for territorial status. In the following weeks, Texans awaited the news from Washington, but each day's delay increased both their anxiety and their irritation. President Houston made no secret of his misgivings, and at one point permitted himself to speculate that if annexation failed, Texas would become a rival power to the United States, possessing the western half of the American continent. At last, his patience nearly exhausted, he concluded that the United States would not condescend to touch Texas, and told Henderson and Van Zandt in Washington, "We must regard ourselves as a nation to *remain forever separate.*"[44] Others, as if bracing themselves, now contemplated anew the advantages of nationhood. A Matagorda editor admitted that annexation would bring great joy to the country, but resolved that its defeat would not cause Texans to despair or yield to a "debasing alliance" with a monarchical power. "This can never be, while the same true rifles that conquered at San Jacinto can be levelled by men animated by a love of liberty."[45]

The U. S. Senate acted on June 8, 1844. Word of its rejection of the annexation treaty by the stunning vote of thirty-five to sixteen finally reached Texas in July. The subject seemed finished. "The people of Texas have pretty much given up all hopes of annexation, so much so that it is scarcely ever spoken of any where," Christian F. Duerr, a Houston merchant, informed a southern correspondent in August, 1844. "No one here believes that the Senate of the U.S. will under any circumstances ratify a treaty having annexation for its object." Nor would Texas be willing to venture it again, and risk further disturbance of her relations with other countries. Already the armistice with Mexico was broken by that country inasmuch as Texas, against the urgings of Britain and France, had violated the spirit of the agreement. "I much question whether our Government will again listen to overtures from the United States," Duerr later wrote. "The Government as well as the people of Texas are not disposed, again to hazard our relations with foreign Governments by negotiations with the United States."[46]

The U.S. presidential election of 1844 pumped new life into the twice-dead annexation issue. James K. Polk had run on a platform of continental expansionism, including the "reannexation" of Texas. His victory, though narrow, was interpreted as a popular mandate for the Texas treaty. Now the proposal was entirely in the hands of the American government. In December, lame-duck President John Tyler recommended that Congress pass a joint resolution requiring a simple majority of both Houses for the annexation of Texas, obviating the procedure (a two-thirds vote of the

Senate) for the approval of a treaty. In Texas, Sam Houston disgustedly washed his hands of the matter and urged Congress to do the same. He now professed to see a glorious future awaiting the Republic of Texas. "The Pacific alone will bound the mighty march of our race and empire. From Europe and America her soil is to be peopled."[47] Yet indications remained that the people were still eager for annexation, even if their newly elected president, Houston's protégé Anson Jones, should be hostile to it.

In January, 1845, as news of the impending success of an annexation resolution reached Texas, the Senate Committee on Foreign Relations gave an enthusiastic endorsement and expressed a new-found rapture over the blessings of American citizenship.[48] While such a sentiment was not yet shared by some leading men in the country, it presaged the later response of the Texan people when the invitation to join the Union was actually tendered. At this critical point, both the French and British governments prevailed upon the Mexican government to recognize the Texas Republic in order to reinforce the Texan partisans of independence. One strenuous opponent of annexation, the Texan minister to Great Britain, George Terrell, naively reported that London wanted Texas to remain an independent power for her own sake — "she had [in Whitehall's view] manifested so much vigor and so much enterprise as gave certain indications of her becoming in time a great nation. . . ."[49] The view, of course, was purely selfish. Annexation would deal a crushing blow to the ambitions of both Britain and France in North America and must be blocked at all costs. Urgently they persuaded President Jones to refrain from any hasty action until a formal peace treaty between Texas and Mexico could be worked out.[50]

Back in Washington, the annexation resolution moved through Congress with surprising swiftness. It passed both Houses in February and was ready for President Tyler's signature on March 1, 1845. The terms of the resolution were considerably more generous than those of the previous year's treaty. Texas was to be admitted directly to statehood, and while the new State would assume the Republic's debt, it would retain the public lands of Texas as a means of making repayment. On March 3, Tyler in his last day in office dispatched Andrew Donelson to Texas with the approved annexation papers in his satchel.

GLORIOUS NEWS! TEXAS ANNEXED! WELCOME INTELLIGENCE! the San Augustine *Red-Lander* headlined on March 15. Overnight, the news dispelled all doubts and silenced all dissent as the people almost in one voice declared for annexation. "The news of the victorious battle of San Jacinto scarcely excited such general and enthusiastic rejoicing," exulted the *Telegraph and Texas Register*.[51] Throughout the nation, for the next three months, annexation meetings accompanied by boisterous celebrations were held to express the popular will.[52] The force of public sentiment all but overwhelmed the last of the diehards, including President Jones, who dashed Britain's plan to stay the measure by moving up his timetable for ratification. He called a special session of the Ninth Congress for June 16, 1845 and issued a proclamation for the election of delegates to meet in a constitutional convention at Austin on July 4.

When Congress convened, the Senate promptly rejected the proposed Mexican treaty of recognition and both Houses unanimously accepted the American offer of annexation. On July 4, 1845, the Convention adopted by a vote of 55 to 1 an ordinance of annexation. For the next two months the members toiled in undershirts in the blistering Texas heat and finally drafted, after lengthy and often exhausting debate, a new state constitution. On October 13, both the ordinance and the constitution were submitted to the people for ratification and approved by votes of 4,254 to 257 and 4,174 to 312 respectively. Over the next several weeks, the U.S. Congress consented to the Texas Constitution and passed the Texas Admission Act, which President Polk signed on December 29, 1845, making Texas a State of the Union.

Yet there was sorrow. Ready though they might be to adopt American citizenship and salute the Stars and Stripes, Texans did not take lightly the relinquishment of their nationality. As late as September 23, 1845, the chairman of the Senate Committee on Foreign Relations took umbrage at the casual assumption of the U.S. State Department that the Republic was no more. He scolded Secretary of State Buchanan for dismissing the Texan chargé at Washington. "Texas is as yet an independent Republic," he insisted. "Texas maintains her independent and separate attitude and *will continue to do so* until the final consummation of the measure of annexation." The stationing of General Zachary Taylor's troops in the country, he maintained, did not mean that Texas had surrendered sovereignty. Their presence was permitted only "by invitation of . . . the *owners of the soil,* the *people of Texas.*"[53]

From first to last, the "owners of the soil" remained supremely jealous of their sovereignty. Once they were in the Union their own particular interpretation of state rights informed their relations with the federal government. Their allegiance to the Lone Star would supersede any other loyalty, and Texas would remain in many a sense a country within a country. The eulogies offered to the Republic could not express the emotions of the people who had struggled against all odds to establish a nation. "Her days were brief, yet glorious — her people have given to the world's history one of its brightest pages," as one editorialist put it.

"The bravery of her sons needs no panegyrist – they have been true to her and equal to every emergency."[54] Perhaps the scene in Austin on February 19, 1846, which witnessed the changing of the guard as President Anson Jones lowered the Lone Star flag and raised the Stars and Stripes over Texas, depicted all that could ever be spoken. There, in the eerie stillness of that gloomy winter day, sat many a weary Texan, listening silently to the fife and bugle corps as the drummers rolled off the death of their nation. "With the glories of the Republic in mind, and apprehensive of the future," a diarist recorded, they wept bitterly. "Their vindication: time and events."[55]

CHAPTER SIX

Federal-State Relations:
The New Mexico Boundary Dispute

The 2nd of March is close at hand. Shall we hail its return with those demonstrations of joy which the anniversary of a nation's birthday should ever excite in patriotic hearts? Or do the names of Alamo, of Goliad, of San Jacinto, fall stillborn on our ears, and no longer arouse in our bosom a lively recollection of the deeds of our fathers, and of the stirring events and incidents connected with the story of the Texan revolution? Or have the names of Milam, of Travis, Crockett and Bonham; of Fannin, Wharton, Smith and their compatriots, ceased to awaken in our minds that enthusiasm of admiration, or failed to kindle that fire of martial excitement, which they were once wont to produce? [1]

The Texans now lived under two flags, and the Stars and Stripes flew above the Lone Star — a reminder of the national supremacy. Sam Houston was pleased. After all his doubts about annexation, he felt enormously relieved that Texans were once again Americans. "We are a state now," he wrote, "and I hope will rank a *Stately* State with our elder sisters."[2]

The task of launching Texas as a state fell to James Pinckney Henderson, the indefatigable diplomat of the Republic. Slender, frail, and sickly, Henderson had nevertheless displayed such gusts of energy that his more robust countrymen turned to him for leadership. As first governor of the state, the former North Carolinian told his compatriots at the somber ceremonies of February 19, 1846 that the fortunes of Texas were inescapably linked to those of the American nation. As Americans together they would enjoy common triumphs, endure common hardships, and share a common destiny. Let the friends of Texas annexation, he urged, have "no reason to regret their efforts in our behalf."[3] If Henderson inadvertently struck a negative note, it was because Texans, while prepared to acquit themselves as loyal Americans, were yet wary of possible encroachments by the federal government. That suspicion would remain a persistent theme in Texas statehood.

Most Texans were aware that annexation was likely to embroil the United States in a war with Mexico. All Mexican factions — centralists, federalists, monarchists, rich landholders, the clergy, and the military — agreed on one point: that the American government had from the beginning aided and abetted Texas in its independent course; in severing that rebel province from the Republic, it committed an act tantamount to war. A proud nation, Mexico had no choice but to fight for what was hers, and domestic political considerations required nothing less. The Texans, whose land might once again be the battleground, took up the gauntlet without hesitation. "Indeed there is nothing we so hope for," the Clarksville *Northern Standard* declared in the summer of 1845, "as that 3000 United States troops may meet 10 or 12,000 Mexicans. . . . Twenty five thousand men, can easily raise the flag of our common country over the National Palace of Mexico."⁴ When war broke out in April, 1846, intense excitement gripped Texas. Her fighting men might now satisfy their cravings for revenge and demonstrate their valor and patriotism. "To the west then, to the glorious west," trumpeted the *Telegraph and Texas Register.* "Let the Star of Texas shine forth once more, until the filthy buzzard of Mexico cowers again before its glorious beams."⁵

From all parts of the state men rallied to arms, and the legislature granted Governor Henderson a leave of absence to take personal command of all Texas troops mustered into the federal service. The Texans distinguished themselves at Monterrey and Buena Vista, earned a reputation for incredible daring wherever they fought, and displayed an *esprit de corps* that expressed itself against not only the enemy but at times other regiments as well. "On the day of battle I am glad to have Texas soldiers with me for they are brave and gallant," General Zachary Taylor commented, "but I never want to see them before or afterwards, for they are too hard to control."⁶ Notorious they were, among fellow-Americans, for abusing unarmed civilians. Commentators usually attributed their arrogance to memories of Mexican atrocities in the Revolution and treachery in the treatment of prisoners taken in the abortive Santa Fe and Mier capers. No sooner did Texans enter Mexico, according to historian Stephen B. Oates, than they proceeded to raid villages, pillage farms, shoot at peon farmers, "open fire with savage pleasure on little brown boys running barefoot through the streets of Matamoros," and hang grown-ups for amusement. When not in battle they took advantage of every opportunity to settle old scores: "Rumor say's several Mexicans killed," noted a Texan ranger in camp after the surrender of Monterrey. "Texians done it of course," he remarked. General Taylor was appalled at this behavior and looked forward to "a restoration of quiet and order in Monterey" once they had departed. Later in the war he swore he had never met troops of such a "licentious char[ac]ter" and accused them of frequently killing Mexican citizens for no apparent reason. In the field, Texans who went on expeditions in search of Mexican guerrilla parties almost never took prisoners. Having hunted them down, they simply shot them on the spot.⁷

As the American war machine ground its way over the central plains of Mexico to final victory in the fall of 1847, snuffing out the last vestiges of guerrilla resistance while occupying the Halls of Montezuma, Governor Henderson lauded his charges "for the important services rendered their country, and the noble manner in which they have sustained the honor and chivalry of their State." American patriotism, in his view, precluded dissent against any war entered into by the government, whether in defense of Texas "or in the protection of the spinning jennies of the abolitionists." He hoped and believed there was no citizen of Texas "whose mind is so deeply imbued with treason as to be opposed to the vigorous prosecution of this war."[8] Henderson had little to fear. The patriotism of Texans for the Stars and Stripes soared, as well it might. In some quarters of the nation, the war was condemned as naked aggression, but in Texas hardly a murmur of protest was heard. "Whoever looks to us for sympathy for a foreign foe, in a contest with our own countrymen, will assuredly be mistaken," the *Northern Standard* averred. Should some call it an "unjust war," we in Texas "go for 'our country, right or wrong' . . . clinging to her against the world in arms."[9]

Almost overlooked on the wider scene was the movement of a small American army into the Santa Fe region of Texas. As Texan volunteers plunged southward to meet the enemy at Palo Alto, Resaca de la Palma, Monterrey, Buena Vista, Vera Cruz, Cerro Gorda, and Mexico City, the "Army of the West" under General Stephen W. Kearny had advanced on New Mexico with 1,700 troops. On August 18, 1846, the Americans entered Santa Fe. Kearny proceeded to occupy the town and the surrounding countryside without a fight, absolving the inhabitants of their allegiance to Mexico and establishing a temporary territorial government. Under "Kearny's Code," drawn up with suggestions from President Polk and the secretary of state, provisions were made for a standing paid militia, a system of secular public schools, the collection of taxes, and separation of church and state. New Mexico would have an elected assembly, three district judges, and a governor; for local government, Kearny created counties.[10] All this was done without the consent of Texas and without acknowledgment of the state's longstanding territorial claim.

This claim had originated with the Boundary Act of December, 1836, by which the Republic of Texas appropriated to itself all the towns and territory of New Mexico situated east of the Rio Grande. During nationhood, the Texans stubbornly insisted on their sovereignty over the vast region west of the Pecos, even though they made no settlements of consequence beyond the Nueces River and met a shattering defeat in the Santa Fe Expedition's attempt to establish Texan authority. Nevertheless, the United States did not question the Texan title to eastern New Mexico when annexation was negotiated. The American government was eager, no doubt, to incorporate as much of Mexico's province as circumstances allowed. All that was said of boundaries was a vague mention of federal responsibility for settling any border disputes with other states or nations. That was strictly *pro forma.* The annexation resolution (which specified that Texas might carve as many as four states out of her territory) actually sustained the Texan claim to the upper Rio Grande by stipulating that if the state was ever divided, slavery could exist only south of the Missouri Compromise line of 36° 30'. The purported boundaries of the Republic had extended northward to the forty-second parallel. That the United States had no intention of contesting the Texan claim is further indicated by President Polk's assurances that Texan rights in New Mexico would be respected and by the government's establishment on December 31, 1845 of a United States customs district west of the Nueces. Since that territory was yet to be seized from Mexico and occupied by American troops, the act of Congress amounted to a confirmation of the Texas title.[11]

Almost at the commencement of statehood, the legislature, as if to leave nothing to chance, reaffirmed by a joint resolution the rights of the state to the entire area claimed by the Republic.[12] Thus, when General Kearny established civil government in Santa Fe, Texans viewed the move as an infraction of their sovereignty. Initially, they hailed the conquest of New Mexico as an important step toward the subjugation of Mexico's entire western territory. But when Kearny departed for California with 300 dragoons at the end of September, leaving hundreds of American troops in Santa Fe to stand guard, appointing a native merchant as chief justice, two Missourians for the posts of solicitor general and marshal, and a local American, Charles Bent, as governor, the Texans began to fret. Why had *their* government not been consulted? Why had a Texan not been appointed to the command? In June, 1847, Governor Henderson — once again at his desk in Austin — addressed these queries to Secretary of State James Buchanan, remonstrating that Santa Fe belonged to Texas. By this time, Bent had been assassinated in the Taos Rebellion (an uprising of Indian civilians against American rule) and the Army was assuming governmental duties. Buchanan tried to soothe the ruffled governor, telling him that the military would not alienate Texan jurisdiction; but a final resolution of the question rested with Congress.[13] Was there then a "question"? Buchanan was subtly intimating that there was.

At the conclusion of the Mexican War early in 1848, Texans looked apprehensively to the situation in Santa Fe, expecting (or hoping) that the "temporary" government would now be terminated in favor of state jurisdiction. When nothing happened, members of the legislature and the new governor, George T. Wood, expressed alarm. Texan nationalists, even in the afterglow of victory, were ready to impugn American motives. A legislative committee on the Affairs of State baldly accused the United States of threatening to make war on the rights of Texas. It recommended immediate and unilateral state action: the organization of county govern- ment and a judicial district in New Mexico. In a rousing flourish that might have created some doubts about their fealty to the American flag, the committee exhorted the legislature to:

discharge our duty to our country [Texas] . . . Let us show ourselves worthy of our country! Let us show to the world that the blood of the Alamo has not been shed in vain! That Texians will ever sustain the honor of their martyred heroes . . . that our banner has been unfurled, and that we will never yield one inch of soil on this side of the Rio Grande.[14]

A clenched-teeth performance, it bode ill for the nation.

The legislature went quickly to work, styling the entire area between the Rio Grande and the Pecos as Santa Fe county. Larger than any other state of the Union, the new county was designated the 11th judicial dis- trict of Texas. With a population of nearly 60,000 brown faces (approxi- mately one-half the number of the white population of Texas), it was allowed only one member in the House of Representatives. The lawmakers evidently were afraid that a substantial Spanish-speaking Mexican element might gain a voice in Austin. Less than a week later they instructed the Texas senators in Congress, Generals Houston and Rusk, to oppose any American peace treaty with Mexico that violated state territorial rights. Simultaneously, on March 20, 1848, the legislature authorized state offi- cers to take over the reins of government at Santa Fe, and asked the United States to sustain (with its army) the Texan civilian personnel. Presumptuously, they sent Judge Spruce M. Baird to Santa Fe to organize the county and serve as judge.

The Treaty of Guadalupe Hidalgo, officially ending the Mexican War on July 4, 1848, presented new difficulties for Texas. Mexico agreed to relinquish all claims to Texas north of the Rio Grande and to cede the entire New Mexico territory and upper California to the United States. The treaty completely ignored the Texas claim. Texan fears were at once confirmed by the failure of Washington to restore the eastern district. In October, 1848, Governor Wood offered President Polk a lesson in Texas history, explaining the origin of the title to Santa Fe and the resolve of the Texan people to sustain it. The Rio Grande boundary, he pointed out, was inseparable from the very principles of the 1836 revolution, "and in the darkest hour of that uneven struggle, a spirit so craven was not to be found in our ranks, who would have been satisfied with less."[15] What the argument lacked in logic it made up for in sheer emotion. Polk knew the problem would not be his; he was not going to run for another term. But such lieutenants as Buchanan, Robert J. Walker, William L. Marcy, and some members of the Congress should have taken heed: proud Texas promised trouble.

When Judge Baird arrived in Santa Fe in November, 1848, he hardly got his foot in the door. Already the locals had been alerted to Texan objectives and told to reject the notion of "Santa Fe County." The military were busily encouraging citizens to sign petitions for making New Mexico a federal territory. Baird was then rudely received by Colonel John McRae Washington, the commanding officer. In an eyeball-to-eyeball confrontation, Washington stated, in effect, that only across his dead body would Texas take over the government of New Mexico. Baird took a room in town and stayed on for several months, hoping to convince the military to change their minds. The Americans did not listen. He tried to make conversation in the saloons and cafes, but with the Lone Star pinned to his lapel, few would talk to him. He had no choice, finally, but to report the failure of his mission.

The election to the presidency of Whig General Zachary Taylor in 1848 did not help matters. Until then, with the Democrats in power, Texans had national officials in basic sympathy with their aspirations. Whigs, on the other hand, and particularly those in the North, had been hostile to Texas annexation. In Zachary Taylor, the Texans had a confessed enemy. Taylor had had his fill of Texan volunteers in the late war. Unable to control the rangers under his command, he not only sighed with relief when they were finally discharged but denounced them with every epithet he could think of. While the rangers were stoutly defended by Sam Houston in Congress, Houston's Texas constituents gave the Democratic candidate, Lewis Cass, a lopsided victory in the presidential vote. Taylor did not forget this either, and once in office he removed many Texans from federal posts who happened to be Democrats, including the sterling Indian agent, Robert Simpson Neighbors. So little love was lost between Zachary Taylor and the Lone Star, and to make matters worse, the new President favored granting statehood to New Mexico. Within months of his inauguration, hopes of statehood were gaining ground in Santa Fe, where it was believed that "as a state we could best resist the encroachments of Texas. . . ." New Mexico's declaration in favor of becoming a free state was one way, according to Howard R. Lamar, of expressing "a bitter anti-Texan feeling."[16] Such sentiments were quite in line with those of the President. If Texas did not move fast, the province would be swallowed up.

Governor George T. Wood under most circumstances was a moderate, even-tempered, reasonable man. One might also say modest: he never boasted about his heroic feats at Monterrey in the Mexican War, where he commanded the 2nd Texas Mounted Volunteers. Fifty-four years old in 1849, he had lived in Texas for nearly ten years with his wife and four children, serving in the Congress of the Republic, the Annexation Convention of 1845, and the state legislature. A solidly-built six-footer, Wood was the successful operator of a large East Texas plantation, a convivial host to his many friends, and a jovial family man. Traveling to and from Austin by mule, his saddle-bags were always stuffed with presents for his children after a trip, and he never failed to distribute candy to the slaves upon his return. He entertained the black children and his own with ghastly stories about his Indian fights in the Creek War, displaying the scars on his knees as he bounced the little ones into the air.[17]

Now at the end of his two-year term, the Governor had lapsed into a gloomy frame of mind. Defeated for reelection by a former Texan ranger because of his failure to take a stronger stand on the Santa Fe matter, Wood was cutting loose at last. In his final message to the legislature on November 6, 1849, he charged the federal government with duplicity on the subject of Texan rights. The time for friendly persuasion was past. The new governor must be fully empowered to contest the issue against the United States, "not by demonstrating in argument the justice of our claims, not by reference to our statutes, but with the whole power and resources of the State."[18] Wood's address was enthusiastically received by the press, and one paper went so far as to contemplate severing connections with "a Union that embraces but to crush and destroy." Then, when word arrived from Santa Fe late in 1849 that the New Mexicans were sending their own delegate to Congress, explosions of temper could be heard in editorial rooms and in the halls of the legislature. James C. Wilson spoke for nearly all of his colleagues in the Texas House of Representatives when he vowed that the people would "live or die by Texas, as she was, as she is and ever has been, with her limits unimpaired." Both the legislature and the press, with wrathful indignation, threatened to recall the Texas delegation in Washington if the New Mexican representative was seated.[19]

The inauguration of Peter H. Bell as the third governor of Texas on December 21, 1849 occasioned further public airing of the Santa Fe question, and Governor Wood, in his valedictory, challenged his countrymen to defend every bit of that territory "to the last extremity." "If ever surrendered," he said, invoking memories of the Alamo, "it must be when she has no soldier to defend it: there will be no messenger of her defeat."[20] The new governor, Peter Hansborough Bell, had come to Texas from Virginia in 1836 to fight in the Revolution, arriving in time to participate in the Battle of San Jacinto. Like a good many American volunteers, Bell stayed in Texas once the war was over, remaining in the ranks of the Republic's army until 1839. After a year's leave, he was back in the saddle as a ranger, and in 1842 was commissioned a major in the Somervell Expedition to the Rio Grande. By the time of the Mexican War, Bell's entire occupation in Texas was soldiering, and he had won the gratitude of his countrymen by scouring the Southwest with other rangers in search of "redskins" and "greasers." When war erupted in 1846, he joined the United States Army, and was among the several Texans who earned high honors at the battle of Buena Vista. During Wood's administration, he commanded a regiment of rangers along the Rio Grande border. Despite his total want of political experience, Bell made a distinguished-looking candidate. Tall and lean, he had a memorable face — long and wolfish with shaggy dark hair reaching to his collar and bushy whiskers highlighting an already prominent nose and penetrating eyes. He was a thirty-seven-year-old bachelor at the time of his election, and when the voters pulled him from his military duties to preside over the state's affairs, they clearly wanted a fighting governor who would not back down in the face of federal bayonets.

In his inaugural address, Bell assured the American people that Texans had "no want of patriotic feeling and devoted kindness" for the Union. But he reaffirmed the determination of Texas to defend her rights. Referring to the state as "our country," he reviewed the "brilliant and soul-stirring scenes" of the Texas Revolution and threw a familiar challenge at his compatriots: "Fellow-citizens! The price of liberty in Texas was dearly paid in the blood of her patriot sons. Let that be held in grateful remembrance, and to us, and to those who are to succeed us, it should be the highest incentive to virtue, patriotism, and honor." Five days later, in his first message to the legislature, Bell minced no words. In order to support the civil authorities of Santa Fe, Texas, so that they might execute the laws of the state, the governor should have authorization to dispatch a military force. Should there be a collision between Texas and the U.S. Army, "the fault will not be hers."[21]

But the legislature, for all its fist-shaking, somehow lost its nerve. Not wanting to bring matters to a head, the members would vindicate the state's honor and reassert its authority by redrawing the New Mexico district. Laying out their maps, they reduced the size of Santa Fe county and carved from the rest of it three new counties—Presidio, El Paso, and Worth. The four counties together remained as the 11th judicial district but were designated a senatorial district as well; Santa Fe county kept its lone representative in the House and the other three were jointly allowed a single member. It was a dilatory tactic that expressed a continuing wait-and-see attitude. Then Governor Bell, by authority of an act passed on January 3, 1850, appointed Robert S. Neighbors of San Antonio as commissioner to Santa Fe. His task was to organize the four new counties and secure recognition of the state's jurisdiction. (See Map 4, p. 47).

The governor could not have chosen a more judicious or courageous individual to execute such a dubious assignment. An inveterate plainsman, this tall, muscular fellow had criss-crossed thousands of miles of Texas Indian country while serving for several years as an agent. Schooled in the diplomacy of the Comanche, a measure of his tact was his very survival and his emergence as one of the few Texans whom the Indians entirely trusted. Following his unfortunate dismissal from the Indian service in 1849, he set out with ranger John S. Ford to blaze a new trail to El Paso. Hardly had he completed the return trip to Austin when Governor Bell presented him with his new commission, instructing him to act in such a manner with the New Mexicans as to "remove all prejudices which may heretofore have existed in respect to the government, and our people as a race."[22] Neighbors had a dry sense of humor, and for this job, he would need every bit of it.

The year 1850 opened with Neighbors starting out gamely on the one hundred day journey to El Paso and Santa Fe, while two thousand miles to the east, President Taylor was telling Congress to admit New Mexico as a state and let the Supreme Court settle the boundary question. In Washington, meanwhile, the national government was strained nearly to the breaking point over a host of divisive issues. The explosive Wilmot Proviso of 1846 had forced Congress to face the once-unmentionable subject of slavery, now that new territories were being added to the Union's domain. As talk of disunion spread among the southern states, it was easy to imagine that this would be a year heavy with significance for the future of the American Republic. Senator Thomas J. Rusk received an anguished letter from one constituent, Benjamin Rush Wallace, that shed much light on the state of mind in Texas. Wallace saw Texas standing alone, isolated from the sectional issues agitating the rest of the country. On one thing at least, he believed, North and South were united: in "conspiring to dispossess Texas of Santa Fe." Texas had already sacrificed much for the sake of the Union, and should not be obliged to preserve it at the cost of her own sovereignty. "Jesus could be composed under insult, but the people of Texas are of a different breed: they will not submit to a government that divests them of what they prize higher than they do the

Union itself."[23]

As the nation's statesmen prepared to grapple with the problems arising from the Mexican Cession, the Texas boundary dispute was only one of several issues that threatened to split the country, and to most Americans, it was the least compelling. In Texas, men talked of boundaries — but everywhere else the talk was of slavery.

The debates in Congress beginning with Senator Henry Clay's compromise resolutions of January 29, 1850 are well known, and need not be described here. For the next eight months the eyes of the nation were fixed upon Capitol Hill. Among Clay's proposals was an adjustment of the Texas-New Mexico boundary, whereby the federal government would assume the Texas debt in exchange for the state's territorial claim to Santa Fe. Each of Clay's other measures, including the admission of California as a free state, dealt squarely with slavery. When the debates reached an impasse in April, the resolutions were referred to a select Committee of Thirteen. On May 8, the Committee reported the Texas bill in roughly the same form as Clay had suggested, filling in the outlines with facts and figures. The federal government would pay Texas a flat $10 million to defray the debt still accumulating from the financing of the Republic. This would not prejudice in any way the state's ownership of its public lands. In return, Texas would relinquish its claim to the trans-Pecos region, about 125,000 square miles. The Committee was responding to the demands of Texas bondholders in the United States who were beginning to despair of ever again seeing their loans. The Missouri merchants' lobby, which long had controlled the trade of the Santa Fe Trail, also enjoyed a sympathetic ear in Congress and was loath to share any of its revenues with the ambitious Texans. Furthermore, the howls of protest from the Lone Star State were not to be taken lightly, and the Committee saw the expediency of buying peace with Texas. This tack was decided upon as the least costly means of preserving the Union, even though many members of Congress resented the pretensions of Texas and regarded its claim a tenuous one at best. Texas, they argued, had shown no capacity, either as a republic or a state, to establish its authority in New Mexico. The American army, not the Texan, had conquered the province, and the New Mexicans themselves, separated from Austin by six hundred miles of wilderness, dreaded any closer contact with the Lone Star.[24]

But the Texans refused to see it this way. To part with New Mexico for dollars would be to sell the blood of their martyred heroes, to bring shame upon the name of Texas. There was, too, the vast economic potential of New Mexico, "valuable lands, timbers and salines . . . also rich and productive mines of the precious metals," and the possibility for a transcontinental railroad that would greatly enrich the state.[25] The plan of the

Committee of Thirteen hit a stone wall when introduced to Texas in June, 1850. The Austin *Texas State Gazette* declared that "not even for the preservation of the Union itself" would Texas agree to a compromise that stripped her of the trans-Pecos area, "and we are confident that our position will be sustained by the unpurchased and unpurchasable votes of our fellow citizens from the Sabine to the Rio Grande and from Red River to the Gulf."[26]

Meanwhile, the dogged Major Neighbors had kept his appointment in New Mexico. He arrived with his entourage first at the Anglo outpost of Franklin (present-day El Paso) and proceeded to organize El Paso county without resistance. Moving on to Santa Fe, the Neighbors party warily rode into town on April 15. Here they encountered trouble, as expected. Missouri merchants on hand spread rumors of another Texan invasion, trying to incite mob action, and the populace vented its hostility. Neighbors could feel the cold stares from leering passers-by and could not deal at all with New Mexico's civilian leaders, both native and Missourian. With President Taylor's blessing, they were at that moment absorbed in efforts to establish a state government. Neighbors knew he was beaten, and when Colonel John Munroe, now military governor of New Mexico, ordered him to leave, he saw no choice but to retrace his steps to Austin and report to the governor.

News of Neighbors's rejection, coming on the heels of the obnoxious Congressional proposal, fired the people, the press, and the politicians into a frenzy. "We must," raged the *State Gazette,* "either submit to the insulting and tyrannical pretensions of the United States [and] to a loss of about one third of the territorial area of the State, or we must protect our rights by that last resort of an injured people — the force of arms." The realization had come. Texans, with no wish to commit corporate suicide (the Alamo tradition notwithstanding), saw themselves cornered by a deceitful federal government. From June to September, 1850, they castigated that government on every issue imaginable. The angry indictment included not only the New Mexico outrage but also federal neglect in frontier defense, in mail facilities, and in river and harbor improvements. An alliance with the South was struck on the slavery question and some now openly regretted the event of annexation itself. Editors called for armed resistance to federal usurpation in New Mexico and a swift suppression of the rebellious inhabitants. They talked of a war to the death, they preferred annihilation to surrender, and a few even dared think, with God and the right on their side, that David's match with Goliath might be reenacted on the plains of New Mexico. Let us battle, the LaGrange *Texas Monument* cried, manfully to the last, and if we must fail in a just cause . . . let us die with arms in our hands, with our eyes turned in the last moments of existence upon the *star* which rose above the political horizon in 1836, still shining with undimmed lustre and glory upon the last battlefield of Texas.[27]

The bugle blared everywhere in the land. From county to county mass meetings in packed halls voiced the sentiment of the people. The citizens of Travis were the first to convene, calling upon state officials to seize Santa Fe by force. Throughout the state, these heated gatherings spewed a venom of hate. Protests against federal power, laments over annexation, threats of secession, and promises of revenge poured forth. The people everywhere announced their readiness to arm themselves and march to New Mexico. "Many of our young men," Governor Bell learned from Collin County, "are all exceedingly anxious for the trip. . . . Santa Fe fever rages very high in this County." The Washington *Ranger* reported that "nearly every man is willing to shoulder his gun, and demand the rights of Texas at the cannon's mouth," while the *Texas State Gazette* estimated that 5,000 men were eager to join an expedition. Only one county in the entire State passed a resolution to delay a military campaign.[28] In Congress, Senator Houston tried to help his colleagues understand the Texas mind. "We have not been a warlike people," he explained rather disingenuously, "but we have resisted aggression and repelled injury. . . . We have no sword to strike but at our assailants."[29]

President Zachary Taylor carried a sword of his own, and he vowed to maintain federal authority in New Mexico if he had to lead the Army of the United States into battle against Texas himself. The President's threat to meet force with force only hardened the determination of the Texans. Early in July, Governor Bell impudently demanded a full explanation of the government's intentions in New Mexico, intimating his readiness to spill American blood. Before the Chief Executive had a chance to reply, he fell sick watching an Independence Day parade, and five days later, he was dead. The reaction in Texas to Taylor's demise was one of smug indifference. "We did not put our paper in mourning," went the standard explanation, "for the simple fact that we and the community in which we live felt no sorrow, and did not regard his death as a National calamity, but if any thing, quite the reverse of that."[30] Governor Bell, barely pausing to take note of his correspondent's sudden departure, issued a call for a special session of the legislature starting August 12. By that date, he resolved, unless Congress agreed to return the New Mexico territory to Texas, he would ask for an army to send to Santa Fe.

The new President, Millard Fillmore of New York, endorsed Clay's compromise plan, which Taylor had tried to scuttle, but offered no hope that his position toward Texas would be any more lenient. By no means a military man, Fillmore did not promise to take command of the Army, but like Taylor, he was prepared to defend American interests in New Mexico. As the August deadline approached, Texas and the United States appeared to be headed toward open hostilities. In Washington, as Allan Nevins describes it, the Senate was devoting a part of each day's work to New Mexico. "Since the Texas legislators, with fire in their eyes and six-shooters on their hips, were preparing to assemble in special session . . . no time was to be lost."[31] Texan passions were sent even higher, if possible, by New Mexico's adoption of a constitution for the proposed state with boundaries so extended as to include some territory indisputably Texan. As the legislators departed from their homes for the journey to Austin, they knew that if Texas did not act decisively and at once, the separate existence of New Mexico as a federal territory or state would be accomplished.[32]

Governor Bell addressed the legislature on August 13, 1850, standing solemnly before the body like the president of his country about to ask for a declaration of war. The federal challenge to Texan sovereignty "must be met boldly, and fearlessly and determined," not by supplication or discussion, "but by action — manly and determined action on our part, by a prompt assertion of our rights and a practical maintenance of them with all the means we can command, 'at all hazards and to the last extremity'." He paused to a thunderous ovation. Texas, he continued, must occupy Santa Fe "with a force ample to quell the arrogant and rebellious spirit now prevailing there, and to enable us to extend and firmly establish the jurisdiction and laws of the State over it." The Governor thereupon requested authority to raise a minimum of two regiments of mounted volunteers for the proposed expedition. Because of the scarce financial resources of the state, Bell insisted that the volunteers mount, arm, and equip themselves, believing Texans to be "patriotic enough to enrol themselves under the banner of their State . . . without expecting any advance of pay for their services. . . ."[33]

On August 15 a select Committee on Santa Fe presented a resolution to the legislature incorporating the Governor's very words, and a week later reported favorably on measures to raise three thousand rangers plus a large reserve, presumably for home defense. The atmosphere was charged by the boom of cannon in the streets of Austin, and public excitement rivaled that which had marked the outbreak of the Mexican War. Never had it seen, the *Texas State Gazette* exclaimed, "so much unanimity and enthusiasm as prevails at this time among men and boys, maids and matrons, upon the subject of the enforcement of jurisdiction over

Santa Fe."[34]

Back in Washington, Congress had been working late into the nights to find a peaceable solution to the Texas question. It found one at last in the shape of a bill presented by Senator James A. Pearce of Maryland. Pearce's measure would compromise the disputed territory east of the Rio Grande, giving Texas some 33,000 square miles (an area about the size of Maine) more than had been designated by the Committee of Thirteen, and extending her westernmost point to El Paso del Norte. (The boundaries of Texas as they stand today are those drawn by the Pearce plan.) In return for the remaining land claimed by Texas, the federal government would still pay to the state ten million dollars. The entire Texas delegation in Congress endorsed the Pearce bill, considering it the best bargain Texas could hope for and seeing little virtue in a suicidal military caper that could destroy both Texas and the Union. The plan also had the support of moderate men North and South, in whose minds compromise was uppermost as they juggled a series of bills concerning slavery. Word of Pearce's proposal traveled quickly to Texas via newspaper reports, reaching Austin just as the legislature was about to launch an expeditionary force. The timing was dramatic. At the last hour the movement to New Mexico was stayed to allow consideration of this latest intelligence. Then, for the next three months, Texans debated the merits of the compromise.

Many bellicose citizen-soldiers, vexed by the delay, felt robbed of an occasion for heroism and glory. Some called the Pearce bill a fraud, others thought it an outright bribe, no different in principle from the proposal of the Committee of Thirteen. State representative Guy M. Bryan ranted for two days in the sultry house chamber against the apparent desertion of Texian principles. "Is all of our standing and dignity as a State gone, and to be risked upon a mere newspaper rumor of dollars and cents....?

If so, farewell to the glories of the past; let a dark line be drawn between the State and the Republic of Texas; all the splendors which encircle the Lone Star, belong to the past; nothing will be left to the present, but dishonor and shame and base submission. Speak not of Texas – her gallantry in the field, or her wisdom in the Cabinet, they belong to another day and another people. . . . Trail your banner, and reverse your arms, for you are no longer worthy of a freeman's name – the name of gallant Texians.[35]

State senator John H. Moffett informed Senator Rusk, following Bryan's vitriolic speech, that friends of Governor Bell were adamant against the sale of any part of Texas to the United States. "A dissolution of the union is evidently wished for, and contemplated by many persons in this State."[36] A survey of the state's press shows initial opposition to the Pearce bill overwhelming, and throughout the month of September and into October, many papers sounded much as they had during the summer. Still at issue, in their view, was the honor and tradition of Texas, the understandings of annexation, the sovereign rights of the state, and even the rights of the South.[37] Public meetings in several parts of the state were again hostile to any agreement with the federal government. At Gilmer in Upshur County the citizens implored Governor Bell to call out the militia and crush the revolt at Santa Fe. At Matagorda they damned the Texas delegation in Washington and praised the Governor, while a gathering at Brenham burned Fillmore and Pearce in effigy. At a meeting in Marshall, "A very strong an [sic] Enthusiastic demonstration was given — Anti Everything," recorded one observer — "Condeming the United States Congress Cursing our Senators & Representatives — Swearing that they were bribed . . . Condeming the Legislature for not acting and for not sustaining Gov Bell et al." The *Texas State Gazette*, a leading spirit of nationalist forces throughout the crisis, expressed the animating sentiment of the many who now rued the day of annexation:

> Above all and through all, we shall never lose sight of the peculiar and paramount duty we owe to Texas. Our first allegiance and warmest love are due to her. For more than ten years we have stood side by side, in war and peace, with those who have been ready to sacrifice life itself for her glory and prosperity.[38]

But the outbursts and protests were beginning to give way to reason. Psychologically, if the Pearce bill was anything, it was a face-saving measure for Texans. They could still boast of their land extending from the Sabine to the Rio Grande. They could still envision a transcontinental railroad stretching eight hundred miles across the state. Here was a case, after all, in which men could both resist surrender and embrace compromise. And beneath all the sound and fury, there remained a core of Union sentiment in Texas, whatever the willingness to fight about almost anything. As the southern states and the rest of the country began to coalesce around the "Compromise of 1850," the Texans in substantial numbers drifted back to the Stars and Stripes, not wishing to be the spoilers of the American Republic. "The people in this section," Benjamin Rush Wallace now reported from East Texas, "can not appreciate that kind of patriotism that would lead any to seek . . . an angry collision with their native country," and George W. Smyth, a devoted unionist, judged Texas the strongest pro-Union state in the South because "we know its value by contrast — we know what it is to be out of the Union."[39]

A strong case could be made for the Pearce bill on its own merits.

FEDERAL-STATE RELATIONS

"It is doubtful whether ten years' trading would give Texas a better bargain than she can now make," the LaGrange *Intelligencer* observed. "It must be admitted that a majority of our people would rather transfer the settled part of New Mexico to the United States, on honorable terms, than to retain it." The unsettled part left to Texas would someday be populated by hardy Anglo-Americans. After all, who really wanted a large Mexican electorate for Texan citizens? Likewise, the Victoria *Advocate* preferred to be "rid forever of a mongrel population, the mass of whom are peons . . . certainly not fitted, by intelligence or morality, to have extended to them the rights of suffrage." Former Governor George T. Wood, from his plantation porch, now thought it much to the honor and benefit of Texas to approve the land swap and take the money. Ten million dollars was nothing to sniff at. It would remove the burdensome yoke of the Republic's debt and open a new era of prosperity: "Texas under the salutary influences of this policy must & will soon become the Empire State of this great Confederacy."[40]

The Pearce bill was scheduled for a statewide referendum in November. By the date of the plebiscite, the cooling of tempers had made the results anticlimactic. With fewer than half of the eligible voters participating, the plan was approved by a margin of three to one. Winter was approaching, the northers were already cascading down the high plains, and an escapade to New Mexico was no longer a warming prospect. The popular decision was endorsed by the legislature in special session, and on November 25, 1850, Governor Bell signed the act of acceptance.

The New Mexico boundary settlement proved a vulnerable link in the fragile Compromise of 1850. While the boundary would remain intact, just as the Union ultimately did, it took the Civil War to convince Texans that New Mexico was not to be theirs. Various Texas leaders in El Paso were bent on annexing New Mexico to the Lone Star State once secession was carried out. "It was evident," writes Howard R. Lamar, "that Texas pride still rankled over the disaster of 1841 and the failure to secure the Rio Grande as a border in 1850." The Confederate army in the Southwest consisted entirely of Texans; a Texan frontier editor, John R. Baylor, won a few battles at the outset and declared himself governor of the Confederate Territory of Arizona; another Texan, William Pelham, enjoyed brief glory as Confederate governor of New Mexico, where he raised the Lone Star banner along with the Stars and Bars. These Texan triumphs in 1861, executed by three regiments which had marched hundreds of miles from San Antonio, were short-lived. Union columns from Colorado and California came to the rescue of the splintered federal forces and drove the Texas army back to the Rio Grande. In rallying New Mexicans to their own defense, Union Governor Henry Connelly, a resident of the Southwest for nearly forty years, knowingly stressed the name "Texan" rather than "Confederate" in defining the enemy. By the summer of 1862, the despised Texans had retreated to El Paso, where they remained to defend their own soil. According to Donald W. Meinig, the initial military thrust as far west as Tucson and the seizure early in the war of Albuquerque and Santa Fe "was more a reassertion of Texas imperialism than an integral part of Confederate strategy."[41] It was, clearly, an admixture of imperialism and a still-throbbing nationalism.

Epilogue

With a territory containing more square miles than many of the governments of Europe; possessing by nature nearly every element... with a large public domain unequalled for diversity... and a climate adapted to the production of all the necessaries and most of the luxuries of life, with a vast mineral wealth... we have it in our power... to lay the foundation for those public improvements and institutions which will hereafter rank Texas as the first State in the American Union.[1]

... Justice and equal rights, under the federal constitution, was the sanction of the [annexation] treaty, and so long as that is maintained, Texas will be loyal.... But if the compact is violated ... Texas has an empire and a history of her own. She can fall back upon her exhaustless, perennial resources. Her magnificent soil, climate, and productions, with a brave people to defend them, will secure independence, freedom, and happiness under the glorious Lone Star Flag.[2]

It does not require too great a stretch of the imagination to see Texas as an independent nation in the twentieth century.[3] Larger in size and less convulsed by history than any Western nation, Texas could probably have maintained itself alongside the United States. Blessed with an abundance of natural resources, a diversity of soils, and an extended frontage on the sea, Texas as a separate republic might well have prospered. As a leading oil producing state in this century, Texas might even have become a major power. Had Texas remained a nation, it probably could not have reclaimed New Mexico or any former parts of the Republic given up in 1850. The United States commanded the continent. Nor does it seem likely that the Americans would have acted aggressively against a daughter republic. Just as the United States enjoyed cordial relations with the Dominion of Canada, an English-speaking neighbor, there is every reason to believe that Washington would have exchanged olive branches with Austin.

EPILOGUE

Whether an independent Texas could have advanced southward and annexed portions of its hereditary enemy, Mexico, is problematical. There can be little doubt that the leaders of the Republic would have tried. In the 1850s, faced with perennial border clashes, Texans demanded a United States protectorate over all Mexico to put that country's revolutionary governments to rest. American suzerainty, they believed, would finally quell the border strife that troubled the Rio Grande valley from Brownsville to Eagle Pass.[4] In the absence of a federal initiative, Texans were about to take matters into their own hands when the Civil War intervened.

The imperialist designs of such prominent Texans as John S. Ford and Sam Houston had been inadvertently promoted by a renegade Texan of Mexican blood. This was Juan Cortina, who undertook a series of daring border raids at the end of the decade. A self-appointed paladin, Cortina instigated a personal war against Texas to avenge insults suffered by his people, long dominated by the Anglos. "His people" were Mexicans both humble and well-born living on either side of the Rio Grande. Cortina's activities could be traced to 1846 when he served locally with the Mexican army opposing General Taylor at the battles of Palo Alto and Resaca de la Palma. After the war, he gathered a band of followers devoted to freebooting and cattle rustling at the expense of the Texan ranchers. During the fifties, Cortina's men (among others) helped to convince many Texans that the Treaty of Guadalupe Hidalgo did not apply to the Lone Star State. By 1859, he was ready to launch a heads-on assault. Entering Brownsville in September with a sizeable force, he raided the jail, shot four men including the jailor, and released the Mexicans held prisoner. Thus commenced a border war that would rage for the next six months, striking terror into the inhabitants and confounding the combined Anglo forces of Texan volunteers and U. S. Army regulars.[5]

At the close of 1859, Colonel John S. Ford and his Texan rangers saw the destruction of many ranches in the region. "Nearly all owned by Americans," he reported, "have been burnt in whole or in part." The American portion of the valley was rapidly depopulating as "disorder, confusion, violence, and blood shed prevail everywhere." Ford sensed a widespread disaffection among the Mexican population of southern Texas. Unable to procure from them reliable information as to Cortina's whereabouts, he suspected them of furnishing him with supplies. "The only friends we have are among those who have something to lose, and they constitute a very small minority." Another ranger, Captain William G. Tobin, informed Governor Houston that Cortina was resolved to fight to the death. "The question appears to me to be one of supremacy of races on the Rio Grande."[6]

Before Cortina could finally be driven into retreat, Houston was demanding a massive federal army, ostensibly to secure the border but in all likelihood to force his pet plan of a protectorate on the Mexicans.[7] If the United States would not cooperate he was prepared to ask the state legislature for appropriations to support 5,000 Texan rangers.[8] The force of Texans already mobilized on the Rio Grande had greater ambitions than merely the suppression of Cortina. "Some of the Rangers who came here under patriotic pretences," charged the Brownsville *American Flag*, "really came here to rob and plunder our people." Texas Secretary of State Eber W. Cave acknowledged it to be well known in Austin "that Ford has organized with the purpose of fillibustering before he left here." Aided and abetted by the Knights of the Golden Circle, a secret expansionist organization bent on the conquest of Mexico, the rangers were likely, Cave anticipated, "to have a foray into Mexico." Already Tobin's company was "burning, hanging, shooting, and amusing themselves generally." "Recent accounts show," the Secretary added, "that unless the disgraceful course of our troops is stopped, there will be no end of war."[9] Even after U. S. troops under Major S. P. Heintzelman and Texan rangers led by Ford delivered successive blows to Cortina's guerrillas in 1860, driving them back to their mountain retreats, sentiment in Texas for a penetration into Mexico remained strong.[10] Only the crisis of the Union diverted the strike. Revenge against Mexico, one ranger later commented, "was far sweeter to the pioneer of western Texas than the wealth of an Astor or a Vanderbilt."[11] For good reason, many Mexicans to this day habitually regard Texas as a separate province and Texans as a people apart. (They are "Tejanos" rather than "Americanos.")

The advent of the Civil War presented Texas with the opportunity to reassume its place in the society of nations. A substantial portion of the men prominent in public affairs from the days of the Republic wanted to take advantage of it. Perhaps a nostalgia for bygone days seemingly more glorious tugged at them. Not all were elder statesmen, however, and a groundswell among the rank and file could be discerned. "I wish to see Texas resume her Nationality, in case she goes out [of the Union]," wrote B. F. Burton of San Augustine to former Governor Elisha M. Pease in February, 1861. "We can acquire enough territory from Mexico to make her the strongest Republic in the world." With the United States about to subdivide, such a forecast was not entirely fanciful. Most of the advocates of Texas nationhood regretted the rupture of the Union. At the same time, they stood unalterably opposed to membership in a southern confederacy. "If the Union must be dissolved," George W. Smyth advised, "let Texas stand alone in her independence. Let her fall back upon her 'Constitution of the Republic'."[12]

Following the election of Lincoln in November, 1860, secession fever swept the state. If carried out of the Union, the sovereign state of Texas could either join its sister slave states in a southern nation or become once more independent. The same options obtained for all the seceding states but only Texas entertained nationhood. The others, of course, had no national history to draw upon and the idea of a separate nation-state never dawned on them. Their sole alternative to the Union was the Confederacy. For the majority of Texans, a revival of the Republic in 1861 seemed untimely and quixotic. But its appeal was unmistakable. The state Democratic party had actually anticipated this possibility in its platform of April, 1860: Texas "possesses the full right as a sovereign State to annul the [annexation] compact, to revoke the powers she has delegated to the government of the United States, to withdraw from the confederacy, and resume her place among the powers of the earth as a sovereign and independent nation." Dr. Gideon Lincecum spoke for many of the leading men of Texas at the close of 1860 when he accused the United States of failing to comply with the articles of annexation, particularly on the subject of border defense. "We have been wishing for an excuse for separation for five or six years," he declared. "We are very capable of sustaining an independent government and with our very abundantly rich resources, a very wealthy one."[13]

Had the crisis not been so grave, had the momentum of the seceding southern states toward confederation not been so irreversible, had the exigencies of the moment not called for swift and expedient measures, Texan nationalists might have prevailed. For months after Lincoln's victory the Lone Star flag was paraded and displayed without a companion banner.[14] Orators seized upon the occasion to recall the Texas Republic. Events, however, moved too fast in the winter of 1860-61 for Texans to unite and reassert their nationhood. Safety seemed the main desideratum and neutrality in a war between the states promised little security. An alliance with sympathetic neighbors in the name of state rights made sense. It was, to most Texans, the honorable and manly commitment.

The forces of unionism were melting away. In his bravest battle, Governor Sam Houston, aided by a mere handful of supporters in the legislature, pleaded for the Union and did all in his power to stave off secession. Fully a third of the populace still agreed with the Governor's unionist principles. But once the secession ordinance was approved by the voters in February, 1861, Houston took a different tack. He now argued against membership in any confederacy. Better that Texas be an independent nation, non-aligned and free to pursue its own policies. In the back of his mind was the vision held by many of the advocates of a Texas republic: the conquest of Mexico and lower California to give the Lone Star a commanding presence in the Caribbean and on the Pacific.[15] Ironically, the cause of Texas nationhood was probably damaged at this critical juncture by Houston's identification with it. Suspicious of the Hero's motives, partisans of secession may have viewed his case for a Republic of Texas as an artifice. A neutral Texas under Sam Houston would only give comfort to the estranged Union government.[16] And so the firebrands made their pact with the South, the Governor was deposed, and the last chance for a Texas nation was lost.

In the twenty-five years after Independence, writes Donald W. Meinig, "Texans had strongly asserted and the nation had in some degree readily accepted the idea of Texas as a highly individual place and Texans as a distinctive people."[17] The Lone Star symbolized their position as a people geographically removed and culturally isolated from the rest of America. For a century or more since 1836, the Lone Star mystique has been the essential psychology of Texas — a maverick nation, standing alone. Much of the nationalist sentiment was nourished in the crucible of separateness. Texans saw theirs as a distinct civilization born of a singular history. Even in modern times, the spirit of independence remains and something of the Texas nation is perpetuated. The vestiges are evidenced in a hundred ways. Most striking in its omnipresence is the Lone Star. The flag of Texas is itself ubiquitous and gives the state the flavor of a separate sovereignty. At the very least, visitors to Texas learn quickly that the state government is a co-equal partner with the federal government. The five-pointed star appears centered on Texas car license plates and the plate is to Texans like a fraternal badge. The Lone Star has also been appropriated as the symbol for countless Texas-made products.

Everywhere one is reminded of the Texas past as it merges with the present. The heroes of the Alamo — Travis, Bowie, Bonham, Crockett — the leaders of the Republic — Houston, Lamar, Burnet, Rusk, and many more — are invoked to represent banks, schools, and other institutions. Their names grace the streets, parks, and playgrounds of cities and towns throughout the state. Many of the counties are named for old Indian fighters and rangers. Perhaps no state citizenry is made as conscious of its heritage as the Texan. Texas history is an integral part of the public school curriculum and is even a required subject at some of the state's colleges. Texas History Week (May 5 to 11), proclaimed in 1970, offers annual lessons to citizens of every age. The venerable Texas Philosophical Society (founded 1837) still devotes itself to the question of "Texas civilization." Monuments from the 1936 Centennial and statuary in public squares and on university campuses provide additional inspiration. Patriotic societies such as the Sons or the Daughters of the Republic of Texas express a pride in ancestry while stressing Texan nationality. And the unwary visitor might well be startled by the lively observances of Texas

Independence Day (March 2) and San Jacinto Day (April 21), featuring artillery fire and bonfire.

One sees other gestures of nationalist feeling or a strong wish to identify with the state. The examples are legion, some noble, some fatuous.[18] The famed U. S. Army 36th Division of World War II, largely recruited from the Lone Star State, reportedly dubbed itself the Texas Army. To prove their point, the Texan G. I.s carried the Lone Star flag onto the beaches of Sicily. On the other hand, the Texas White House of Lyndon Baines Johnson produced some embarrassing moments. One lady coming to LBJ's inaugural in 1965 stepped off the plane at Washington with electric letters in her hair that lit up and spelled out TEXAS.[19] President Johnson himself could not be detached from his Texan identity. No American president has made so much of his state citizenship (or had so much made of it by others). Thus, it surprised no one that he should make a present to other heads of state of a finely illustrated book called *The Republic of Texas*.[20] In Bethesda, Maryland, the President's daughter, Lynda Bird, had her husband bring her a spadefull of Texas earth to be placed under her hospital bed in time for the delivery of their daughter. This would preserve the Johnson family tradition of being born over Texas soil.

On a more solemn occasion, Governor John B. Connally unwittingly reduced the American historian, Walter Prescott Webb, to Texas proportions in his memorial proclamation of March 11, 1963: "He embodied the best characteristics of a Texan in his personal qualities, and he devoted a lifetime to helping the remainder of the world understand the uniqueness of Texas." These words would not have been comforting to a man who viewed history from a broad perspective of time and space. Other Texan spokesmen, including historians, have betrayed a like provincialism. "The great difference between Texas and every other state in the 20th century," writes T. R. Fehrenbach, "was that Texas had a history."[21] Perhaps with that history in mind, Governor Price Daniel attempted to combat the United States in an ongoing dispute between Texas and the federal government over ownership of the oil-bearing tidelands. He "reactivated" the Texas Navy as "a patriotic organization to preserve the rights and boundaries of this state" by requesting the owners of 286,000 pleasure boats in Texas "to ready their craft as ready [sic] for emergency service at any time."[22] This buffoonery came to naught but easily revived memories of the deadly serious New Mexico boundary conflict a century before.

The most that can be said for these chauvinistic acts is that they are typically and uniquely Texan. Without diffidence or false modesty, the Texan expects that the world will recognize him. He swells to giant proportions and luxuriates in his identity. There is surely a strain of exhibitionism in this. "One great fault of the Texians," thought a bemused

Englishman in 1839, "is that they try to do everything at once, & having done very little & that badly, they imagine they have succeeded."[23] Americans may find that a shrewd observation today, given the prevailing stereotype. One is left to wonder whether the brash, boastful, extravagant Texan or the ardent nationalist draws attention to himself and his state to compensate for an ineffable sense of inadequacy.

It may well be that the remnants of Texan nationalism serve a need more psychological than real. There is always a lag between actual achievement and self-fulfillment. For some, both individuals and nations, the gap is never bridged. The third largest state in the Union in population, the second largest in area, Texas *is* the expanding, thriving, influential, and virile country that the founders of the Republic wanted it to be. Perhaps Texans will not be content until theirs is the empire state of America. The day may not be long in coming, but in the meantime, Texans can stand tall and take pride in what they have accomplished. They no longer require the shopworn stepladder of caricature or an outmoded nationalism to propel them forward.

Notes

Introduction

1. Hugh H. Haynie to Edward Burleson, Jr., January 9, 1860, Edward Burleson, Jr. Papers, UT; John J. Sinnicksen to Elisha M. Pease, March 10, 1846. Elisha M. Pease Letters, ATCC. For similar expressions, see Dorman H. Winfrey, *Julien Sidney Devereux and his Monte Verdi Plantation* (Waco, 1962), 61; John W. Ames, "Leaving Texas," *The Overland Monthly,* XII (February, 1874), 132; Mary Baylor, "Reminiscences, 1827-1840," UT.
2. See David M. Potter, *People of Plenty: Economic Abundance and the American Character* (Chicago, 1966 ed.), 16; also Lewis Nordyke, "The Truth About Texas," *The Rotarian,* XCII (February, 1958), 54.
3. David M. Potter, *The South and the Sectional Conflict* (Baton Rouge, 1968), 41-42.
4. See Anthony D. Smith, *Theories of Nationalism* (New York, 1972 ed.), 153-227.
5. Charles P. Roland and Richard C. Robbins, eds., "The Diary of Eliza (Mrs. Albert Sidney) Johnston," *SHQ,* LX (April, 1957), 482; Viktor Bracht, *Texas in 1848,* trans. Charles Frank Schmidt (San Antonio, 1931), 222; James Hall Bell, Speech Against Secession delivered at the Capitol, December 1, 1860, p. 4. General Albert Sidney Johnston once refused to give up his Texan citizenship even though he stood to gain financially by doing so. "When I die," he told a compatriot, "I want a handful of Texas earth on my breast." Quoted in Charles P. Roland, *Albert Sidney Johnston: Soldier of Three Republics* (Austin, 1964), 3-4. See also White to Pryor, March 4, 1861, Francis Menefee White Papers, UT; Sam Houston, "To the People of Texas" [Broadside], March 16, 1861. The following letter, dated December 3, 1969, was sent to the author by Mr. Richard Martin, a Columbia University graduate student: "I was reading (haltingly) a book on medieval theology in German with the following dedication: 'Dem Andenken Meiner Grossmutter Amaline Moorhead-Martin, geb. Smith,

NOTES

geb. 11. Februar 1842 zu Mexia, Republik von Texas; gest. 21. Januar 1922 zu Gorman, Bundesstaat Texas'. Incongruous in a German book on theology, it seems rather indicative of the power of Texas allegiance, even to the point of providing information which is not customarily included in a dedication."

6. On state loyalties, see Daniel J. Elazar, *The American Partnership: Intergovernmental Co-Operation in the Nineteenth Century United States* (Chicago, 1962), 319-320; Dixon Wector, *The Hero in America* (New York, 1941), 2; James Truslow Adams, *The Founding of New England* (Boston, 1949 ed.), 1-2; Carl L. Becker, *Everyman His Own Historian* (Chicago, 1966 ed.), 1-28.

7. Potter, *South and the Sectional Conflict*, 69-70.

8. See Nackman, "Anglo-American Migrants to the West," *WHQ*, V (October, 1974), 442-455. Page 16 of ch. 2 and pp. 35-40 of ch. 3 are based on this article. Permission has been granted by the editors of *WHQ*.

9. Mrs. Viele, *"Following the Drum": A Glimpse of Frontier Life* (New York, 1858), 142 ff.

10. [Anon.], *A Visit to Texas* (New York, 1834), 214; Edward Stiff, *The Texan Emigrant* (Cincinnati, 1840), 48-49; Chamberlain quoted in W. Eugene Hollon, *The Southwest: Old and New* (Lincoln, 1968 ed.), 163.

11. Saligny to Molé, March 6, 1839, quoted in Nancy N. Barker, "The Republic of Texas: A French View," *SHQ*, LXXI (October, 1967), 186; J. Nicholson to S. Nicholson, June 6, 1839, James Nicholson Papers, UT; British diplomat quoted in Joseph Leach, *The Typical Texan* (Dallas, 1952), 78; Bracht, *Texas in 1848*, 66-67; Wavell quoted in Justin H. Smith, *The Annexation of Texas* (New York, 1941 ed.), 34.

12. See Marilyn M. Sibley, *Travelers in Texas, 1761-1860* (Austin, 1967), 88-110.

13. Leach, *Typical Texan*, passim; J. Frank Dobie, *The Flavor of Texas* (Dallas, 1936), 107-09. On the propagation of the Texan tall tale, see William R. Hogan, *The Republic of Texas* (Austin, 1969 ed.), 160-164.

14. S. A. Maverick to M. A. Maverick, January 4, 1846, in Rena M. Green, ed., *Samuel Maverick, Texan: 1803-1870* (San Antonio, 1952), 311; George W. Terrell to W. D. Miller, January 20, 1845, Washington D. Miller Papers, TSL.

15. Charles Hooten, *St. Louis' Isle* (London, 1847), 15.

16. *Niles' Register* quoted in Jennie W. Floyd, "An Annotated Bibliography on Texas Found in American Periodicals before 1900" (unpublished master's thesis, Southern Methodist University, 1927), xxxiv-xxxv; Thomas Hughes, ed., *G.T.T. Gone to Texas* (London, 1884), v; Leach, *Typical Texan*, 29; Anson Jones, *Memoranda and Official Correspondence* (New York, 1859), 8; Opelousas *Gazette* quoted in Floyd, "Annotated Bibliography on Texas," xxxiv-xxxv. As Frederick Law Olmsted observed, "'G.T.T.' (gone to Texas) was the slang appendage . . . to every man's name who had disappeared before the discovery of some rascality. Did a man emigrate thither, every one was on watch for the discreditable reason to turn up." *A Journey Through Texas* (New York, 1857), 124.

17. *Sun* quoted in Matagorda *Bulletin*, February 21, 1839; Greeley and Hone quoted in Leach, *Typical Texan*, 28, 31; Hartford *Courant*, September 27, 1844 and October 1, 1844; cartoon reproduced in Stephen B.

Oates, ed., *The Republic of Texas* (Palo Alto, 1968), 50.
18. Austin to T. F. Leaming, September 25, 1830, Thomas F. Leaming Papers, UT; *Telegraph and Texas Register*, May 26, 1841. See also James P. McKinney to Walker Austin, June 21, 1837, Thomas F. McKinney Papers, UT; Matagorda *Bulletin*, February 21, 1839; Brazoria *Brazos Courier*, September 15, 1840; Henry Thompson *Oration* (Houston, 1839, 8; James Reily to W. D. Miller, September 16, 1844, Miller Papers.
19. W. E. Channing, *A Letter to the Hon. Henry Clay, on the Annexation of Texas to the United States* (Boston, 1837); G. L. Hammeken, "Brief Remarks on Dr. Channing's Letter to Hon. Henry Clay" (1837), UT, 2-4.
20. Wharton to S. F. Austin, December 11, 1836, *The Diplomatic Correspondence of the Republic of Texas*, ed. George P. Garrison (3 vols., Washington, 1908-1911), II, 75; George W. Bonnell, *Topographical Description of Texas* (Austin, 1840), 121; Houston *Morning Star*, June 13, 1844; Bryan to Hayes, January 23, 1843, "The Bryan-Hayes Correspondence," ed. Ernest W. Winkler, *SHQ*, XXV (October, 1921), 104; *Intelligencer*, February 28, 1846.
21. *The Weekly Despatch*, June 22, 1844.
22. *William Bollaert's Texas*, eds. W. Eugene Hollon and Ruth L. Butler (Norman, 1956), 234n; broadside quoted in "Riding Line" (Texas State Historical Association publication, March, 1971), 15.

Chapter 1

1. Eugene C. Barker, *The Life of Stephen F. Austin* (Austin, 1969 ed.), 34-37.
2. Austin to Leaming, February 1, 1828, Thomas F. Leaming Papers, UT; *Documents of Texas History*, eds. Ernest Wallace and David M. Vigness (Austin, 1963), 47.
3. *Documents*, 50; H. N. P. Gammel, comp., *The Laws of Texas, 1822-1897* (10 vols., Austin, 1898), I, 97-106. A conversion to Catholicism was seldom necessary, in practice, for the acquisition of land. Anglo-Texas was almost untouched by the established church, owing to the limited number of priests in the region, and the settlers could worship as they pleased. See I. Ingram to R. Ingram, May 29, 1830, Ira Ingram Papers, UT; Smyth to Gregg, May 22, 1835, George W. Smyth Papers, UT; James M. Day, comp., *The Texas Almanac, 1857-1873* (Waco, 1967), 206.
4. Mattie Bell, "The Growth and Distribution of the Texas Population" (unpublished master's thesis, Baylor University, 1935), 75; Eugene C. Barker, "Notes on the Colonization of Texas," *SHQ*, XXVII (October, 1923), 116-17; Douglass C. North, *The Economic Growth of the United States, 1790-1860* (New York, 1966), 187.
5. Quoted in Samuel H. Lowrie, *Culture Conflict in Texas, 1821-1835* (New York, 1932), 46.
6. See Constitution of Coahuila y Texas, March 11, 1827, articles 145-148, 159, 160, 164, in *Documents*, 62; Seymour V. Connor, "The Evolution of County Government in the Republic of Texas," *SHQ*, LV (October, 1951), 164-65; Lester G. Bugbee, "The Texas Frontier, 1820-1825," *PSHA*, IV (March, 1900), 108.

NOTES

7. Smyth, January 20, 1835, Smyth Papers.
8. Charles S. Potts, "Early Criminal Law in Texas," *TLR*, XXI (April, 1943), 395-96; Eugene C. Barker, *Mexico and Texas, 1821-1835* (New York, 1965 ed.), 91; Ray Allen Billington, *The Far Western Frontier, 1830-1860* (New York, 1962 ed.), 121.
9. In Eugene C. Barker, "The Government of Austin's Colony, 1821-1831," *SHQ*, XXI (January, 1918), 247-48.
10. Terán to Guadalupe Victoria, June 30, 1828, in Alleine Howren, "Causes and Origin of the Decree of April 6, 1830," *SHQ*, XVI (April, 1913), 395; also *The Texas Gazette* (San Felipe), January 23, 1830, August 29, 1830.
11. José María Sánchez, "A Trip to Texas in 1828," *SHQ*, XXIX (April, 1926), 260-61.
12. Howren, "Causes and Origin of the Decree," 416.
13. Austin to Leaming, May 13, 1829, Leaming Papers.
14. *Texas Gazette*, April 10, 1830; also Austin to Leaming, February 1, 1828, Leaming Papers; Noah Smithwick, *The Evolution of a State* (Austin, 1900), 9-10.
15. William H. Wharton, October 3, 1832, *Proceedings of the General Convention* (Brazoria, 1832), 14.
16. Austin to Leaming, July 14, 1830, July 17, 1830, Leaming Papers; *Texas Gazette*, September 25, 1829, March 6, 1830, March 27, 1830. For a colonist's viewpoint, see I. Ingram to R. Ingram, May 29, 1830, Ingram Papers.
17. John W. S. Dancy, August 2, 1838, "Diary of the Travels of John W. Dancy," UT; Smythe, January 20, 1835, Smyth Papers: Terán to Guadalupe Victoria, June 30, 1828, in Howren, "Causes and Origin of the Decree," 395-98.
18. Smyth, December 29, 1832, in Elbert J. Myers, "Life of George W. Smyth" (unpublished master's thesis, University of Texas, 1931), 38.
19. *Texas Gazette*, September 25, 1830; Jonas Harison, October 6, 1832, *Proceedings of the General Convention*, 27.
20. Austin to Terán, June 27, 1832, Thomas W. Streeter Texas Collection, YU. The reaction of Texans to these attacks was mixed. A Matagorda citizens' committee deplored the Anahuac affair but warned Mexico that "the employment of a military force to check that which should be left solely to the energetic opperation of the Law might frustrate our pacific determinations and make us a party to the proceedings we now condemn." S. R. Fisher, S. J. Poit, and J. Norton to Don Rámon Múzquis, June, 20, 1832, "Domestic Correspondence" TSL.
21. John Austin, October 1, 1832, *Proceedings of the General Convention*, 7. See Turtle Bayou resolutions, June 13, 1832, in *Documents*, 73; *Communication Forwarded from San Felipe de Austin Relative to Late Events in Texas* (Mobile, 1832), 3-4; toasts at Matagorda citizens' dinner, August 22, 1832, Samuel E. Asbury Papers, UT.
22. *Documents*, 79. The delegates decried the perilous condition of such towns as San Antonio and Goliad, and rebuked the Mexican government for failing to provide defense against the Comanches, Wacoes, and "other insignificant bands of savages, whom a well organized local government would soon subdue and exterminate." In James T. DeShields, *Border*

NOTES

Wars of Texas (Tioga, 1912), 95-97; also David B. Edward, *The History of Texas* (Cincinnati, 1836), 207.

23. S. F. Austin to H. Austin, April 19, 1833, in Barker, *Mexico and Texas*, 119.
24. I. Ingram to R. Ingram, July 23, 1833, Ingram Papers.
25. Austin quoted in Edward, *History of Texas*, 211.
26. Smyth, January 20, 1835, Smyth Papers.
27. Milam quoted in *Heroes of Texas* (Waco, 1964), 121.
28. (Anon.), *Texas in 1837*, ed. Andrew F. Muir (Austin, 1958), 134-35.
29. Travis quoted in Forrest E. Ward, "Pre-Revolutionary Activity in Brazoria County," *SHQ*, LXIV (October, 1960), 227. Even Travis was not original. He was parroting the very words of John Adams. See Richard B. Morris, *Seven Who Shaped Our Destiny: The Founding Fathers as Revolutionaries* (New York, 1973), 96; see also Forbes to Miller, July 21, 1835, "Domestic Correspondence"; Smith to Chambers, September 2, 1835, Don Carlos Barrett Papers, UT; Barker, *Mexico and Texas*, 138-39, 145, 155-61; Eugene C. Barker, "The Texan Declaration of Causes for Taking Up Arms Against Mexico," *QTSHA*, XV (January, 1912), 174.
30. N. T. Byars (1835), in D. W. C. Baker, comp., *A Texas Scrap-Book* (New York, 1875), 440; also *Telegraph and Texas Register* (San Felipe), October 17, 1835.
31. Lawrence H. Gipson, *The Coming of the Revolution, 1763-1775* (New York, 1962 ed.), 232; Austin to Leaming, March 15, 1831, Leaming Papers.
32. Smithwick, *Evolution of a State*, 101.
33. Reported in New Orleans *Bee*, October 14, 1835, in Annie L. Middleton, "Studies Relating to the Annexation of Texas by the United States" (unpublished doctoral dissertation, University of Texas, 1938), 29.
34. Austin to Leaming, August 23, 1835, Leaming Papers.
35. In Joshua James, comp., *A Journal of a Tour in Texas* (Wilmington, N.C., 1835), 15.
36. The movement for Texas independence appears to confirm David M. Potter's contention that a conflict of interest is likely to be a greater threat to national unity than cultural diversity. When the state "acts against what the group conceives to be its fundamental welfare, there is a question whether loyalty can survive," he writes. "The disruptive potentials inherent in cultural diversity remain latent until conflicts of interest bring them into play." *The South and the Sectional Conflict* (Baton Rouge, 1968), 80. The Texas Revolution was clearly not an internal social revolution. Still in its first generation, Texas society was relatively classless and land ownership was widespread. There was no cause to interfere with property relations since Mexican property holdings were nil, and after independence was achieved, many Spanish and Mexican land titles were confirmed by Texas courts and legislatures. See Gerald Ashford, "Jacksonian Liberalism and Spanish Law in Early Texas," *SHQ*, LVII (July, 1953), 28. On the historiography of the Texas Revolution, see Seymour V. Connor, *Texas: A History* (New York, 1971), 118-122; Paul L. Hendrix, "A Historiographical Study of the Texas Revolution" (unpublished master's thesis, University of Houston, 1961), 27.
37. William H. Wharton, "Freemen of Texas. To Arms!!! To Arms!!!!"

NOTES

(Brazoria, September 3, 1835), Streeter Collection.
38. John Henry Brown, *Life and Times of Henry Smith* (Austin, 1935), 106. Texas histories, for the most part, accept the anti-revolutionary view because the ostensible aim was merely to restore rights and privileges denied by Mexico's central government. See, for example, William C. Binkley, *The Texas Revolution* (Baton Rouge, 1952), 119.
39. Branch T. Archer, November 3, 1835, in Gammel, *Laws of Texas,* I, 511.
40. Houston quoted in Richard R. Stenberg, "The Texas Schemes of Jackson and Houston, 1829-1836," *SSSQ,* XV (December, 1934), 242.
41. *Telegraph and Texas Register,* October 26, 1835, December 2, 1835, March 24, 1836; also Burleson to Austin, December 10, 1835, Edward Burleson Papers, UT; Nacogdoches *Texean and Emigrant's Guide,* December 26, 1835; Henry Smith, "Texas Expects Every Man to Do His Duty" (Broadside, February, 1836) Streeter Collection; Austin to Leaming, April 30, 1836, Leaming Papers.
42. Wharton to Archer, November 28, 1835, in Brazoria *Texas Republican* (n.d.); *The Goliad Declaration of Independence,* December 20, 1835 (Brazoria, 1835), 5; also H. Austin to Holley, November 27, 1835, Henry Austin Papers, UT.
43. E. Warren to H. Warren, December 25, 1835, Streeter Collection; William F. Gray, *From Virginia to Texas* (Houston, 1909), 61-62; Austin to Leaming, February 16, 1836, Leaming Papers.
44. Pease to Father, March 4, 1836, Elisha M. Pease Papers, UT; Brigham to Howes, March 12, 1836, Asa Brigham Papers, UT.
45. Austin to Holley, March 29, 1836, Henry Austin Papers; also D. G. Burnet quoted in New Orleans *True American,* April 7, 1836, in (Anon.), *A Visit to Texas* (New York, 1836 ed.), 258.

Chapter 2

1. May 9, 1853, James B. McIntyre Letter, UT.
2. February 5, 1856, in Jane Frances Leathers, ed., "Christopher Columbus Goodman," *SHQ,* LXIX (January, 1966), 363.
3. Rusk to Lamar, May 12, 1836, Thomas Jefferson Rusk Papers, UT; J. R. Jones to children, July 17, 1836, John Rice Jones, Jr. Papers, UT.
4. Ann Raney Thomas Coleman Reminiscences, UT, pt. 1, p. 151; William Fairfax Gray, *From Virginia to Texas* (Houston, 1909), 134, 152; also Harriet A. Ames Reminiscences, UT, p. 14.
5. E. M. Pease to Father, May 26, 1836, Elisha Marshall Pease Papers, UT.
6. W. Hale to P. S. Hale, April 11, 1836, Philip Smith Hale Papers, UT; S. T. Allen to T. T. Allen, May 18, 1836, in Marc S. Simmons, ed., "Samuel T. Allen and the Texas Revolution," *SHQ,* LXVIII (April, 1965), 487.
7. Branch T. Archer, November 3, 1835, *Journals of the Consultation* (Houston, 1838), 7.
8. Johnnie Belle McDonald, "The Soldiers of San Jacinto" (unpublished master's thesis, University of Texas, 1922), 23-24.
9. J. W. Hassell to Father, June 21, 1836, Samuel E. Asbury Papers, UT; Holland quoted in Leo Hershkowitz, "'The Land of Promise': Samuel

NOTES

Swartwout and Land Speculation in Texas, 1830-1838," *NYHSQ*, XLVIII (October, 1964), 318; Crockett to children, January 9, 1836, Asbury Papers.

10. I. Ingram to R. Ingram, May 10, 1834, Ira Ingram Papers, UT.

11. Elgin Williams, *The Animating Pursuits of Speculation* (New York, 1949), 28, 16 ff; Felloseby to Mary Anna, March 27, 1836, John Felloseby Letter, UT; also G. Paschal to T. J. Rusk, September 23, 1837, Rusk Papers; William R. Hogan, *The Texas Republic* (Austin, 1969 ed.), 82-87.

12. Douglass C. North, *Economic Growth of the United States, 1790-1860* (New York, 1966), 189-190; A. Brigham to Friends, February 28, 1832, Asa Brigham Papers, UT.

13. McAlister to G. W. Smyth, September 9, 1835, George W. Smyth Papers, UT; Hamilton to Rusk, February 8, 1836, Rusk Papers.

14. Ray Allen Billington, *The Far Western Frontier, 1830-1860* (New York, 1962), 119; Brigham to S. Howe, March 8, 1835, Brigham Papers; Smyth to J. Gallagher, May 23, 1835, Smyth Papers; *Texean [sic] and Emigrant's Guide*, December 26, 1835.

15. *Telegraph and Texas Register* (San Felipe), October 31, 1835; Brigham to Howe, March 8, 1835, Brigham Papers; J. P. McKinney to W. Austin, January 8, 1837, Thomas F. McKinney Papers, UT; Tarleton to *Journal*, April 22, 1836, Asbury Papers.

16. Smyth to "Sir," Smyth Papers; M. A. Maverick to Mother, August 25, 1838, and S. A. Maverick to M. A. Maverick, November 19, 1845, in Rena M. Green, ed., *Samuel Maverick, Texan: 1803-1870* (San Antonio, 1952), 77, 222; Leeper to David Walker, February 17, 1854, David Walker Papers, UT.

17. Mary Austin Holley, *Texas* (Lexington, Ky., 1836), 137; (Anon.), *Texas in 1837*, ed. Andrew F. Muir (Austin, 1958), 60-61; also David Woodman, Jr., *Guide to Texas Emigrants* (Boston, 1835), 175; John M. Nance, ed., "A Letter Book of Joseph Eve," *SHQ*, XLIII (October, 1939), 212.

18. In Joshua James, comp., *A Journal of a Tour in Texas* (Wilmington, N. C., 1835), 14-15.

19. Kaufman to McCullough, March 20, 1838, Henry Sayles, Jr. Papers, SWC; Hamilton to Pakenham, January 3, 1840, *The Diplomatic Correspondence of the Republic of Texas*, ed. George P. Garrison (3 vols., Washington, 1908-1911), II-3, 884. For other expressions of boosterism, see *Telegraph and Texas Register*, September 13, 1836, May 12, 1841; Pease to Father, August 4, 1837, Elisha M. Pease Papers, UT; J. Nicholson to S. Nicholson, June 6, 1839, James Nicholson Papers, UT; *Texas Emigrant*, August 31, 1839; Jayne to Wife, June 7, 1840, Brewster H. Jayne Letter, UT; Pancoast to Family, December 11, 1845, Josiah Pancoast Papers, UT.

20. Francis C. Sheridan, *Galveston Island* (Austin, 1954 ed.), 105; also Ferdinand Roemer, *Texas* (San Antonio, 1935 ed.), 32-33.

21. North, *Economic Growth*, 199-203; Samuel Rezneck, "The Social History of an American Depression, 1837-1843," *AHR*, XL (July, 1935); Malcolm J. Rohrbough, *The Land Office Business* (New York, 1968), 301-02.

NOTES

22. Samuel Hammett Adams [pseud. Philip Paxton], *A Stray Yankee in Texas* (New York, 1854), ix.

23. Jones to Lamar, October 16, 1838, *The Papers of Mirabeau Buonaparte Lamar*, ed. Charles Adams Gulick (6 vols., Austin, 1920-1927), II, 253-54; James Norman Smith, "Autobiography, 1798-1860" (4 vols., UT), III, 107-110.

24. I. M. Freeman to I. T. Freeman, September 16, 1839, Ira M. Freeman Papers, UT; Gordon to Lamar, April 14, 1839, *Lamar Papers*, II, 528.

25. *Evening Post*, May 8, 1840, *Tribune*, July 21, 1841, quoted in Berenice S. Cook, "Texas as Seen in the New York Press from 1835 to 1845" (unpublished master's thesis, Columbia University, 1935), 45; Edward Stiff, *The Texan Emigrant* (Cincinnati, 1840), 76-77; William E. Sawyer, ed., "A Young Man Comes to Texas in 1852," *Texana*, VII (Spring, 1969). 23; Dorman H. Winfrey, *Julien Sidney Devereux and His Monte Verdi Plantation* (Waco, 1962), 28-31, 57-58. The fact that Texas became a haven for debtors was mirrored in the laws of the Republic: "No person shall be imprisoned for debt in consequence of inability to pay," guaranteed the Declaration of Rights in the 1836 Constitution. This protection was repeated in the state Constitution of 1845. Another security was the Texas Homestead Law of 1839, which defended a household against seizure for default. It too was affirmed by the 1845 Constitution, which empowered the legislature to protect from forced sale property not exceeding 200 acres of farmland or a town lot not exceeding $2,000 in value. See H. N. P. Gammel, comp., *The Laws of Texas, 1822-1897* (10 vols., Austin, 1898), II, 1894; Ernest Wallace and David M. Vigness, eds., *Documents of Texas History* (Austin, 1963), 105, 130.

26. Force to Family, July 10, 1837, William A. Force Papers, UT; H. N. P. Gammel, comp., *The Laws of Texas, 1822-1897* (10 vols., Austin, 1898), II, 35-36.

27. Paschal to Rusk, September 23, 1837, Rusk Papers; Force to Family, July 10, 1837, Force Papers; J. Nicholson to S. Nicholson, June 6, 1839, Nicholson Papers.

28. James V. Reese, "The Worker in Texas, 1821-1876" (unpublished doctoral dissertation, University of Texas, 1964), 102; Noah Smithwick, *The Evolution of a State* (Austin, 1900), 10; T. H. B. Hockaday to J. Campbell, January 10, 1860, Jack Campbell Papers, UT; H. V. Scott to B. Slade, January 13, 1846, Harriet Virginia Scott Papers, UT.

29. C. Chamberlain to E. J. Munson, April 28, 1838, Force Papers; I. M. Freeman to I. T. Freeman, June 15, 1840, Freeman Papers, 26-27; J. R. Jones to S. D. Mullowny, December 28, 1846, Jones Papers; Patricia Mercer, "Diary, 1840-1841," UT. An Englishwoman visiting in 1844 saw money-grubbing as a national characteristic of Texans: "Every thought and every idea here resolves itself into . . . dollars, and how to obtain them, seems their one sole and engrossing thought." Matilda C. Houstoun, *Texas and the Gulf of Mexico* (2 vols., London, 1844), II, 109.

30. Austin to Holley, November 21, 1838, Henry Austin Papers, UT; R. Sanders to J. Sanders, November 25, 1841, Robert Sanders Letter, UT; Jones to Brady, December 1, 1842, Jones Papers.

31. Irion to Henderson, March 20, 1838, *Diplomatic Correspondence*, II-3, 849; Lamar to Congress, November 12, 1839, *Lamar Papers*, III, 164;

Committee on Finance, n.d., *Journal of the Senate of the Fourth Congress of the Republic of Texas, 1839-1840,* ed. Harriet Smither (Austin, n.d.), 36n; George W. Bonnell, *Topographical Description of Texas* (Austin, 1840), 150.

32. *Telegraph and Texas Register,* March 6, 1839, November 9, 1842, quoted in Maybelle V. G. Stone, "Immigration to Texas, 1836-1845" (unpublished master's thesis, University of Texas, 1938), 18, 66.

33. *Telegraph and Texas Register,* July 21, 1841, quoted in Walter P. Webb, *The Great Plains* (Boston, 1931), 181; Swartwout to Houston, December 26, 1841, "Domestic Correspondence," TSL.

34. Birdsall to Bullman, March 19, 1838, "Domestic Correspondence."

35. Seymour V. Connor, *Texas: A History* (New York, 1971), 137; Lamar to Congress, November 3, 1841, *Journal of the Senate of the Sixth Congress of the Republic of Texas, 1841-1842,* ed. Harriet Smither (Austin, 1940), 20.

36. See act of January 4, 1841, authorizing the Peters Colony "for the purpose of colonizing and settling a portion of the vacant and unappropriated lands of the republic. . . . " Legislation of February 5, 1842 provided similarly for other colonization companies. Gammel, *Laws of Texas,* II, 554-57.

37. James K. Pike, *Scout and Ranger* (Princeton, 1932 ed.), 15.

38. Henry Thompson, *Oration* (Houston, 1839 [sic]), 9; *Telegraph and Texas Register,* July 21, 1841.

39. Connor, *Texas,* 148.

40. Smith to Bee, October 17, 1843, Barnard E. Bee Papers, UT; also Miller to Houston, February 9, 1842, Washington D. Miller Papers, TSL.

41. Walter P. Webb and H. Bailey Carroll, eds., *Handbook of Texas* (2 vols., Austin, 1952), I, 308.

42. *Handbook,* I, 7-8, II, 181; Lota M. Spell, *Music in Texas* (Austin, 1936), 35.

43. W. C. Holden, "Immigration and Settlement in West Texas," *WTHAYB,* V (June, 1929), 66; also Emma Jean Walker, "The Contemporary Texan: An Examination of Major Additions to the Mythical Texan in the Twentieth Century" (unpublished doctoral dissertation, University of Texas, 1966), 18, 173-74.

44. Rupert N. Richardson et al., *Texas the Lone Star State* (Englewood Cliffs, 1970 ed.), 148; W. Eugene Hollon, *The Southwest: Old and New* (Lincoln, 1968 ed.), 187; Connor, *Texas,* 169-70. On the other hand, the U. S. Graduation Act of 1854 lowered the price of lands that had gone begging. All unsold public lands on the market for ten to fifteen years were reduced to $1.00 per acre; from fifteen to twenty years, to 75 cents per acre; from twenty to thirty years, to 25 cents per acre; over thirty years, to 12.5 cents per acre. Preemption (squatter's rights) was extended to all lands subject to graduation. Roy M. Robbins, *Our Landed Heritage* (Lincoln, 1962 ed.), 170.

45. Paul W. Gates, "Frontier Estate Builders and Farm Laborers," in *The Frontier in Perspective,* eds. Walker D. Wyman and Clifton B. Kroeber (Madison, 1957), 157-58.

46. J. De Cordova, *Texas: Her Resources and Her Public Men* (Philadelphia, 1858), 353.

NOTES

47. Smith to Brother, May 19, 1850, Ann Raney Thomas Coleman Papers, UT; Oberthier to Scruggs, March 12, 1852, Thomas W. Streeter Collection, YU; William E. Sawyer, ed., "A Young Man Comes to Texas in 1852," *Texana*, VII (Spring, 1969), 24; *Chronicle* quoted in *The Texas Ranger*, February 2, 1854.

48. George Blackburn and Sherman L. Ricards, Jr., "A Demographic History of the West: Manistee County, Michigan, 1860," *JAH*, LVII December, 1970), 603-04; *The Texas Gazette*, August 9, 1830; Marion D. Mullins, *The First Census of Texas, 1829-1836* (Washington, D.C., 1959), 1-6; *Seventh Census of the United States: 1850* (Washington, 1853), xlii; *Population of the United States in 1860* (Washington, 1864), xvii, xxix, xxxiii, 592-93, 598, 616-619; Mattie Bell, "The Growth and Distribution of the Texas Population" (unpublished master's thesis, Baylor University, 1935), 80. See also D. W. Meinig, *Imperial Texas* (Austin, 1969), 35; Stone, "Immigration to Texas," 66-67; Frederic Gaillardet, *Sketches of Early Texas and Louisiana* (Austin, 1966 ed.), 73.

49. William W. White, "Migration into West Texas, 1845-1860" (unpublished master's thesis, University of Texas, 1948), 11; Bell, "Growth and Distribution of Texas Population," 80, 142; Harold D. Woodman, ed., *Slavery and the Southern Economy* (New York, 1966), 14-15.

50. Quoted in Averam B. Bender, *The March of Empire* (Lawrence, 1952), 4; J. De Cordova, "The Cultivation of Cotton in Texas: The Advantages of Free Labour" (London, 1858), 44.

51. Olmsted, *A Journey Through Texas* (New York, 1857), 244; J. Burnam to W. Burnam, November 28, 1852, Lottie Holman Card Papers, SWC.

52. Cordova, *Texas*, 21; *Lecture on Texas* (Philadelphia, 1858), 7; *The Texas Immigrant and Traveller's Guide Book* (Austin, 1856); *The Cultivation of Cotton in Texas* (London, 1858).

53. Bell to Legislature, December 22, 1851, *Journal of the House of Representatives of the State of Texas*, Fourth Legislature (Austin, 1852), 368-69; J. D. B. DeBow, *The Industrial Resources, Etc. of the Southern and Western States* (3 vols., New Orleans, 1853), III, 326; also Melinda Rankin, *Texas in 1850* (Boston, 1850), 24; Mr. Walker, January 18, 1860, *Journal of the Senate of the State of Texas*, Eighth Legislature (Austin, 1860), 292-94.

54. Austin to Leaming, February 1, 1828, Thomas F. Leaming Papers, UT. Austin was less eager for European emigrants. "They will not in general possess the enterprise, perseverence and morality so indispensible to settle a wilderness." In Reese, "The Worker in Texas," 22.

55. Committee on Public Lands, January 20, 1853, *Journals of the House of Representatives of the State of Texas*, Fourth Legislature – Extra Session (Austin, 1853), 123; Mr. Murrah, December 9, 1857, *Journal of the House of Representatives of the State of Texas*, Seventh Biennial Session (Austin, 1857), 309; also Mr. Walker, 1857, January 25, 1858, *Journal of the Senate of Texas*, Seventh Biennial Session (Austin, 1857), 274, 419.

56. Pike, *Scout and Ranger*, 4.

NOTES

Chapter 3

1. Edward Stiff, *The Texan Emigrant* (Cincinnati, 1840), 48.
2. Philip Paxton [pseud.], *A Stray Yankee in Texas* (New York, 1854), ix.
3. Dill to Martínez, January 31, 1822, "Domestic Correspondence," TSL; Milam to J. Poinsett, August 28, 1825, Joel Roberts Poinsett Papers, UT.
4. Carl Solms-Braunfels, *Texas, 1844-1845* (Houston, 1936 ed.), 137-38; Smyth to "Sir" (ca. 1833), George W. Smyth Papers, UT; *The Texas Gazette*, August 21, 1830.
5. Quoted in Charles M. Andrews, *The Colonial Background of the American Revolution* (New Haven, 1967 ed.), 211-212.
6. Marilyn M. Sibley, *Travelers in Texas, 1761-1860* (Austin, 1967), 111-112.
7. C. L. Sonnichsen, *Ten Texas Feuds* (Albuquerque, 1957), 14.
8. The Abbe Domenech, *Missionary Adventures in Texas and Mexico* (London, 1858), 227-228.
9. Aldridge to Mrs. John Jackson, April 28, 1837, William B. Aldridge Papers, UT; I. M. Freeman to I. T. Freeman, September 16, 1839, Ira M. Freeman Papers, UT.
10. John Q. Anderson, ed., *Tales of Frontier Texas, 1830-1860* (Dallas, 1966), 140, 215, 275; also William R. Hogan, *The Texas Republic* (Austin, 1966 ed.), 160-64; Hennig Cohen and William B. Dillingham, eds., *Humor of the Old Southwest* (Boston, 1964), ix-xxiii; Elton Miles, *Southwest Humorists* (Austin, 1969), 1-10; Constance Rourke, *American Humor* (Garden City, 1953 ed.), 37-69.
11. Francis C. Sheridan, *Galveston Island* (Austin, 1954 ed.), 113; Galveston *Texas Times*, October 19, 1842, in *William Bollaert's Texas*, eds. W. Eugene Hollon and Ruth L. Butler (Norman, 1956), 80; also Thomas D. Clark, *The Rampaging Frontier* (Bloomington, 1954 ed.), 183, 186, 196-97; Everett Dick, *The Dixie Frontier* (New York, 1964 ed.), 333; George Dangerfield, *The Era of Good Feelings* (New York, 1952), 112; John Hope Franklin, *The Militant South, 1800-1861* (Cambridge, 1956), 190.
12. Ferdinand Roemer, *Texas* (San Antonio, 1935 ed.), 48; Thompson to Lamar, September 5, 1839, in *The Papers of Mirabeau Buonaparte Lamar*, ed. Charles Adams Gulick (6 vols., Austin, 1920-1927), III, 102; Gustav Dresel, *Houston Journal* (Austin, 1954 ed.), 33.
13. *Heroes of Texas* (Waco, 1964), 17, 29; Travis letter of February 24, 1836 in *Documents of Texas History*, eds. Ernest Wallace and David M. Vigness (Austin, 1963), 96.
14. Robert H. Williams, Jr., "Travis – A Potential Sam Houston?" *SHQ*, XL (October, 1936), 159. The average age of the Alamo defenders was 28.2. Archie P. McDonald, "The Young Men of the Texas Revolution," *Texana*, III (Winter, 1965), 342.
15. Cloud letter, December 28, 1835, quoted in McDonald, "The Young Men of the Texas Revolution," 344; Travis to Henry Smith, February 12, 1836, quoted in *Heroes of Texas*, 136; Travis letter of March 3, 1836, in *Documents*, 97.
16. Fannin to Joseph Mims, March 13, 1836, Thomas F. McKinney Papers, UT.
17. "Hymn of the Alamo" by Robert M. Potter, October, 1836, in

NOTES

A. Garland Adair and M. H. Crockett, eds., *Heroes of the Alamo* (New York, 1956), 77. See also Alex Dienst, "Contemporary Poetry of the Texan Revolution," *SHQ,* XXI (October, 1917), 156-184.
18. Pease to Father, March 29, 1836, Elisha M. Pease Papers, UT; Giddings quoted in Stephen B. Oates, ed., *The Republic of Texas* (Palo Alto, 1968), 25; Robinson to Convention, March 4, 1836, *Journals of the General Convention of 1836* (Houston, 1838), 34; Lamar quoted in Herbert P. Gambrell, *Mirabeau Buonaparte Lamar* (Dallas, 1934), 87.
19. *Texas Republican,* September 26, 1835; J. H. Jenkins, III, ed., *Recollections of Early Texans* (Austin, 1958),   39; Ernest W. Winkler, ed., "The Bryan-Hayes Correspondence," *SHQ,* XXV (October, 1921), 98.
20. See Mark E. Nackman, "The Making of the Texan Citizen Soldier, 1835-1860," *SHQ,* LXXVIII (January, 1975), 231-253.
21. Seguin quoted in Jennie W. Floyd, "An Annotated Bibliography on Texas Found in American Periodicals Before 1900" (unpublished master's thesis, Southern Methodist University, 1927), xliii-xliv; Houston to Congress, November 27, 1837, *Journal of the House of Representatives of the Republic of Texas,* Called Session of September 25, 1837, and Regular Session, Commencing November 6, 1837 (Houston, 1838),160; also Sam Houston, "A General Call to Arms," March 10, 1842, in *The Writings of Sam Houston,* eds. Amelia W. Williams and Eugene C. Barker (8 vols., Austin, 1938-1943), II, 490-91; Joseph Eve to J. J. Crittenden, April 3, 1842, in John M. Nance, ed., "A Letter Book of Joseph Eve," *SHQ,* XLIII (January, 1940), 371-72. "The sacred memory of those immortal heroes, the martyrs of the Alamo and the victors at San Jacinto," a visitor to Texas concluded, "will incite them by deeds of noble courage and reckless daring to honor those noble men who with their blood purchased liberty in the fairest and richest country on earth." Viktor Bracht, *Texas in 1848* (San Antonio, 1931 ed.), 76; also Charles De Morse, May 20, 1874, in D. W. C. Baker, comp., *A Texas Scrap-Book* (New York, 1875), 212.
22. Harvey A. Adams Papers (2 vols., UT), II, 5-6; J. C. Parmenter, "Texan Hymn," in Baker, comp., *Texas Scrap-Book,* 395.
23. Emile Durkheim, *Suicide* (New York, 1951 ed.), 217-240.
24. Of the 359 members of the Texas conventions and congresses from 1832 to 1845 whose deaths are accounted for, no less than five committed suicide. This is a suicide rate among the leadership of nearly 1.4 per hundred. See profiles in *Biographical Directory of the Texan Conventions and Congresses, 1832-1845* (Austin, 1941). This compares alarmingly with Durkheim's statistics for "anomic suicide" in Italy between 1864 and 1877, which range from 29 to 40.6 suicides per *million.* Durkheim, *Suicide,* 244.
25. Quoted in letter from J. A. Rogers to M. B. Lamar, July 12, 1838, *Lamar Papers,* II, 183.
26. Walter P. Webb and H. Bailey Carroll, eds., *The Handbook of Texas* (2 vols., Austin, 1952), I, 377; Stanley Siegel, *A Political History of the Texas Republic, 1836-1845* (Austin, 1956), 98. Collinsworth's demise may not have been entirely unexpected. Acquaintances reported that he had been drinking heavily during the week preceding his leap. T. F. McKinney to S. M. Williams, October 13, 1838, in Hogan, *The Texas Republic,* 44.

NOTES

27. Cornelia Hood in Webb and Carroll, eds., *Handbook*, I, 338-39.
28. Herbert Gambrell in Webb and Carroll, eds., *Handbook*, I, 922-23.
29. See, for example, letter of October 14, 1838, in Lois F. Blount, "A Brief Study of Thomas J. Rusk Based on His Letters to His Brother, David, 1835-1856," *SHQ*, XXXIV (April, 1931), 280-81. A rare glimpse into the private man is given in a letter from Rusk to his four boys upon his election to the United States Senate: "I have had my share of trouble in this world and the most which I have suffered has proceeded from three causes 1st Getting in debt 2nd Becoming Security for others 3rd Intemperance These three courses are the rocks upon which I have wrecked most of my earthly happiness and which I would warn my sons against. Debt beyond the means of paying to a sensitive mind is perfect slavery and will eventually destroy the brightest Intellect It cramps and destroys the best feelings of human nature and added to intemperance will make earth a hell. . . . Be industrious — honest sober kind to the unfortunate and distressed Speak evil of none and associate only with those of principles and reputation. . . . " February 22, 1846, Thomas Jefferson Rusk Papers, UT.
30. Henry Thompson, *Texas* (Philadelphia, 1839), 54-55.
31. *Dictionary of American Biography* (20 vols., New York 1928-1936), XVI, 236-37; Noah Smithwick, *Evolution of a State* (Austin, 1900), 146, 151; Francis R. Lubbock, *Six Decades in Texas* (Austin, 1968 ed.), 82; Blount, "A Brief Study of Thomas J. Rusk," *SHQ*, XXXIV, 181-202, 271-290.
32. See Stanley Elkins and Eric McKitrick, "A Meaning for Turner's Frontier," *PSQ*, LXIX (September, 1954), 321-353, (December, 1954), 565-602; Ray Allen Billington, *America's Frontier Heritage* (New York, 1966), 131, 134.
33. J. Eve to C. A. Wickliffe, December 26, 1842, in Nance, ed., "Letter Book of Joseph Eve," *SHQ*, XLIV (July, 1940), 107.
34. Ralph A. Wooster, "Membership in Early Texas Legislatures, 1850-1860," *SHQ*, LXIX (October, 1965), 164n-165; James V. Reese, "The Worker in Texas, 1821-1876" (unpublished doctoral dissertation, University of Texas, 1964), 177.
35. Alfred Thomas Howell to Father, June 7, 1852, in William E. Sawyer, ed., "A Young Man Comes to Texas in 1852," *Texana*, VII (Spring, 1969), 21. The foregoing statistics on the conventional and congressional membership from 1832 to 1845 are derived from the author's compilation and analysis of the 482 biographical profiles in the *Biographical Directory of Texan Conventions and Congresses*.
36. Gambrell, *Lamar*, 55-57; Lubbock, *Six Decades*, 43, 79, 92.
37. Herbert Gambrell, *Anson Jones* (Garden City, 1948), 22-24, 42-43; Anson Jones, *Memoranda and Official Correspondence* (New York, 1859), 9, 11. Jones expressed the following opinions in 1839. On Sam Houston: "No man is more completely master of the art of appropriating to himself the merit of others' good arts, and shifting on to others the odium of his bad ones. . . . " On Mirabeau B. Lamar: "It is strong evidence of the poverty of worth or talent [in Texas], when such a man as L. is called for the head of a country. He is a very weak man, and governed by petty passions which he cannot control, and by prejudices which are the result of ignorance (of the world). Obstinacy he possesses, and what his friends call

146

honesty. " On David G. Burnet: "He has every kind of sense but common sense, and consequently will never do for a statesman." *Memoranda,* 32, 35.
38. James M. Day, comp., *The Texas Almanac, 1857-1873* (Waco, 1967), 17-19.
39. Day, comp., *Texas Almanac,* 60-61.
40. Alvy L. King, "Louis T. Wigfall: The Stormy Petrel" (Ph.D. dissertation, Texas Technological College, 1967), 76.
41. Ben H. Procter, *Not Without Honor: The Life of John H. Reagan* (Austin, 1962), 17, 41.
42. Smyth to Chambers, February 10, 1830, quoted in Elbert J. Myers, "Life of George W. Smyth" (unpublished master's thesis, University of Texas, 1931), 5.
43. John S. Ford in Stephen B. Oates, ed., *Rip Ford's Texas* (Austin, 1963), 9 ff.
44. Charles P. Roland, *Albert Sidney Johnston* (Austin, 1964), 54.
45. Dorman H. Winfrey, *Julien Sidney Devereux and His Monte Verdi Plantation* (Waco, 1962), 28-31.
46. Day, comp., *Texas Almanac,* 467.

Chapter 4

1. Bell to Legislature, December 22, 1851, *Journal of the House of Representatives of the State of Texas,* Fourth Legislature (Austin, 1852), 368.
2. Speech of Guy M. Bryan before Texas Veterans Association, May 14, 1873, in D. W. C. Baker, comp., *A Texas Scrap-Book* (New York, 1875), 184.
3. Lamar to Congress, November 1, 1840, *The Papers of Mirabeau Buonaparte Lamar,* ed. Charles A. Gulick (6 vols., Austin, 1920-1927), III, 469.
4. W. W. Newcomb, *The Indians of Texas* (Austin, 1969 ed.), 338; also Joseph Leach, *The Typical Texan* (Dallas, 1952), 61; Joe B. Frantz, "The Lone Star Mystique," in *The Republic of Texas,* ed. Stephen B. Oates (Palo Alto, 1968), 9; W. H. Hutchinson, "Bear Flag and Lone Star: Two Imperial Powers and their Stereotypes," *SHQ,* LXXII (October, 1968), 149.
5. Houston to Congress, May 5, 1837, *Journal of the House of Representatives of the Republic of Texas,* First Congress, Second Session (Houston, 1838), 16.
6. Brigham to Howe, March 9, 1836, Asa Brigham Papers, UT.
7. See correspondence in Josephine K. Hunley, "A Documentary History of Texan Sentiment for Annexation to the United States, 1835-1838" (unpublished master's thesis, University of Texas, 1937), 13-14, 19, 76; S. F. Austin to "Gentlemen," June 14, 1836, Thomas W. Streeter Texas Collection, YU; S. T. Allen to T. T. Allen, May 18, 1836, in Marc S. Simmons, ed., "Samuel T. Allen and the Texas Revolution," *SHQ,* LXVIII (April, 1965), 487-88; also Joseph W. Schmitz, *Texan Statecraft, 1836-1845* (San Antonio, 1941), 24, 35; George P. Garrison, "The First Stage of the Movement for the Annexation of Texas," *AHR,* X (October, 1904), 74.
8. Lamar, October 22, 1836, *Journals of the House of Representatives of the Republic of Texas,* First Congress, First Session (Houston, 1838),

NOTES

89; Rusk to Houston, August 11, 1836, Thomas Jefferson Rusk Papers, UT.

9. H. V. Scott to B. Slade, January 13, 1846, Harriet V. Scott Papers, UT.

10. James T. DeShields, *They Sat in High Place* (San Antonio, 1940), 35; *Lamar Papers*, I, 11.

11. Austin to Holley, November 8, 1836, December 9, 1836, Henry Austin Papers, UT.

12. D. G. Burnet to Congress, October 4, 1836, *Journals of the House, First Congress, First Session*, 12.

13. Committee on Foreign Relations, November 12, 1836, in Hunley, "Documentary History," 40-41.

14. Austin to Wharton, November 18, 1836, Austin to Meigs, November 7, 1836, in Hunley, "Documentary History," 26-29, 44, 47-48.

15. Perry to Leaming, February 1, 1837, Thomas F. Leaming Papers, UT. Similar reports are given in *Telegraph and Texas Register*, December 30, 1836; Pease to Father, January 8, 1837, in Katherine Hart and Elizabeth Kemp, eds., "E. M. Pease's Account of the Texas Revolution," *SHQ*, LXVIII (July, 1964), 80; *Morning Courier and New York Enquirer*, February 24, 1837, in Berenice S. Cook, "Texas as Seen in the New York Press from 1835 to 1845" (unpublished master's thesis, Columbia University, 1935), 48-49.

16. Houston to Jackson, November 20, 1836, *The Writings of Sam Houston, 1813-1863*, eds. Amelia W. Williams and Eugene C. Barker (8 vols., Austin, 1938-1943), I, 488.

17. Wharton to Austin, December 11, 1836, *The Diplomatic Correspondence of the Republic of Texas*, ed. George P. Garrison (3 vols., Washington,' 1908-1911), II-1, 152. Many Southerners also welcomed the admission of Texas as a new slave state. "They will force their Government to adopt us," wrote the Texan minister in Washington, "or they will create a new order of things." Hunt to Irion, July, 1837, *Diplomatic Correspondence*, II-1, 238. According to Wharton, President Jackson told him in the strictest confidence that Texas must "claim the Californias on the Pacific in order to paralyze the opposition of the North and East to Annexation. That the fishing interest of the North and East wish a harbour on the Pacific; that this claim of the Californias will give it to them and will diminish their opposition to annexation." Wharton to Rusk, January, 1837, *Diplomatic Correspondence*, II-1, 193-94.

18. (Anon.), *Texas in 1837*, ed. Andrew F. Muir (Austin, 1958), 3-4, 42; Francis R. Lubbock, *Six Decades in Texas* (Austin, 1968 edn.), 60-61.

19. William F. Gray, *From Virginia to Texas* (Houston, 1909), 219.

20. Perry to Leaming, June 4, 1837, Leaming Papers.

21. Irion to Hunt, June 26, 1837, December 11, 1837, *Diplomatic Correspondence*, II-1, 233-35, 279; Catlett to Henderson, May 25, 1837, *Diplomatic Correspondence*, II-1, 220.

22. M. Ruter to R. Ruter, December 15, 1837, Martin Ruter Papers, UT.

23. Henderson to Irion, October 14, 1837, *Diplomatic Correspondence*, II-3, 814-15; Irion to Henderson, January 5, 1838, *Diplomatic Correspondence*, II-3, 837; also Irion to Hunt, September 20, 1837, December 31, 1837, *Diplomatic Correspondence*, II-1, 262, 279. "Texas, an

infant nation," declared the *Telegraph and Texas Register* on October 7, 1837, "requests an intimate connexion with a kindred republic; if that republic, forgetful of the ties of consanguinity, refuse the connexion *now*, if refuses *forever;* for the infant, left a neglected foundling upon the world, will never *again* seek his kindred . . . but exalting in his *own* strength and urged on by his high destiny, the conquest of the Modern Stymphalus shall be among the least of his glorious achievements." In Hunley, "Documentary History, " 92.

24. Kaufman to McCullough, March 20, 1838, Henry Sayles, Jr. Papers, SWC; Smith to Bee, March 21, 1838, Barnard E. Bee Papers, UT; Rusk to Citizens, January 10, 1838, Rusk Papers.

25. Matagorda *Bulletin,* March 28, 1838.

26. Francis C. Sheridan, *Galveston Island* (Austin, 1954 ed.), 115. "There is in the character of the Anglo-American race," a visiting Frenchman observed, "a marvelous facility for espousing . . . the land upon which their wandering feet come to rest, and for cutting off all ties with their former homeland." Frederic Gaillardet, *Sketches of Early Texas and Louisiana* (Austin, 1966 ed.), 69-70. This does not mean that Texans ceased to admire American institutions. The Fourth of July was still celebrated and Texans felt a kinship with the American people. See Lubbock, *Six Decades,* 84; Kaufman to Food, November 25, 1840, *Journals of the House of Representatives of the Republic of Texas,* Fifth Congress, First Session (Austin, 1841), 157-58; Pease to Mother, July 20, 1841, Elisha M. Pease Letters, ATCC; Smyth to Simmans, June 22, 1844, George W. Smyth Papers, UT; Houston *Morning Star,* July 4, 1844.

27. Gustav Dresel, *Houston Journal* (Austin, 1954 ed.), 60; Pease to Father, September 10, 1836, February 5, 1837, Elisha M. Pease Papers, UT; Aldridge to Jackson, April 28, 1837, William B. Aldridge Papers, UT; Bryan to Joel, March 29, 1839, in Fannie B. Sholars, "Life and Services of Guy M. Bryan" (unpublished master's thesis, University of Texas, 1930), 19.

28. Lipscomb to Bee, August 8, 1840, Bee Papers; *Democratic Review* (1845) in Jennie W. Floyd, "An Annotated Bibliography on Texas Found in American Periodicals Before 1900" (unpublished master's thesis, Southern Methodist University, 1927), lii; Lamar Inaugural, December 10, 1838, *Documents of Texas History,* eds. Ernest Wallace and David M. Vigness (Austin, 1963), 126.

29. Chamberlain to Munson, April 28, 1838, William A. Force Papers, UT; Chairman Everitt in Hunley, "Documentary History," 117-18; Bryan to Father, February 11, 1839, Moses Austin Bryan Papers, UT.

30. Irion to Henderson, August 7, 1838, November 28, 1838, *Diplomatic Correspondence,* II-3, 864-65, 1218; also Henderson to Molé, November 12, 1838, *Diplomatic Correspondence,* II-3, 1236-37.

31. Lamar, December 10, 1838, *Lamar Papers,* II, 319-321.

32. Gaillardet, *Sketches of Early Texas,* 70. As long as Texans were confident of their ability to maintain independence, thought two British visitors, they would not surrender their national status. Sheridan, *Galveston Island,* 115-116n; Arthur Ikin, *Texas* (London, 1841), 62.

33. Lamar to Congress, December 21, 1838, *Lamar Papers,* II, 367-68.

NOTES

34. Kaufman, November 11, 1839, *House Journal of the Fourth Congress of the Republic of Texas, 1839-1840*, ed. Harriet Smither (Austin, n.d.), 2; Anderson, November 1, 1841, *Journals of the Sixth Congress of the Republic of Texas, 1841-1842*, ed. Harriet Smither (3 vols., Austin, 1944), II, 4-5.
35. Sheridan, *Galveston Island*, 98-99n.
36. [A. B. Lawrence], *A History of Texas* (New York, 1845 ed.), 229; Ikin, *Texas*, 16; also Gaillardet, *Sketches of Early Texas*, 4; Saligny to House, November 17, 1840, *Journals of the House of Representatives of the Republic of Texas*, Fifth Congress, First Session (Austin, 1841), 103-04; Justin H. Smith, *The Annexation of Texas* (New York, 1941 ed.), 50-51.
37. Lubbock, *Six Decades*, 36-37; [Lawrence], *History of Texas*, 230-31; Letter of December 8, 1838, Bee Papers.
38. Gray, *From Virginia to Texas*, 244; Joseph Eve to R. P. Letcher, November 30, 1841, in John M. Nance, ed., "The Letter Book of Joseph Eve," *SHQ*, XLIII (October, 1939), 212-13; also Joseph Eve to C. A. Wickliffe, December 26, 1842, *ibid.*, XLIV (July, 1940), 107.
39. Houston *Telegraph and Texas Register*, May 26, 1841, July 28, 1841; Brazoria *Brazos Courier*, June 9, 1840, June 16, 1840, September 15, 1840.
40. Austin *Texas Democrat*, February 4, 1846.
41. Henry Thompson, *Oration* (Houston, 1839 [sic]), 8.
42. Childress, March 11, 1836, *Journals of the General Convention* (Houston, 1838), 70.
43. *Northern Standard*, April 13, 1843, in Harvey L. Graham, "The Northern Standard, 1842-1848: A Texas Frontier Newspaper" (unpublished master's thesis, University of Texas, 1928), 109-110.
44. Dorman H. Winfrey, "Mirabeau B. Lamar and Texas Nationalism," *SHQ*, LIX (October, 1955), 188.
45. In *The Texas Almanac for 1858* (Galveston, 1857), 175-76. When Texans entered the Union in 1845, most of their new countrymen began calling them "Texans." Many Texian diehards did not suffer lightly this presumption, and the fight for "Texian" continued until the Civil War. See, for example, the LaGrange *Texas Monument*, a highly chauvinistic paper, in John Q. Anderson, ed., *Tales of Frontier Texas, 1830-1860* (Dallas, 1966), 85-86.
46. David M. Potter, *The South and the Sectional Conflict* (Baton Rouge, 1968), 53.
47. Preamble in *Telegraph and Texas Register*, January 13, 1838; Lamar to Congress, December 21, 1838, *Lamar Papers*, II, 348-49; Lamar to Congress, November 12, 1839, *Lamar Papers*, III, 179-181. The need for a Texas education was also stressed in statehood. See Pease to Legislature, December 23, 1853, *Journal of the Senate of the State of Texas*, Fifth Legislature (Austin, 1853), pt. 2, 13-15; Wigfall report, January 16, 1858, *Journal of the Senate of Texas*, Seventh Biennial Session (Austin, 1857), 348-49; Committee on Education, December 20, 1859, *Journal of the House of Representatives*, Eighth Legislature (Austin, 1860), 253.
48. The promotion of Texan culture through nationalism was an ongoing process. At the moment of statehood in 1846, a legislative committee

moved to establish the "Texas Monumental and Historical Association" to commemorate the revolutionary struggle. See Committee on Affairs of State, April 27, 1846, *Journals of the House of Representatives of the First Legislature of the State of Texas* (Clarksville, 1848), 545. In 1849 the House Committee on Education urged the preservation of all Texas newspapers in the capitol: "The stirring times in which they were published, and the remarkable events chronicled by them, make these papers . . . valuable reference books for the future historian of the 'Lone Star'." Report of December 7, 1849, *Journals of the House of Representatives of the State of Texas,* Third Session [Third Legislature, Regular Session] (Austin, 1849), 240. In 1850, the legislature authorized the governor to procure a slab of native marble or granite (or, if possible, a chunk of stone from the walls of the Alamo) and have carved a five-pointed star with the word "Texas" inscribed. This would be sent to the nation's capital and placed in the new Washington Monument. Act of January 3, 1850, in H. P. N. Gammel, comp., *The Laws of Texas, 1822-1897* (10 vols., Austin, 1898), III, 463-64. Eight years later, a select committee recommended translation into English of Spanish documents pertaining to the Texas Revolution. Its chairman, José Antonio Navarro, born in Spanish Texas in 1795, called for the perpetuation of "everything that will throw light upon our early history." Report of January 11, 1858, *Official Journal of the House of Representatives of the State of Texas,* Seventh Biennial Session (Austin, 1857), 522. Simultaneously, the committee on state affairs discovered that an Alamo Monument carved in 1853 had been sold at auction in New Orleans. "This beautiful specimen of art should belong to the State," chairman Hamilton P. Bee demanded, "commemorative as it is of that event which rivals in history the devoted sacrifice made for their country by the Spartans at Thermopylae." Their heartstrings plucked, the committee put forward an ambitious project:

> On the same spot where the spirit of those Texan patriots ascended to their God, there should be a monument towering to the skies, and inscribed on its broad base should be but the simple sentence: "REMEMBER THE ALAMO."

Report of January 12, 1858, *Journal of the House of Representatives,* Seventh Session, 538-39. Three years later, when Louisiana seceded from the Union and adopted a five-pointed star, Texans reminded their neighbor of that symbol's exclusivity "to the national flag of Texas." While conceding that the single star flag had been used before in history as a banner of revolution, the Texas spokesman insisted that "this wandering, Revolutionary Star is . . . no longer liable to national appropriation. It finished its sublimest achievement, when it conquered for freedom the vast and fertile empire of Texas." See Caleb G. Forshey to H. K. Elgee, February 22, 1861, *Journal of the Secession Convention of Texas, 1861,* ed. Ernest W. Winkler (Austin, 1912), 103-05.
49. Miller to Walker, February 17, 1842, Washington D. Miller Papers, TSL.
50. Thompson, *Oration,* 5, 12.
51. Sheridan, *Galveston Island,* 113; *William Bollaert's Texas,* eds. W.

NOTES

Eugene Hollon and Ruth L. Butler (Norman, 1956), 25-26.
52. Miller to Houston, February 16, 1842, Miller Papers.
53. Gaillardet, *Sketches of Early Texas*, 8-9. Similar experiences are described in Dresel, *Houston Journal*, 31; Brazoria *Brazos Courier*, April 21, 1840.
54. Burnet to Congress, October 4, 1836, *Journals of the House*, First Congress, First Session, 19; Burleson to Citizens, April 2, 1842, *Journals of the Sixth Congress*, III, 46.
55. Commager, "The Search for a Usable Past," in *Historical Viewpoints*, ed. John A. Garraty (2 vols., New York, 1970), I, 171; C. D. Stuart, "Texan Song of Liberty" (1844), in Baker, *Texas Scrap-Book*, 406; also William Barton, "Texas Song of Liberty" (1836), in A. Garland Adair and M. H. Crockett, eds., *Heroes of the Alamo* (New York, 1956), 79; "The Texas Soldier's Address to His Flag" (1840), "Ode to San Jacinto" (1841), W. E. Graham, "Texas — Our Home" (n.d.), in Baker, *Texas Scrap-Book*, 387, 397, 402.

Chapter 5

1. Max Savelle, *Seeds of Liberty* (Seattle, 1965 ed.), 13.
2. John Q. Anderson, ed., *Tales of Frontier Texas, 1830-1860* (Dallas, 1966), 7-8; D. W. Meinig, *Imperial Texas* (Austin, 1969), 39; Arthur Ikin, *Texas* (London, 1841), 32.
3. Irion to Hunt, December 31, 1837, *The Diplomatic Correspondence of the Republic of Texas*, ed. George P. Garrison (3 vols., Washington, 1908-1911), II-1, 279-80; also Irion to Henderson, March 20, 1838, *Diplomatic Correspondence*, II-3, 852; Lamar to Congress, November 1, 1840, *The Papers of Mirabeau Buonaparte Lamar*, ed. Charles A. Gulick (6 vols., Austin, 1920-1927), III, 464.
4. Wharton to Austin, December 31, 1836, *Diplomatic Correspondence*, II-1, 167.
5. Austin to Benton, November 19, 1836, in Josephine K. Hunley, "A Documentary History of Texan Sentiment for Annexation to the United States, 1835-1838" (unpublished master's thesis, University of Texas, 1937), 50; Wharton to Rusk, January, 1837, *Diplomatic Correspondence*, II-1, 190.
6. In John Milton Nance, *After San Jacinto* (Austin, 1963), 174.
7. Nance, *After San Jacinto*, 182; War Department Broadside, Austin, June 6, 1840, YU; Seguin to Lamar, December 26, 1840, "Domestic Correspondence;" TSL; Campbell to Burnet, December 28, 1840, "Domestic Correspondence;" Dimitt to Executive Department, January 9, 1841, "Domestic Correspondence."
8. Burnet in James M. Day, comp., *The Texas Almanac, 1857-1873* (Waco, 1967), 408-09; *Texas in 1837*, ed. Andrew F. Muir (Austin, 1958), 103; Parmenter in D. W. C. Baker, comp., *A Texas Scrap-Book* (New York, 1875), 396. A negative view of the Mexican character has persisted to recent times, as expressed by two Texan-bred historians of the American West: "There is a cruel streak in the Mexican nature, or so the history of Texas would lead one to believe," wrote Walter P. Webb. "He won more

victories over the Texans by parley than by force of arms. For making promises — and for breaking them — he had no peer." Webb, *The Texas Rangers* (Cambridge, 1935), 14. States W. Eugene Hollon: "The great majority of Mexican settlers [in Texas] were placid, illiterate, and superstitious." *The Southwest: Old and New* (Lincoln, 1968 ed.), 107.

9. Brazoria *Brazos Courier,* October 6, 1840; Clarksville *Northern Standard,* April 13, 1843. See also [Anon.] to Friends, April 10, 1843, Norman Woods Papers, UT; Barkley to Woods, May 8, 1843, in L.U. Spellmann, ed., "Letters of the 'Dawson Men' from Perote Prison," *SHQ,* XXXVIII (April, 1935), 252; Webb to Bee, February 20, 1839, *Secret Journals of the Senate of the Republic of Texas, 1836-1845,* ed. Ernest W. Winkler (Austin, 1911), 153-54; Bryan to Hayes, December 21, 1843, in Ernest W. Winkler ed., "The Bryan-Hayes Correspondence," *SHQ,* XXV (October, 1921), 109; San Augustine *Red-Lander,* June 22, 1844.

10. *Telegraph and Texas Register,* December 17, 1836; Anthony Ganilh, *Mexico versus Texas* (Philadelphia, 1838), preface; Miller to Houston, February 16, 1842, March 5, 1842, Washington D. Miller Papers, TSL. See also Henderson to Irion, October 14, 1837, *Diplomatic Correspondence,* II-3, 817-19; *Telegraph and Texas Register,* January 13, 1838; Gustav Dresel, *Houston Journal* (Austin, 1954 ed.), 101; Francis C. Sheridan, *Galveston Island* (Austin, 1954 ed.), 66-67.

11. Austin to Rusk, January 7, 1836, Thomas Jefferson Rusk Papers, UT; Rusk to Clay, August 3, 1836, *ibid.; Telegraph and Texas Register,* September 6, 1836; Mosely Baker, November 10, 1836, *Journals of the House of Representatives of the Republic of Texas,* First Congress, First Session (Houston, 1838), 142; Wharton to Austin, December 11, 1836, *Diplomatic Correspondence,* II-1, 153; also Hunt to Henderson, May 30, 1837, *Diplomatic Correspondence,* II-1, 222; Burnet to Congress, October 4, 1836, *Journals of the House,* First Congress, First Session, 142.

12. George Washington Morgan Papers, UT, 8-9; Charles P. Roland, *Albert Sidney Johnston* (Austin, 1964), 64, 75-76; S. Maverick to M. Maverick, March 13, 1838, in Rena Maverick Green, ed., *Samuel Maverick, Texan* (San Antonio, 1952), 66; Hunley, "Documentary History," 78-79; also J. Nicholson to W. Thompson, July 10, 1839, James Nicholson Papers, UT.

13. See Pease to Father, February 5, 1837, Elisha M. Pease Papers, UT; Irion to Henderson, January 5, 1838, *Diplomatic Correspondence,* II-3, 838; M. B. Lamar, December 10, 1838, *Documents of Texas History,* eds. Ernest Wallace and David M. Vigness (Austin, 1963), 126; W. H. Jack, December 3, 1839, *House Journal of the Fourth Congress of the Republic of Texas, 1839-1840,* ed. Harriet Smither (Austin, n.d.), 103; Hamilton to Pakenham, January 3, 1840, *Diplomatic Correspondence,* II-3, 884; Richard S. Hunt and Jesse F. Randel, *Guide to the Republic of Texas* (New York, 1839), 50.

14. *Telegraph and Texas Register,* September 16, 1837; also Matagorda *Bulletin,* January 17, 1838, in Joe B. Frantz, "Newspapers of the Republic of Texas" (unpublished master's thesis, University of Texas, 1940), 142; Austin *Texas Sentinel,* February 12, 1840.

15. Irion to Hunt, December 31, 1837, *Diplomatic Correspondence,* II-1, 227; Hunt to Irion, January 31, 1838, April 13, 1838, *Diplomatic Correspondence,* II-1, 288, 324.

16. John Scoble, *Texas* (London, 1839), 42-43; Edward Everett Hale, *A Tract for the Day* (Boston, 1845), 4.

17. Brazoria *People*, April 18, 1838; Pease to Father, July 10, 1838, Pease Papers; Lamar to Congress, December 21, 1838, *Documents*, 127.

18. Report of April 13, 1839, *Documents*, 132; also Lamar to Congress, November 12, 1839, *Lamar Papers*, III, 160. See Act of Incorporation, December 27, 1839, in H. N. P. Gammel, comp., *The Laws of Texas, 1822-1897* (10 vols., Austin, 1898), II, 386-391.

19. J. W. Harris, December 3, 1839, *House Journal of the Fourth Congress*, 119.

20. Frederic Gaillardet, *Sketches of Early Texas and Louisiana* (Austin, 1966 ed.), 57.

21. Dunlap to Lamar, May 16, 1839, in Nance, *After San Jacinto*, 181, and William C. Binkley, *The Expansionist Movement in Texas, 1836-1850* (Berkeley, 1925), 37. The Senate Foreign Relations Committee also favored the purchase of territory. See report of December 18, 1839, *Secret Journals of the Senate*, 162.

22. Burnet to Treat, August 9, 1839, *Secret Journals of the Senate*, 156; Lipscomb to Treat, June 13, 1840, *Diplomatic Correspondence*, II-2, 644.

23. Burnet to Congress, December 16, 1840, *Journals of the House of Representatives of the Republic of Texas*, Fifth Congress, First Session (Austin, 1841), 292-93; also Burnet to Congress, December 19, 1840, December 30, 1840, *Journals of the House*, Fifth Congress, First Session, 315, 387-88.

24. *Brazos Courier*, October 20, 1840; also Matagorda *Colorado Gazette and Advertiser*, July 10, 1841. District Judge Anderson Hutchinson lambasted the Lamar administration: "With millions of debt piled upon us thro the course of so many wars, invasions & projected counter invasions, embassies & negotiations, armies & navies, special legions for the development of special military genius & glory, and expeditions without appropriations — we shall be fortunate indeed if we shall be enabled to preserve nationality." Hutchinson to Miller, July 28, 1841, Miller Papers.

25. Joint Committee report, December 18, 1840, *Journals of the House*, Fifth Congress, First Session, 300-301; Select and Joint Committee report, January 12, 1841, *Journals of the House*, Fifth Congress, First Session, 478.

26. Lamar to Congress, November 12, 1839, *Lamar Papers*, III, 182.

27. *Address to the Citizens of Santa Fe*, April 14, 1840 (Austin, 1841), 13.

28. *Address to Citizens*, June 5, 1841, 4-5; Binkley, *Expansionist Movement*, 73-74.

29. Roberts to Commissioners, June 15, 1841, *Letters of the Secretary of State to Commissioners to Santa Fe* (Austin, 1841), 7.

30. Jackson to Houston, May 25, 1842, Jesse Grimes Papers, UT.

31. Report of November 22, 1841, *Journals of the Sixth Congress of the Republic of Texas, 1841-1842*, ed. Harriet Smither (3 vols., Austin, 1844), II, 59-62; also report of December 6, 1841, *Journals of the Sixth Congress*, II, 99 ff.

32. Report of January 10, 1842, *Journals of the Sixth Congress*, II, 363 ff; also speech of Mr. Fowler, December 15, 1841, *Journals of the Sixth Congress*, II, 157.

NOTES

33. Houston to Congress, February 1, 1842, *Journals of the Sixth Congress,* II, 434-35.

34. Houston to Santa Anna, March 21, 1842, *The Writings of Sam Houston, 1813-1863,* eds. Amelia W. Williams and Eugene C. Barker (8 vols., Austin, 1938-1943), II, 526-27. For reaction to the invasion, see Miller to Houston, March 7, 1842, March 17, 1842, Miller Papers; C. G. Bryant to S. Bryant, September 25, 1844, Charles G. Bryant Papers, UT.

35. Sullivan to Huston, March 23, 1842, Thomas W. Streeter Texas Collection, YU; Burnet to Huston, January 18, 1842, Streeter Collection; Burleson to Citizens, April 6, 1842, *Journals of the Sixth Congress,* III, 44-45; Eve to Southgate, May 5, 1842, in John M. Nance, ed., "A Letter Book of Joseph Eve," *SHQ,* XLIII (April, 1940), 493-94.

36. Report of July 4, 1842, *Journals of the Sixth Congress,* II, 111; Houston to House, July 22, 1842, *Houston Writings,* III, 116-124.

37. As one captive described the march, he was "driven before the bayonet many hundred miles and that two [sic] without a blanket or a coat to sheald him from the weather [and]fedd on the refused Flower that was full of Bugs and worms with a small quantity of Beef." [Anon.] to Friends, April 10, 1843, Woods Papers.

38. Van Zandt to Jones, November 30, 1843, *Diplomatic Correspondence,* II-2, 228; Francis Paul Prucha, *The Sword of the Republic* (New York, 1969), 378.

39. Houston to Congress, January 10, 1843, *Secret Journals of the Senate,* 270-75; Van Zandt to Jones, March 13, 1843, *Diplomatic Correspondence,* II-2, 133-34; Smith to Jones, March 31, 1843, *Diplomatic Correspondence,* II-3, 1428-29; Mayfield to "Gentlemen," June 13, 1843, "Domestic Correspondence"; Maverick to Weir, August 15, 1843, in Green, ed., *Sam Maverick,* 258.

40. Houston to Jones, June 10, 1843, *Houston Writings,* III, 407-08.

41. Bryan to Hayes, December 21, 1843, in Winkler, ed., "Bryan-Hayes Correspondence," 109-110. See Houston to Eve, February 17, 1843, *Diplomatic Correspondence,* II-2, 128; Van Zandt to Jones, September 18, 1843, *Diplomatic Correspondence,* II-2, 210; William R. Hogan, *The Republic of Texas* (Austin, 1969 ed.), 93-102. For a personal glimpse at one financially depressed young man, see Kuykendall to Huff, July 1, 1843, James H. Kuykendall Papers (2 vols., UT), II, 12.

42. Houston to Congress, January 20, 1844, *Secret Journals of the Senate,* 294-95.

43. "You say you dread to hear from Texas for fear of getting some bad news," wrote a Houston resident to a friend in the States. "You may rest assured that things are greatly exaggerated in the U. S. papers & that [Sam] Houston is *not* about giving this country up to England. . . . For myself I am very glad that the notion of Houston's wanting to sell Texas to England is gaining ground in the U. S., for it may possibly induce your Government to admit us into the Union & self interest may effect what sympathy could not." Duerr to Dell, January 8, 1844, Christian F. Duerr Papers, UT, 108-09. For a random sample of Texas opinion, see S. Maverick to M. Maverick, January 14, 1844, and Maverick to Simpson, February 27, 1844, in Green, ed., *Sam Maverick,* 264, 267-68; Morgan to Storms, January 26, 1844, James Morgan Papers, UT; LaGrange *Intelli-*

gencer, February 1, 1844; *The Civilian and Galveston Gazette*, April 17, 1844; *Red-Lander*, May 11, 1844; Smyth to Simmans et al., June 22, 1844, Thomas F. McKinney Papers, UT; Bryan to Hayes, July 1, 1844, in Winkler, ed., "Bryan-Hayes Correspondence," 113-14.

44. Houston to Murphy, May 6, 1844, *Houston Writings*, IV, 322-23; Houston to Van Zandt and Henderson, May 17, 1844, *Diplomatic Correspondence*, II-2, 282.

45. Matagorda *Weekly Despatch*, June 22, 1844; also Houston *Morning Star*, June 11, 1844; *Northern Standard*, June 19, 1844.

46. Duerr to Dell, August 11, 1844, September 27, 1844, Duerr Papers, 131, 155.

47. Houston to Congress, December 9, 1844, *Houston Writings*, IV 403-04.

48. Report of January 20, 1845, *Journals of the Senate of the Ninth Congress of the Republic of Texas* (Washington, 1845), 181-89.

49. Terrell to Smith, February 13, 1845, *Diplomatic Correspondence*, II-3, 1180.

50. See terms of the proposed treaty in Ashbel Smith, March 29, 1845, *Correspondence Relating to a Treaty of Peace Between Mexico and Texas* (Washington, 1845), 5.

51. *Telegraph and Texas Register*, March 26, 1845; also *Red-Lander*, March 15, 1845, March 22, 1845, April 12, 1845; *Intelligencer*, March 22, 1845, April 7, 1845; *Morning Star*, March 22, 1845.

52. See *Telegraph and Texas Register*, April 2, 1845, May 7, 1845; Washington *Texas National Register*, April 24, 1845; Allen to Smith, May 10, 1845, *Diplomatic Correspondence*, II-3, 1194; *Northern Standard*, May 13, 1845; Rusk to Phillips, June 13, 1845, Rusk Papers; Francis R. Lubbock, *Six Decades in Texas* (Austin, 1968 ed.), 164-69.

53. Kaufman to Buchanan, September 23, 1845, *Diplomatic Correspondence*, II-2, 402-06. On the stationing of American troops, see resolution of Texas constitutional convention, July 7, 1845, in Lucien E. Peevy, "The First Two Years of Texas Statehood, 1846-1847" (unpublished doctoral dissertation, University of Texas, 1948), 716.

54. Austin *Texas Democrat*, January 21, 1846.

55. W. A. Droddy Diary, UT, 129; also *Texas Democrat* ("Extra"), February 20, 1846; Peevy, "First Two Years of Statehood," 74-75.

Chapter 6

1. Letter, *The Northern Standard* (Clarksville), February 25, 1846.

2. Houston to Gillespie, January 23, 1846, Henry Sayles, Jr. Papers, SWC.

3. Henderson to Legislature, February 19, 1846, *Journals of the House of Representatives of the First Legislature of the State of Texas*, (Clarksville, 1848), 20.

4. *Northern Standard*, August 9, 1845.

5. *Telegraph and Texas Register* (Houston), May 6, 1846, June 10, 1846; also *Northern Standard*, May 13, 1846, November 7, 1846, January 16, 1847; Austin *Texas Democrat*, May 20, 1846; Galveston *News*, May 30,

NOTES

1846, in Lucien E. Peevy, "The First Two Years of Texas Statehood, 1846-1847" (unpublished doctoral dissertation, University of Texas, 1948), 770; La Grange *Far West*, March 20, 1847.

6. In Victor T. Lewis, "Texas and the Nation, 1845-1860" (unpublished master's thesis, East Texas State Teachers College, 1940), 28.

7. Stephen B. Oates, "Los Diablos Tejanos! [The Texan Devils!]," *AW*, II (Spring, 1965), 42-43, 47, 49; James K. Holland, "Diary of a Texan Volunteer in the Mexican War," *SHQ*, XXX (July, 1926), 27; Lewis, "Texas and the Nation," 41, 43; Taylor to Wool, July 14, 1847, Taylor MS, YU.

8. In Peevy, "First Two Years of Texas Statehood," 802; Henderson to Legislature, December 15, 1847, *Journals of the Senate of the State of Texas*, Second Legislature (Houston, 1848), 9-10.

9. *Northern Standard*, October 23, 1847.

10. Howard Roberts Lamar, *The Far Southwest, 1846-1912* (New York, 1970 ed.), 63-64, 66.

11. Rupert N. Richardson et al., *Texas, the Lone Star State* (Englewood Cliffs, 1970 ed.), 138.

12. Joint Resolution, April 29, 1846, in H. N. P. Gammel, comp., *The Laws of Texas, 1822-1897* (10 vols., Austin, 1898), II, 1461.

13. Lamar, *Far Southwest*, 64, 68-70; Richardson, *Texas*, 138.

14. Report of February 28, 1848, *Journals of the Senate*, Second Legislature, 438-39.

15. Wood to Polk, October 6, 1848, *Journals of the Senate of the State of Texas*, Third Legislature, Third Session — Regular (Austin, 1849), 24.

16. Lamar, *Far Southwest*, 75; also Kenneth F. Neighbours, "The Taylor-Neighbors Struggle Over the Upper Rio Grande Region of Texas in 1850," *SHQ*, LXI (April, 1958), 452-53.

17. S. H. German, Louella S. Vincent, "Governor George Thomas Wood," *SHQ*, XX (January, 1917), 260-276; Matamoros *American Flag*, September 29, 1847.

18. Wood to Legislature, November 6, 1849, *Journals of the Senate*, Third Legislature, Third Session, 14, 17.

19. Mr. Wilson, November 29, 1849, in W. F. Weeks, *Debates in the House of Representatives on the Santa Fe Question* (Austin, 1849), 4 ff; William C. Binkley, *The Expansionist Movement in Texas, 1836-1850* (Berkeley, 1925), 175; Clarence A. Bridges, "Texas and the Crisis of 1850" (unpublished master's thesis, University of Texas, 1925), 108.

20. Wood to Legislature, December 21, 1849, *Journals of the Senate*, Third Legislature, Third Session, 272-73.

21. Bell to Legislature, December 21, 1849, *Journals of the Senate*, Third Legislature, Third Session, 274-79; Bell to Legislature, December 26, 1849, *Journals of the Senate*, Third Legislature, Third Session, 286.

22. Webb to Neighbors, January 8, 1850, in Binkley, *Expansionist Movement*, 179.

23. Wallace to Rusk, January 16, 1850, Thomas Jefferson Rusk Papers, UT.

24. See, for example, Mr. Baldwin of Connecticut, *Speech in the Senate of the United States on the Claim of Texas to New Mexico*, July 25, 1850. Even state representative Benjamin E. Tarver admitted to these facts. See speech of December 3, 1849 in Weeks, *Debates on the Santa Fe Question*,

NOTES

20-21.

25. Austin *Texas State Gazette*, August 24, 1850.

26. *Texas State Gazette*, June 1, 1850.

27. *Texas State Gazette*, June 8, 1850, June 15, 1850, June 29, 1850, July 6, 1850, July i3, 1850, August 10, 1850, August 17, 1850; *Texas Monument*, July 20, 1850, July 31, 1850; *Northern Standard*, July 13, 1850, July 20, 1850, August 3, 1850; Marshall *Texas Republican*, July 20, 1850, August 3, 1850, August 10, 1850; Victoria *Advocate*, June 21, 1850, and Colorado *Tribune*, July 5, 1850, in Bridges, "Texas and the Crisis of 1850," 111-12. "Perhaps we may be considered enthusiastic on this subject," the *Northern Standard* of July 20 admitted, "but it must be remembered that to us Texas is the dearest word in life. . . . We know no other land, nor do we wish to so long as she is herself."

28. Bridges, "Texas and the Crisis of 1850," 110; Fitzhugh to Bell, August 16, 1850, Peter H. Bell Papers, UT; *Ranger* (n.d.) quoted in *Texas Republican*, August 3, 1850; *Gazette* in Binkley, *Expansionist Movement*, 192; *Texas Monument*, August 14, 1850.

29. Mr. Houston, June 13, 1850, *The Congressional Globe*, First Session, Thirty-First Congress, Appendix (Washington, 1850), 866.

30. *Northern Standard*, September 7, 1850.

31. Allan Nevins, *Ordeal of the Union* (4 vols., New York, 1947-1950), I, 341.

32. Richardson, *Texas*, 140; Guir to Miller, August 11, 1850, Washington D. Miller Papers, TSL.

33. Bell to Legislature, August 13, 1850, *Journals of the Senate of the State of Texas*, Third Legislature – Extra Session (Austin, 1850), 10-12.

34. *Texas State Gazette*, August 24, 1850; Holman Hamilton, *Prologue to Conflict* (New York, 1966 ed.), 151.

35. *Speech of Hon. Guy M. Bryan . . . on the Santa Fe Question*, August 27 and 28, 1850 (Austin, 1850); also "ALAMO" in *Texas Republican*, August 24, 1850.

36. Moffett to Rusk, August 28, 1850, in Nancy Ann Head, "State Rights in Texas: The Growth of an Idea, 1850-1860" (unpublished master's thesis, The Rice Institute, 1960), 27; also Hamilton, *Prologue to Conflict*, 153.

37. See *Texas State Gazette*, August 31, 1850, September 7, 1850, September 14, 1850, September 21, 1850, October 19, 1850; *Northern Standard*, August 31, 1850; *Texas Republican*, September 21, 1850, September 28, 1850, October 19, 1850; *Texas Monument*, October 9, 1850, October 30, 1850; Marshall *Star State Patriot*, *Cherokee Sentinel*, Houston *Gazette*, and *Nueces Valley* quoted in *Texas State Gazette*, August 31, 1850, September 21, 1850, October 5, 1850.

38. Holland to Miller, October 3, 1850, Miller Papers; *Texas State Gazette*, August 24, 1850; also Hamilton, *Prologue to Conflict*, 152.

39. Wallace to Smyth, October 21, 1850, George W. Smyth Papers, UT; Smyth to Rusk, November 30, 1850, Rusk Papers; also Houston to Senate, July 3, 1850, *The Writings of Sam Houston, 1813-1863*, eds. Amelia W. Williams and Eugene C. Barker (8 vols., Austin, 1938-1943), V 191-92; *Northern Standard*, September 28, 1850.

40. *Intelligencer*, August 28, 1850; *Advocate*, August 30, 1850; Wood to

NOTES

"General," September, 1850, Miller Papers; also *Texas Monument,* September 4, 1850; *Advocate,* October 10, 1850.
41. Lamar, *Far Southwest,* 113-17; D. W. Meinig, *Imperial Texas* (Austin, 1969), 42.

Epilogue

1. Elisha M. Pease to Legislature, December 21, 1853, *Journal of the Senate of the State of Texas,* Fifth Legislature (Austin, 1853), Pt. 2, p.4; also Pease to Legislature, December 23, 1853, *ibid.,* 25. For similar expressions see J. W. Henderson to Legislature, December 22, 1851, *Journal of the House of Representatives of the State of Texas,* Fourth Legislature (Austin, 1852), 371; A. S. Johnston to W. P. Johnston, June 15, 1854 in Charles P. Roland, *Albert Sidney Johnston* (Austin, 1964), 164; William L. Yancey to Louis T. Wigfall, April 16, 1858, Louis Trezevant Wigfall Papers, UT.
2. *The Texas Almanac for 1861.*
3. See, for example, MacKinlay Kantor, *If the South Had Won the Civil War* (Cleveland, 1961 ed.), 85-112.
4. See John S. Ford to Edward Burleson, Jr., February 15, 1856, Edward Burleson, Jr. Papers, UT; speech of Sam Houston, April 24, 1858, *The Congressional Globe,* First Session, Thirty-Fifth Congress (Washington, 1858), 1680.
5. A well-documented account of "Cortina's War" is Clarence C. Clendenen, *Blood on the Border* (New York, 1969), 16-44; also T. R. Fehrenbach, *Lone Star: A History of Texas and the Texans* (New York, 1968), 507-521; Walter P. Webb and H. Bailey Carroll, eds., *The Handbook of Texas* (2 vols., Austin, 1952), I, 416-18.
6. Ford to Houston, December 29, 1859, "Transcripts from the Office of the Adjutant-General," UT, p. 60; Tobin to Houston, January 2, 1860, *ibid.,* 63-64.
7. Llerena B. Friend, *Sam Houston: The Great Designer* (Austin, 1969 ed.), 301-03; Walter P. Webb, *The Texas Rangers* (Cambridge, 1935), 183. Houston's plan had enthusiastic backing from a Kentucky congressman who promised to assist him with 5,000 cavalry and artillery troops drawn from Pennsylvania, New Jersey, and other states. Humphrey Marshall to Houston, February 25, 1860, "Domestic Correspondence," TSL.
8. Houston to Legislature, February 8, 1860, *Journal of the Senate of the State of Texas, Eighth Legislature* (Austin, 1860), 545.
9. Brownsville *American Flag,* January 12, 1860; E. W. Cave to C. S. Taylor, January 3, 1860, Charles Stanfield Taylor Papers, UT; also Earl W. Fornell, "Texans and Filibusters in the 1850s," *SHQ,* LIX (April, 1956), 427.
10. For a sampling of opinion, see *Proceedings of the Mass Meeting of the National Democracy of Texas* (Austin, 1860), 9; W. E. Burnet to D. G. Burnet, February 17, 1860, in Raymond Estep, ed., "Lieutenant William E. Burnet Letters," *Chronicles of Oklahoma,* XXXVIII (Winter, 1960), 387; E. Burleson, Jr. to Houston, March 13, 1860, Burleson, Jr. Papers; J. Withers to V. Clay, March 23, 1860, Wigfall Papers; Oreta Turner,

NOTES

"Border Troubles Along the Rio Grande, 1848-1878" (unpublished master's thesis, East Texas State Teachers College, 1940), 51.

11. James Pike, *Scout and Ranger* (Princeton, 1932 ed.), 124-26.

12. Burton to Pease, February 16, 1861, Elisha M. Pease Letters, ATCC; G. W. Smyth to E. H. Cushing, November 12, 1860, George W. Smyth Papers, UT.

13. Ernest W. Winkler, ed., *Platforms of Political Parties in Texas* (Austin, 1916), 82; Lois Wood Burkhalter, *Gideon Lincecum, 1793-1874: A biography* (Austin, 1965), 139-140. For other voices favoring separate nationhood, see H.B. Andrews to E.M. Pease, November 20, 1860, Pease Letters, Dallas *Herald*, November 21, 1860; the Corpus Christi *Ranchero*, November 24, 1860; J. L. Haynes to New Orleans *Picayune*, November 24, 1860, John L. Haynes Scrapbook, UT; Speech of Judge O. M. Roberts, of the Supreme Court of Texas, on December 1, 1860, upon the "Impending Crisis," p. 6; Senator L. T. Wigfall, December 5, 1860, in Edward R. Maher, "Secession in Texas" (unpublished doctoral dissertation, Fordham University, 1960), 118-19; New Orleans *Picayune*, December 11, 1860, in Frank H. Smyrl, "Unionism in Texas, 1856-1861," *SHQ*, LXVIII (October, 1964), 188; D. D. Atchison to E. M. Pease, December 19, 1860, Pease Letters; Allan C. Ashcraft, "East Texas in the Election of 1860 and the Secession Crisis," *ETHJ*, I (July, 1963), 11; Stephen B. Oates, "Texas Under the Secessionists," *SHQ*, LXVII (October, 1963), 168; Jimmie Hicks, "Texas and Separate Independence, 1860-61," *ETHJ*, IV (October, 1966), 86-87, 99-100.

14. E. Barrett to C. S. Taylor, November 9, 1860, Taylor Papers; Marshall *Texas Republican*, November 24, 1860, December 8, 1860; speech of O. M. Roberts, December 1, 1860; James M. Day, comp., *The Texas Almanac, 1857-1873* (Waco, 1967), 485; Ada Warren Cale, "Texas Frontier Problems, 1836-1860" (unpublished master's thesis, St. Mary's University, 1944), 94-95; Ashcroft, "East Texas in the Election of 1860," 11; Hicks, "Texas and Separate Independence," 86; Smyrl, "Unionism in Texas," 186; Oates, "Texas Under the Secessionists," 167.

15. Maher, "Secession in Texas," 129.

16. Hicks, "Texas and Separate Independence," 93.

17. D. W. Meinig, *Imperial Texas*, (Austin, 1969), 62, 124; also W. H. Hutchinson, "Bear Flag and Lone Star: Two Imperial Powers and Their Stereotypes," *SHQ*, LXXII (October, 1968), 149; W. J. Hughes, *Rebellious Ranger: Rip Ford and the Old Southwest* (Norman, 1964), vii; Llerena B. Friend, "The Texan of 1860," *SHQ*, LXII (July, 1958), 1, 17; Emma Jean Walker, "The Contemporary Texan: An Examination of Major Additions to the Mythical Texan in the Twentieth Century" (unpublished doctoral dissertation, University of Texas, 1966), 17, 20; John Q. Anderson, ed., *Tales of Frontier Texas, 1830-1860* (Dallas, 1966), 3; Charles Anderson, *Texas, Before and on the Eve of the Rebellion* (Cincinnati, 1884), 5. For studies of the Texan subculture in the twentieth century, see Evon Z. Vogt, "American Subcultural Continua as Exemplified by the Mormons and Texans," *American Anthropologist*, LVII (December, 1955), 1163-1164; Laurence R. Veysey, "Myth and Reality in Approaching American Regionalism," *American Quarterly*, XII (Spring, 1960), 31-43.

18. For a compendium of Texan foibles, see John Bainbridge, *The Super-*

NOTES

Americans (Garden City, 1961); David Nevin, *The Texans* (New York, 1968); also W. Eugene Hollon, *The Southwest: Old and New* (Lincoln, 1968 ed.), 372, 418.

19. "The Texanization of Washington," *Look*, vol. 29, no. 7, April 6, 1965, 30-34.

20. Stephen B. Oates, ed., *The Republic of Texas* (Palo Alto, 1968).

21. Fehrenbach, *A History of Texas*, 711; also Herbert Gambrell, ed., *Texas: Today and Tomorrow* (Dallas, 1961), 34.

22. Quoted in Bainbridge, *Super-Americans*, 14-15. See Ernest R. Bartley, *The Tidelands Oil Controversy* (Austin, 1953), 79-94, on Texan claims to submerged coastal lands.

23. Francis C. Sheridan, *Galveston Island* (Austin, 1954 ed.), 113.

Bibliography

This is a selective bibliography of sources in Texas history, primarily for the period 1820-1860. General works appearing in Notes or otherwise consulted are not included here.

MANUSCRIPT COLLECTIONS

Unless otherwise indicated, all manuscripts are in the University of Texas Library Archives, Austin.

Adams, Harvey A. Papers, ca. 1815-1844.
Adjutant General of Texas. Transcripts, 1838-1869.
Aldridge, William B. Letters, 1836-1837.
Ames, Harriet A. Reminiscences.
Amster, John C. Papers, 1803-1865.
Arnett, William W. Papers, 1841-1892.
Asbury, Samuel E. Papers, 1920-1948.
Austin, Henry. Papers, 1806-1846.
Barrett, Don Carlos. Papers, 1827-1838.
Baylor, John R. Family Papers, 1838-1906.
Baylor, Mary. Reminiscences, 1827-1840.
Bee, Barnard E. Papers, 1829-1853.
Bee, Hamilton. Papers, 1838-1894.
Bell, Peter H. Papers, 1847-1898.
Brigham, Asa. Papers, 1832-1837.
Brown, Frank. "Annals of Travis County and of the City of Austin (From the Earliest Times to the Close of 1875)." Austin-Travis County Collection, Austin Public Library.
Bryan, Moses Austin. Correspondence, 1839.
Bryant, Charles G. Papers, 1842.
Burleson, Edward. Papers, 1835-1844.
Burleson, Edward, Jr. Papers, 1854-1861.
Campbell, Jack. Letters, 1860-1861.
Card, Lottie Holman. Papers [Jesse Burnam Correspondence, 1852-1862]. Southwest Collection: Lubbock, Texas.

BIBLIOGRAPHY

Carothers, Sam D. Family Papers, 1853–1870.
Coleman, Ann Raney Thomas. Papers, 1810–1892.
Dancy, John Winfield Scott. "Diary of the Travels of John W. Dancy in Texas and the United States, 1838–1839. . . ."
"Domestic Correspondence," 1822–1860. Texas State Library.
Douglass, Kelsey H. Papers, 1837–1840.
Droddy, W. A. Diary, 1846.
Duerr, Christian Friedrich. Diary, March 21, 1839 to December 31, 1844.
Embree, Mrs. J.W. Diary, 1856–1861.
Epperson, B. H. Papers, 1832–1864.
Erskine, Andrew Nelson. Papers, 1845–1862.
Felloseby, John. Letter, 1836.
Force, William A. Papers, 1837–1859.
Freeman, Ira M. Papers, 1836–1864.
Grimes, Jesse. Papers, 1834–1854.
Hale, Philip Smith. Letters, 1836, 1855.
Hammeken, George L. "Brief Remarks on Dr. Channing's letter to Hon. Henry Clay." [1837]
Haynes, John L. Scrapbook (1859–1860).
Herndon, John Hunter. "Diary of Trip from Kentucky to Texas, 1837–1838."
Howard, William E. Papers, 1814–1892. Southwest Collection: Lubbock, Texas.
Ingram, Ira. Papers, 1830–1835.
Jayne, Brewster H. Letter, 1840.
Jones, John Rice, Jr. Papers, 1835–1850.
Kuykendall, James Hampton. Papers (1822–1829; 1836–1860), Sketchbook.
Lamar, Rebecca Ann. "Journal of [Trip] from Georgia to Texas," 1838.
Lang, Willis. Diary, 1860.
Leaming, Thomas F. Papers, 1796–1847.
McClintock, William A. "Journal of a Soldier of the Second Kentucky Regiment: Trip Through Texas and Northern Mexico in 1846-1847."
McIntyre, James B. Letter, 1853.
McKinney, Thomas Freeman. Papers, 1828–1873.
Mercer, Patricia. Diary, 1840–1841.
Miller, Washington D. Papers and Letters, 1837–1861. Texas State Library.
Morgan, George Washington. Papers, 1812–1932 (Memoirs).
Morgan, James. Letters, 1844.
Morrow, Temple Houston. Sam Houston Family Papers, 1836-1939. Southwest Collection: Lubbock, Texas.
Neighbors, Robert Simpson. Papers, 1852–1859.
Nelson, Albert Aldrich. Papers, 1833–1853.
Nicholson, James. Papers, 1838–1845.
Pancoast, Josiah. Letters, 1843–1849.
Pease, Elisha Marshall. Papers, 1834–1854.
Pease, Elisha Marshall. Personal Letters and Letters Received, 1830–1861. Austin-Travis County Collection, Austin Public Library.
Poinsett, Joel Roberts. Papers, 1807–1851.
Rawlins, Roderick. Letters, 1845–1848.
Reding, James W. Family Papers, 1837–1910 [W.R. and Reding Correspondence, 1837–1865].
Rcily, James. Letters, 1838–1852.
Rister, Carl Coke. Papers [Texas, 1818–1866; Robert E. Lee, 1850–1861]. Southwest Collection: Lubbock, Texas.
Robertson, Sterling Clack. Family Papers, 1824–1865.
Rogers, Nathan Foster. Letters, 1849–1854.
Root, George W. Letters, 1858–1862.
Rusk, Thomas Jefferson. Papers, 1834–1857.

BIBLIOGRAPHY

Ruter, Martin. Papers, 1833–1838.
Sanders, Robert. Letter, 1841.
Sayles, Henry, Jr. Papers, 1830–1857. Southwest Collection: Lubbock, Texas.
Scott, Harriet Virginia. Letters, 1846.
Smith, James Norman. Autobiography, 1798–1860 [vols. III and IV].
Smyth, George W. Papers, 1833–1861.
Stewart, Charles Bellinger. Papers, 1836–1876.
Streeter, Thomas W. Texas Collection. Beinecke Library, Yale University.
Tannehill, Jesse C. Papers, 1832–1867.
Taylor, Charles Stanfield. Papers, 1832–1864.
Turner, Amasa. Papers, 1827–1863.
Walker, David. Letters, 1854–1861.
Wellington, Royal Wetherton. Papers, 1835–1875.
White, Francis Menefee. Letters, 1859–1861.
Wigfall, Louis Trezevant. Papers, 1833–1873.
Woods, Norman. Letters, 1843.

GOVERNMENT DOCUMENTS, OFFICIAL AND SEMI-OFFICIAL

U. S. Government Publications

DeBow, J. D. B., Superintendent of the United States Census. *The Seventh Census of the United States: 1850.* Washington, D. C. Robert Armstrong, 1853.
Manufactures of the United States in 1860. Compiled from the Original Returns of the Eighth Census. Washington, D.C.: Government Printing Office, 1865.
Population of the United States in 1860. Compiled from the Original Returns of the Eighth Census. Washington, D.C.: Government Printing Office, 1864.
The Congressional Globe:
First Session, Twenty-ninth Congress. Washington, D.C.: Blair & Rives, 1846.
First Session, Thirtieth Congress, Appendix. Washington, D.C.: Blair & Rives, 1848.
Second Session, Thirtieth Congress. Washington, D.C.: Blair & Rives, 1849.
First Session, Thirty-first Congress. Washington, D.C.: John C. Rives, 1850.
First Session, Thirty-first Congress, Appendix. Washington, D.C.: John C. Rives, 1850.
Second Session, Thirty-first Congess. Washington, D.C.: John C. Rives, 1851.
First Session, Thirty-second Congress. Washington, D.C.: John C. Rives, 1852.
Second Session, Thirty-third Congress. Washington, D.C.: John C. Rives, 1855.
Third Session, Thirty-fourth Congess. Washington, D.C.: John C. Rives, 1857.
First Session, Thirty-fifth Congress. Washington, D.C.: John C. Rives, 1858.
Second Session, Thirty-fifth Congress. Washington, D.C.: John C. Rives, 1859.
Second Session, Thirty-fifth Congress, Appendix. Washington, D.C.: John C. Rives, 1859.
First Session, Thirty-sixth Congress. Washington, D.C.: John C. Rives, 1860.
Second Session, Thirty-sixth Congress. Washington, D.C.: John C. Rives, n.d.
Second Session, Thirty-sixth Congress, Appendix. Washington, D.C.: John C. Rives, 1861.

Texas Government Publications

1. Journals of the House of Representatives, Republic of Texas
   First Congress – First Session. Houston: Office of the Telegraph, 1838.
   First Congress – Second Session. Houston: Telegraph Office, 1838.

BIBLIOGRAPHY

Second Congress – Adjourned Session. Houston: Telegraph Office, 1838.
Called Session of September 25, 1837, and Regular Session, Commencing November 6, 1837. Houston: Niles & Co., 1838.
Regular Session of Third Congress, November 5, 1858. Houston: Intelligence Office, 1839.
Journal of the House of Representatives of the Fourth Congress of the Republic of Texas, 1839-1840. Edited by Harriet Smither. Austin: Von Boeckmann-Jones Co., n.d.
Fifth Congress – First Session (1840-1841). Austin: Cruger and Wing, 1841.
Journals of the Sixth Congress of the Republic of Texas, 1841-1842, II: The House Journal. Edited by Harriet Smither. Austin: Capital Printing Co., 1944.
Seventh Congress. Washington: Thomas Johnson, 1843.
Eighth Congress. Houston: Cruger & Moore, 1844.
Ninth Congress. Washington, Miller & Cushney, 1845.
Ninth Congress, Extra Session. Washington, Miller & Cushney, 1845.
2. *Journals of the House of Representatives, State of Texas.*
First Legislature. Clarkesville: The Standard Office, 1848.
Second Legislature. Houston: Telegraph Office, 1848.
Third Session [Third Legislature, Regular Session]. Austin: Wm. H. Cushney, 1849.
Third Legislature – Third Session. Austin: Texas State Gazette Office, 1850.
Fourth Legislature. Austin: Cushney & Hampton, 1852.
Fourth Legislature – Extra Session. Austin: J.W. Hampton, 1853.
Fifth Legislature. Austin: J.W. Hampton, 1853.
Sixth Legislature. Austin: Marshall & Oldham, 1855.
Sixth Legislature, Adjourned Session. Austin: Marshall & Oldham, 1856.
Seventh Biennial Session. Austin: John Marshall, 1857.
Eighth Legislature. Austin: John Marshall, 1860.
Extra Session of the Eighth Legislature. Austin: John Marshall, 1861.
3. *Journals of the Senate, Republic of Texas*
First Congress, Second Session. Houston: Telegraph Office, 1838.
Called Session of Congress Convened September 25, 1837; and the Regular Session, Convened November 6, 1837. Houston: Niles & Co., 1838.
Second Congress – Adjourned Session. Houston: Telegraph Power Press, 1838.
Third Congress, First Session, 1838. Houston: National Intelligencer Office, 1839.
Journal of the Senate of the Republic of Texas, Fourth Congress, 1839-1840. Edited by Harriet Smither. Austin: Von Boeckmann-Jones, n.d.
Fifth Congress, First Session. Houston: Telegraph Office, 1841.
Journal of the Senate of the Republic of Texas, Sixth Congress, 1841-1842. Edited by Harriet Smither. Austin: Von Boeckmann-Jones Co., 1940.
Seventh Congress, Convened at Washington on the 14th of November, 1842. Washington: Thomas Johnson, 1843.
Eighth Congress. Houston: Couger & Moore, 1844.
Ninth Congress. Washington: Miller & Cushney, 1845.
Ninth Congress – Extra Session. Washington: Miller & Cushney, 1845.
4. *Journals of the Senate, State of Texas*
First Legislature. Clarksville: Standard Office, 1848.
Second Legislature. Houston: Telegraph Office, 1848.
Third Session. Austin: Wm. H. Cushney, 1849.
Extra Session, Third Legislature. Austin: Texas State Gazette Office, 1850.
Fourth Legislature. Austin: Cushney & Hampton, 1852.
Fourth Legislature – Extra Session. Austin: J.W. Hampton, 1853.
Fifth Legislature. Austin: J.W. Hampton, 1853.
Sixth Legislature. Austin: Marshall & Oldham, 1855.
Sixth Legislature – Adjourned Session. Austin: Marshall & Oldham, 1856.

BIBLIOGRAPHY

Seventh Biennial Session. Austin: John Marshall, 1857.
Eighth Legislature. Austin: John Marshall, 1860.
Extra Session of the Eighth Legislature. Austin: John Marshall, 1861.

Miscellaneous

Correspondence Relating to a Treaty between Mexico and Texas. Washington: National Register, 1845.

Debates and Proceedings of the Sixth Legislature of the State of Texas. State Gazette Appendix. Austin: Marshall & Oldham, 1856.

Debates of the Sixth Legislature of the State of Texas. Adjourned Session. State Gazette Appendix. Austin: Marshall & Oldham, 1856.

Debates of the House of Representatives of the Eighth Legislature of the State of Texas. State Gazette Appendix. Austin: John Marshall & Co., 1860.

DeBow, J.D.B. *The Industrial Resources, Etc. of the Southern and Western States.* Vol. III. New Orleans: Merchants Exchange, 1853.

A Digest of the General Statute Laws of the State of Texas; also the Colonization Laws. Prepared by W. S. Oldham and G. W. White. Austin: 1859.

Gammel, Hans Peter Nielsen, comp. *The Laws of Texas, 1822-1897.* 10 vols.[Vols I-IV: 1822-1861]. Austin: The Gammel Book Co., 1898.

Garrison, George Pierce, ed. *The Diplomatic Correspondence of the Republic of Texas.* In American Historical Association Annual Reports for 1907 and 1908. 3 vols. Washington, D.C.: 1908-1911.

The Goliad Declaration of Independence, December 20, 1835. Brazoria, 1835.

Journals of the Consultation [of 1835]. Houston, 1838.

[Journals of] the General Convention [of 1836]. Houston, 1838.

Mullins, Marion Day. *The First Census of Texas, 1829-1836.* [Special Publications of the National Genealogical Society, No. 22]. Washington, D.C.: 1959.

Proceedings of the General Convention [of 1832]. Brazoria, 1832.

Smither, Harriet, ed. *Journals of the Sixth Congress of the Republic of Texas, 1841-1842,* III. Journals Called Session. Austin: Capital Printing Co., 1945.

Wallace, Ernest and Vigness, David M., eds. *Documents of Texas History.* Austin: The Steck Company, 1963.

Weeks, W. F. *Debates in the [Texas] House of Representatives on the Santa Fe Question.* Austin: Southwestern American Office, 1849.

Weeks, W. F. *Debates of the Texas [Constitutional] Convention.* Houston: J.W. Cruger, 1845.

White, Gifford, ed. *The 1840 Census of the Republic of Texas.* Austin: The Pemberton Press, 1966.

Wilson, Right Honorable James Harold. Speech of May 3, 1971. *[Texas] House Journal.* Sixty-second Legislature, Regular Session.

Winfrey, Dorman H., ed. *Texas Indian Papers, 1825-1916.* 4 vols. Austin: Texas State Library, 1959-61.

Winfrey, Dorman H. and Day, James M., eds. *The Indian Papers of Texas and the Southwest, 1825-1916.* Austin: Texas State Library, 1966.

Winkler, Ernest William, ed. *Journal of the Secession Convention of Texas, 1861.* Austin Printing Company, 1912.

Winkler, Ernest William, ed. *Platforms of Political Parties in Texas.* Bulletin of the University of Texas. Austin, 1916.

Winkler, Ernest William, ed. *Secret Journals of the Senate of the Republic of Texas, 1836-1845.* Austin Printing Company, 1911.

BIBLIOGRAPHY

CONTEMPORARY WRITINGS, REPORTS, AND SPEECHES

Almonte, Juan N. "Statistical Report on Texas, 1835." Translated by Carlos E. Castaneda. *SHQ*, XXVIII (January, 1925), 177-222.

Ames, John W. "Leaving Texas," *The Overland Monthly*, XII (February, 1874). 130-137.

Anderson, Charles. *Texas, Before and on the Eve of the Rebellion*. Cincinnati: Peter G. Thompson, 1884.

Anderson, John Q., ed. *Tales of Frontier Texas, 1830-1860*. Dallas: Southern Methodist University Press, 1966.

Anon. *Texas in 1837*. Edited by Andrew F. Muir. Austin: University of Texas Press, 1958.

Anon. (Lawrence, A.B.). *Texas in 1840 or the Emigrant's Guide to the New Republic*. New York: Nafis & Cornish, 1845. 2nd edition. Orig. ed., 1840.

Anon. (Langworthy, Asahel). *A Visit to Texas*. New York: Goodrich & Wiley, 1836.

Anon. *Western Texas, The Australia of America; or the Place to Live*. Cincinnati: E. Mendenhall, 1860.

Austin, Stephen F. Address Delivered in Louisville, Kentucky, on March 7, 1836. New York: William H. Colyer, 1836.

Austin, Stephen F. *The Austin Papers, October, 1834-January, 1837*. Vol. III. Edited by Eugene C. Barker. Austin: University of Texas Press, 1927.

Baker, D.W.C. (comp.). *A Texas Scrap-Book: History, Biography, and Miscellany of Texas and Its People*. New York: A. S. Barnes & Company, 1875.

Baker, Mosely. "To the Hon. John Quincy Adams, and the other Twenty Members of Congress who Addressed 'The People of the Free States of the Union,' Remonstrating Against the Annexation of Texas to the American Union." Houston: October 20, 1843.

Baldwin, Mr., of Connecticut. Speech on the claim of Texas to New Mexico in the Senate of the United States, Thursday, July 25, 1850.

Ballou, Ellen Bartlett, ed. "Scudder's Journey to Texas, 1859." *SHQ*, LXIII (July, 1959), 1-14.

Barrow, John. *Facts Relating to North-Eastern Texas*. London: Simpkin, Marshall, and Co., 1849.

Beckwith, Arthur, contributor. "Texas Letter from John Hemphill to his Brother, James, in Tennessee." *SHQ*, LVII (October, 1953), 222-224.

Bell, James Hall. Speech [against secession] delivered at the Capitol, December 1, 1860.

Blount, Lois Foster. "A Brief Study of Thomas J. Rusk Based on his Letters to his Brother, David, 1835-1856." *SHQ*, XXIV (January, 1931), 181-202; (April, 1931), 271-290.

Bollaert, William. *William Bollaert's Texas*. Edited by W. Eugene Hollon and Ruth L. Butler. Norman: University of Oklahoma Press, 1956.

Bonnell, George W. *Topographical Description of Texas to which is Added an Account of the Indian Tribes*. Austin: Clark, Wing, and Brown, 1840.

Boom, Aaron M., ed. "Texas in the 1850s, as Viewed by a Recent Arrival." *SHQ*, LXX (October, 1966), 281-288.

Bourne, S. A. G. *Observations upon the Mexican Province of Texas*. London: William and Samuel Graves, 1828.

Bracht, Viktor. *Texas in 1848*. Translated by Charles Frank Schmidt. San Antonio: Naylor Co., 1931.

Braman, D. E. E. *Information about Texas*. Philadelphia: J. B. Lippincott & Co., 1857.

Bryan, Guy M. Speech on the Santa Fe Question Delivered in the House of Representatives, August 27 and 28, 1850. Austin: South-Western American Office, 1850.

Buchanan, A. Russell, ed. "George Washington Trahern: Texan Cowboy Soldier from

BIBLIOGRAPHY

Mier to Buena Vista." *SHQ*, LVIII (July, 1954), 60–90.

Burnet, David G. "Proclamation." Velasco, June 20, 1836.

Catlin, George. *Notes for the Emigrant to America.* London: 1848.

Cazneau, Mrs. William L. [pseud. Cora Montgomery]. *Eagle Pass;* or *Life on the Border.* Edited by Robert Crawford Cotner. Austin: The Pemberton Press, 1966. Orig. ed., 1852.

"J.C. Clopper's Journal and Book of Memoranda for 1828." *QTSHA*, XIII (July, 1909), 44–80.

Communication forwarded from San Felipe de Austin Relative to Late Events in Texas. Mobile: Patriot Office, 1832.

DeCordova, J. "The Cultivation of Cotton in Texas: The Advantages of Free Labour." London: J. King and Co., 1858.

DeCordova, J. *Lecture on Texas.* Philadelphia: Ernest Crozet, 1858.

DeCordova, J. *Texas: Her Resources and Her Public Men.* Philadelphia: J. B. Lippincott & Co., 1858.

DeCordova, J. *The Texas Immigrant and Traveller's Guide Book.* Austin: DeCordova & Frazier, 1856.

DeRyee, William and Moore, R. E. *The Texas Album of the Eighth Legislature, 1860.* Austin: Miner, Lambert & Perry, 1860.

Dewees, William B. *Letters from an Early Settler of Texas to a Friend.* Compiled by Cara Cardelle. Louisville: Morton & Griswold, 1852.

Domenech, The Abbe. *Missionary Adventures in Texas and Mexico: A Personal Narrative of Six Years Sojourn in those Regions.* London: Longman *et al.,* 1858.

Dresel, Gustav. *Gustav Dresel's Houston Journal: Adventures in North America and Texas, 1837-1841.* Translated and edited by Max Freund. Austin: University of Texas Press, 1954.

Duval, John C. *Early Times in Texas.* Dallas: Tardy Publishing Co., 1936. Orig. ed., 1892.

Edward, David B. *The History of Texas.* Cincinnati: J. A. James & Co., 1836.

Ehrenberg, Herman. *With Milam and Fannin: Adventures of a German Boy in Texas' Revolution.* Austin: The Pemberton Press, 1968. Originally translated, 1935. Orig. ed: *Texas und Seine Revolution.* Leipsig, 1843.

Estep, Raymond, ed. "Lieutenant William E. Burnet Letters," *CO,* XXXVIII (Autumn, 1960), 274–309; (Winter, 1960), 369–397; XXXIV (Spring, 1961), 15–41.

Field, Joseph E. "Three Years in Texas." In *Magazine of History,* XXVII. Greenfield, Mass: J. Jones, 1836.

Fisher, Orceneth. *Sketches of Texas in 1840.* Springfield, Illinois: Walters & Weber, 1841.

Foote, Henry S. *Texas and the Texans; or the Advance of the Anglo-Americans to the Southwest.* 2 vols. Philadelphia: Thomas, Cowperthwait & Co., 1841.

Ford, John Salmon. *Rip Ford's Texas.* Edited by Stephen B. Oates. Austin: University of Texas Press, 1963.

The French Legation in Texas. Translated and edited by Nancy Nichols Barker. 2 vols. Austin: Texas State Historical Association, 1973.

Gaillardet, Frederic. *Sketches of Early Texas and Louisiana.* Translated by James L. Shepherd, III. Austin & London: University of Texas Press, 1966.

Gaither, George G. "My Texas Tour." *Ballou's Magazine,* II (September, 1855), 243–45.

Ganilh, Anthony. *Mexico versus Texas: A Descriptive Novel, Most of the Characters of Which Consist of Living Persons.* Philadelphia: N. Siegfried, 1838.

Gray, William F. *From Virginia to Texas, 1835.* Houston: Gray, Dillaye & Co., 1909.

Green, Rena Maverick, ed. *Samuel Maverick, Texan: 1803-1870: A Collection of Letters, Journals and Memoirs.* San Antonio: 1952.

Greer, James K., ed. *A Texas Ranger and Frontiersman: The Days of Buck Barry in Texas, 1845-1906.* Dallas: The Southwest Press, 1932.

BIBLIOGRAPHY

Hale, Edward Everett. *A Tract for the Day: How to Conquer Texas Before Texas Conquers Us.* Boston: Redding & Co., 1845.

Hammeken, George L. "Recollections of Stephen F. Austin." *SHQ,* XX (April, 1917), 369–380.

Hammett, Samuel Adams [pseud. Philip Paxton]. *A Stray Yankee in Texas.* New York: Redfield, 1854.

Harris, Lewis Birdsall. "Journal, 1836–1842." *SHQ,* XXV (July, 1921), 63, 71; (October, 1921), 131–146; (January, 1922), 185–197.

Hart, Katherine and Kemp, Elizabeth, eds. "E. M. Pease's Account of the Texas Revolution." *SHQ,* LXVIII (July, 1964), 79–89.

Holland, James K. "Diary of a Texan Volunteer in the Mexican War." *SHQ,* XXX (July, 1926), 1–33.

Holley, Mary Austin. *Texas.* Lexington, Ky.: J. Clarke & Co., 1836.

Holley, Mary Austin. *The Texas Diary, 1835–1838.* Edited by J. P. Bryan. Austin: The University of Texas, 1965.

Holley, Mary Austin. *Texas: Observations, Historical, Geographical and Descriptive.* Baltimore: Armstrong & Plaskitt, 1833.

Hooton, Charles. *St. Louis' Isle, or Texiana.* London: Simmonds and Ward, 1847.

Houston, Sam. "A Lecture on the Trials and Dangers of Frontier Life, as exemplified in the History of Texas," in *Lectures on Popular Subjects.* Philadelphia: T. K. Collins, 1851.

Houston, Sam. "To the People of Texas." Austin, March 16, 1861.

Houston, Sam. *The Writings of Sam Houston, 1813–1863.* 8 vols. Edited by Amelia W. Williams and Eugene C. Barker. Austin: University of Texas Press, 1938–43.

Houstoun, Matilda C. *Texas and the Gulf of Mexico.* 2 vols. London: John Murray, 1844.

Hughes, Thomas, ed. *G. T. T. Gone to Texas: Letters from Our Boys.* London: Macmillan and Co., 1884.

Hunt, Richard S. and Randel, Jesse F. *Guide to the Republic of Texas.* New York: J. H. Colton, 1839.

Ikin, Arthur. *Texas.* London: Sherwood, Gilbert, and Piper, 1841.

James, Joshua. *A Journal of a Tour in Texas.* Wilmington, N. C.: T. Loring, 1835.

Jenkins, J. H. III, ed. *Recollections of Early Texans: The Memoirs of John Holland Jenkins.* Austin: 1958.

Jones, Anson. *Memoranda and Official Correspondence Relating to the Republic of Texas, Its History and Annexation – Including a Brief Autobiography of the Author.* New York: 1859.

Kennedy, William. *Texas: The Rise, Progress, and Prospects of the Republic of Texas.* 2 vols. London: R. Hastings, 1841.

Kuykendall, J. H. "Reminiscences of Early Texans." *QTSHA,* VI (January, 1903), 236–253; (April, 1903), 311–330; VII (July, 1903), 29–64.

Lamar, Mirabeau B. Address to the Citizens of Santa Fe. Austin: Gazette Office, 1841.

Lamar, Mirabeau B. Letter on the Subject of Annexation, Addressed to Several Citizens of Macon, Ga. Savannah: Thomas Purse, 1844.

Lamar, Mirabeau Buonaparte. *The Papers of Mirabeau Buonaparte Lamar.* 6 vols. Edited by Charles Adams Gulick. Austin: A. C. Baldwin & Sons, 1920–1927.

Lathrop, Barnes F., ed. "Texas vs. Louisiana, 1849." *SHQ,* L (July, 1946), 93–97.

Leathers, Frances Jane, ed. "Christopher Columbus Goodman: Soldier, Indian Fighter, Farmer, 1818–1861." *SHQ,* LXIX (January, 1966), 353–376.

Leclerc, Frederic. *Texas and its Revolution.* Translated by James L. Shepherd, III. Houston: The Anson Jones Press, 1950. Orig. ed., 1840.

Lester, C. Edwards. *Sam Houston and His Republic.* New York: 1846.

Letters of Secretary of State to Commissioners to Santa Fe. Austin: G. H. Harrison, 1841.

Linn, John J. *Reminiscences of Fifty Years in Texas.* New York: D. & J. Sadlier & Co., 1883.

BIBLIOGRAPHY

Lockhart, John Washington. *Sixty Years on the Brazos: The Life and Letters of Dr. John Washington Lockhart, 1824-1900*. Edited by Jonnie Lockhart Wallis and Laurence L. Hill. New York: Argonaut Press, 1966.

Lubbock, Francis R. *Six Decades in Texas: The Memoirs of Francis Richard Lubbock, Confederate Governor of Texas*. Austin and New York: The Pemberton Press, 1968. Orig. ed., 1900.

Marcy, Randolph B. *Thirty Years of Army Life on the Border*. New York: Harper & Bros., 1866.

Maverick, Mary A. *Memoirs of Mary A. Maverick*. Edited by Rena Green Maverick. San Antonio: Alamo Printing Co., 1921.

McCalla, W. L. *Adventures in Texas*. Philadelphia: 1841.

Maillard, N. Doran P. *The History of the Republic of Texas*. London: Smith, Elder & Co., 1842.

Montgomery, Corinne (pseud.). *Texas and Her Presidents*. New York: 1845.

Moore, A.W. "A Reconnoissance of Texas in 1846." *SHQ*, XXX (April, 1927), 252-271.

Moore, Francis, Jr. *Map and Description of Texas*. Introduction by James M. Day. Waco: Texian Press, 1965. Orig. ed. Philadelphia: H. Tanner, Jr., 1840.

Morgan, Thomas J. *A Glance at Texas*. Columbus, Ohio: Statesman Office, 1844.

Nance, John Milton, ed. "A Letter Book of Joseph Eve, United States Charges d'Affaires to Texas." *SHQ*, XLIII (October, 1939), 196-221; (January, 1940), 365-377; (April, 1940), 486-510; XLIV (July, 1940), 96-116.

Newcomb, Jas. P. *Sketch of Secession Times in Texas and Journal of Travel from Texas through Mexico to California*. San Francisco: privately published, 1863.

Newell, Chester. *History of the Revolution in Texas*. New York: Wiley & Putnam, 1838.

Newman, John B. *Texas and Mexico in 1846*. In *Magazine of History*, XXIII, no. 3, 5-33. Tarrytown, N.Y.: William Abbatt, 1923. Orig. publ., 1846.

Niles, John M. *South America and Mexico with a Complete View of Texas*. Hartford: H. Huntington, 1837.

Oates, Stephen B., ed. "Hugh F. Young's Account of the Snively Expedition as Told to John S. Ford." *SHQ*, LXX (July, 1966), 71-92.

Olmsted, Frederick Law. *A Journey Through Texas*. New York: Dix, Edwards & Co., 1857.

O'Neill, Neal John. *The Guide to Texas*. Dublin: Joseph Blundell, 1834.

Parker, A. A. *Trip to the West and Texas*. Concord, N.H.: William White, 1836.

Parker, W. B. Notes Taken . . . Through Unexplored Texas [in 1854]. Philadelphia: Hayes & Zell, 1856.

Pike, James. *Scout and Ranger; Being the Personal Adventures of James Pike of the Texas Rangers in 1859-60*. Princeton: Princeton University Press, 1932. Orig. ed., 1865.

Priestly, Philander. "Texas." *The American Farmer*, XIV (June 29, 1832), 126-127.

Proceedings of the Mass Meeting of the National Democracy of Texas. Austin: Southern Intelligencer Office, 1860.

Rankin, Melinda. *Texas in 1850*. Boston: Damrell & Moore, 1850.

Red, William S., ed. "Extracts from the Diary of W. Y. Allen, 1838-1839." *SHQ*, XVII(July, 1913), 43-60.

Reid, John C. *Reid's Tramp; or a Journal of the Incidents of Ten Months Travel Through Texas, New Mexico, Arizona, Sonora, and California*. Selma, Ala.: John Hardy & Co., 1858.

Reid, Samuel C. *The Scouting Expeditions of McCulloch's Rangers*. Philadelphia: G. B. Zieber & Co., 1847.

Roberts, O. M. Speech on December 1, 1860, upon the "Impending Crisis."

Robinson, James W. "Proclamation by the Acting Governor of the Provisional Government of Texas." San Felipe de Austin: Baker and Bordens, February 12, 1836.

Roemer, Ferdinand. *Texas*. Translated by Oswald Mueller. San Antonio: Standard Printing Co., 1935.

BIBLIOGRAPHY

Roland, Charles P. and Robbins, Richard C., eds. "The Diary of Eliza (Mrs. Albert Sidney) Johnston." *SHQ*, LX (April, 1957), 463–500.

Rusk, Mr. T. J. Speech on the Mexican War, Delivered in the Senate of the United States, February 17, 1848. Washington: John T. Towers, 1848.

Sanchez, Jose Maria. "A Trip to Texas in 1828." Translated by Carlos E. Castaneda. *SHQ*, XXIX (April, 1926), 249–288.

Schmitz, Joseph, ed. "Impressions of Texas in 1860." *SHQ*, XLII (April, 1939), 334–350.

Scoble, John. *Texas: Its Claims to be Recognised as an Independent Power, by Great Britain*. London: Harvey and Darton, 1839.

Sheridan, Francis C. *Galveston Island: The Journal of Francis C. Sheridan, 1839–1840*. Edited by Willis W. Pratt. Austin: University of Texas Press, 1954.

Sibley, Marilyn McAdams, ed. "Letters from Sam Houston to Albert Sidney Johnston, 1836–1837." *SHQ*, LXVI (October, 1962), 252–261.

Simmons, Marc S., ed. "Samuel T. Allen and the Texas Revolution." *SHQ*, LXVIII (April, 1965), 481–488.

Smith, Ashbel. *Reminiscences of the Texas Republic*. Austin: The Pemberton Press, 1967. Orig. ed., 1876.

Smith, Edward. *Account of a Journey Through North-Eastern Texas Undertaken in 1849 for the Purposes of Emigration*. London: Hamilton, Adams & Co., 1849.

Smith, Ophia D., ed. "A Trip to Texas in 1855." *SHQ*, LIX (April, 1956), 24–39.

Smithwick, Noah. *The Evolution of a State: or, Recollections of Old Texas Days*. Austin: Gammel Book Co., 1900.

Solms-Braunfels, Carl. *Texas, 1844–1845*. Houston: The Anson Jones Press, 1936.

Sowell, A. J. *Rangers and Pioneers of Texas*. New York: Argosy-Antiquarian Ltd., 1964. Orig. ed., 1884.

Spellmann, L. U., ed. "Letters of the 'Dawson Men' from Perote Prison." *SHQ*, XXXVIII (April, 1935), 246–269.

Stiff, Edward. *The Texan Emigrant*. Cincinnati: G. Conclin, 1840.

Terrell, A. W. "Recollections of General Sam Houston." *SHQ*, XVI (October, 1912), 113–136.

The Texan Emigration and Land Company. *Emigration to Texas*. London: Richardson, 1843.

The Texas Almanac, 1857–1873: A Compendium of Texas History. Compiled by James M. Day. Waco: Texian Press, 1967.

Thompson, Henry. Oration delivered the 2d March 1841 on the Anniversary of the Independence of the Republic of Texas. Houston: National Intelligencer Office, 1839[sic].

Thompson, Henry. *Texas*. Philadelphia: Brown, Bicking & Guilbert, 1839.

Viele (Mrs.). *"Following the Drum": A Glimpse of Frontier Life*. New York: Rudd & Carleton, 1858.

Wharton, William H. *Address Delivered in New York* (April 26, 1836). New York: William H. Colyer, 1836.

Wharton, William H. *Texas: A Brief Account of the Origin, Progress, and Present State of the Colonial Settlements of Texas; Together With an Exposition of the Causes Which Have Induced the Existing War with Mexico*. Austin: The Pemberton Press, 1964. Orig. ed., 1836.

Wigfall, Louis T. Speech, in Reply to those of Generals Houston and Rusk, on June 25, 1849. Marshall: Republican Office.

Wilbarger, Josiah W. *Indian Depredations in Texas*. Austin: Hutchings Printing House, 1888.

Winkler, E. W., ed. "The Bryan-Hayes Correspondence." *SHQ*, XXV (October, 1921), 98–120; (January, 1922), 198–221; (April, 1922), 274–299.

Woodman, David, Jr. *Guide to Texas Emigrants*. Boston: M. Hawes, 1835.

Yoakum, Henderson K. History of Texas from its First Settlement in 1666 to its Annexation to the United States in 1846. 2 vols. New York: Redfield, 1856.

BIBLIOGRAPHY

NEWSPAPERS

The Advocate of the People's Rights (Brazoria), 1834.
The Alamo Express (San Antonio), 1860–1861.
The Alamo Star (San Antonio), 1854–1855.
Austin City Gazette, 1840.
Brazos Courier (Brazoria), 1839–1840.
The Civilian and Galveston Gazette, 1838–1848.
Colorado Gazette and Advertiser (Matagorda), 1841.
The Colorado Herald (Matagorda), 1846.
The Daily Galvestonian, 1840–1841.
Dallas Herald, 1860–1861.
The Far West (LaGrange), 1847.
The Houstonian, 1841.
The Indianola Courier, 1859–1861.
La Grange Intelligencer, 1844–1846
Matagorda Bulletin, 1838–1839.
Mexican Citizen (San Felipe de Austin), 1831.
The Morning Star (Houston), 1841–1846.
The National Vindicator (Washington-on-Brazos), 1843–1844.
The Northern Standard (Clarkesville), 1842–1861.
The Ranchero (Corpus Christi), 1859–1861.
The Red-Lander (San Augustine), 1841–1846.
San Luis Advocate, 1840–1841.
The Southern Intelligencer (Austin, 1859–1861.
Telegraph and Texas Register (Houston, 1835–1850.
The Texas Banner (Huntsville), 1849.
The Texas Democrat (Austin), 1846–1849.
The Texas Emigrant (Washington-on-Brazos), 1839.
The Texas Gazette (San Felipe de Austin), 1829–1831.
The Texas Monument (La Grange), 1850.
Texas National Register (Washington-on-Brazos), 1844-1846.
Texas Planter (Brazoria), 1852–1854.
The Texas Ranger (Washington-on-Brazos), 1849–1856.
The Texas Republican (Brazoria), 1834–1836.
Texas Republican (Marshall), 1849–1861.
Texas Sentinel (Austin), 1840–1841.
Texas State Gazette (Austin), 1849–1861.
The Texas Union (San Augustine), 1849.
Texean and Emigrant's Guide (Nacogdoches), 1835.
The Texian Advocate (Victoria), 1850.
The Texian Democrat (Houston), 1844.
The Weekly Despatch (Matagorda), 1844.

MONOGRAPHS, ESSAYS, PERIODICAL ARTICLES, UNPUBLISHED THESES

Adair, A. Garland and Crockett, M. H., eds. *Heroes of the Alamo.* New York: Exposition Press, 1956.
Adams, Ephraim Douglass. *British Interests and Activities in Texas, 1838-1846.* Gloucester, Mass.: Peter Smith, 1963. Orig. ed., 1910.
Adams, Paul. "Amelia Barr in Texas, 1856-1868." *SHQ,* XLIX (January, 1946), 361–373.

BIBLIOGRAPHY

Ashburn, Karl E. "Slavery and Cotton Production in Texas." *SSSQ*, XIV (December, 1933), 257–271.

Ashcraft, Allan C. "East Texas in the Election of 1860 and the Secession Crisis." *ETHJ*, I (July, 1963), 7–16.

Ashford, Gerald. "Jacksonian Liberalism and Spanish Law in Early Texas." *SHQ*, LVII (July, 1953), 1–39.

Bainbridge, John. *The Super-Americans: A Picture of Life in the United States as Brought into Focus, Bigger than Life, in the Land of the Millionaires — Texas.* Garden City: Doubleday & Co., 1961.

Barker, Eugene C. "The Annexation of Texas." *SHQ*, L (July, 1946), 49–74.

Barker, Eugene C. "The Government of Austin's Colony, 1821-1831." *SHQ*, XXI (January, 1918), 223–252.

Barker, Eugene C. "The Influence of Slavery in the Colonization of Texas." *SHQ*, XXVII (July, 1924), 1–33.

Barker, Eugene C. *The Life of Stephen F. Austin, the Founder of Texas, 1793-1836: A Chapter in the Westward Movement of the Anglo-American People.* Dallas: Cokesbury Press, 1925.

Barker, Eugene C. *Mexico and Texas, 1821-1835.* New York: Russell & Russell, 1965. Orig. ed., 1928.

Barker, Eugene C. "Notes on the Colonization of Texas." *SHQ*, XXVII (October, 1923), 108–119.

Barker, Eugene C. "The Texan Declaration of Causes for Taking Up Arms Against Mexico." *QTSHA*, XV (January, 1912), 173–185.

Barker, Nancy N. "The Republic of Texas: A French View." *SHQ*, LXXI (October, 1967), 181–193.

Barton, Henry W. "The Anglo-American Colonists Under Mexican Militia Laws." *SHQ*, LXV (July, 1961), 61–71.

Barton, Henry W. "The Problem of Command in the Army of the Republic of Texas." *SHQ*, LXII (January, 1959), 299–311.

Beacham, William B. "Travelers' Impressions of Texas and Texans, 1767-1860." M.A. Thesis: Southern Methodist University, 1937.

Bell, Mattie. "The Growth and Distribution of the Texas Population." M.A. Thesis: Baylor University, 1935.

Bender, Averam B. *The March of Empire: Frontier Defense in the Southwest, 1848-1860.* Lawrence: University of Kansas Press, 1952.

Bender, A. B. "The Texas Frontier, 1848-1861." *SHQ*, XXXVIII (October, 1934), 135–148.

Billington, Ray Allen. *The Far Western Frontier, 1830-1860.* New York: Harper & Row, 1962. Orig. ed., 1956.

Binkley, William Campbell. *The Expansionist Movement in Texas, 1836-1850.* Berkeley: University of California Press, 1925.

Binkley, William Campbell. "The Last Stage of Texan Military Operations Against Mexico, 1843." *SHQ*, XXII (January, 1919), 260–271.

Binkley, William Campbell. *The Texas Revolution.* Baton Rouge: Louisiana State University Press, 1952.

Biographical Directory of Texan Conventions and Congresses, 1832-1845. Austin: Book Exchange, 1941.

Bloom, Lansing Bartlett. "Texan Aggressions, 1841-1843." *Old Santa Fe*, II (October, 1914), 143–156.

Boatright, Mody C. "The Myth of Frontier Individualism." In Richard Hofstadter and Seymour Martin Lipset, eds., *Turner and the Sociology of the Frontier.* New York: Basic Books, 1968.

Brack, Gene. "Mexican Opinion and the Texas Revolution." *SHQ*, LXXII (October, 1968), 170–182.

Bridges, Clarence Allan. "Texas and the Crisis of 1850." M. A. Thesis: University of Texas, 1925.

BIBLIOGRAPHY

Brown, John Henry. *Life and Times of Henry Smith, the First American Governor of Texas.* Austin: Steck Co., 1935.

Bugbee, Lester G. "The Texas Frontier, 1820-1825." *PSHA,* IV (March, 1900), 102-121.

Burkhalter, Lois Wood. *Gideon Lincecum, 1793-1874: A Biography.* Austin & London: University of Texas Press, 1965.

Cale, Ada Warren. "Texas Frontier Problems, 1836-1860." M. A. Thesis: St. Mary's University [San Antonio], 1944.

Christian, Asa K. *Mirabeau Buonaparte Lamar.* Austin: Von Boeckmann-Jones Co., 1922.

Clarke, Mary Whately. *David G. Burnet: First President of Texas.* Austin and New York: The Pemberton Press, 1969.

Clendenen, Clarence C. *Blood on the Border: The United States Army and the Mexican Irregulars.* New York: The Macmillan Co., 1969.

Connor, Seymour V. *Adventure in Glory: The Saga of Texas, 1836-1849.* Austin: Steck-Vaughn Co., 1965.

Connor, Seymour V. "The Evolution of County Government in the Republic of Texas." *SHQ,* LV (October, 1951), 163-200.

Connor, Seymour V. "Land Speculation in Texas." *SR,* XXXIX (Spring, 1954), 138-143.

Connor, Seymour V. *Texas: A History.* New York: Thomas Y. Crowell Co., 1971.

Cook, Berenice S. "Texas as Seen in the New York Press from 1835 to 1845." M. A. Thesis: Columbia University, 1935.

Cooper, Maidie. "Texas Colonization Under Mexican Restrictions, 1821-1835." M. A. Thesis: Sam Houston State Teachers College, 1940.

Cottrell, Dorothy. "Texan Reprisals Against New Mexico in 1843." M. A. Thesis: University of New Mexico, 1934.

Davenport, Harbert. "The Men of Goliad." *SHQ,* XLIII (July, 1939), 1-41.

Day, James M. *Jacob de Cordova: Land Merchant of Texas.* Waco: Heritage Society of Waco, 1962.

DeShields, James T. *Border Wars of Texas.* Tioga: The Herald Co., 1912.

DeShields, James T. *They Sat in High Place.* San Antonio: Naylor Co., 1940.

Dixon, Sam Houston and Kemp, Louis Wiltz. *The Heroes of San Jacinto.* Houston: The Anson Jones Press, 1932.

Dobie, J. Frank. *The Flavor of Texas.* Dallas: Dealey and Lowe, 1936.

Dunn, Roy Sylvan. "The KGC [Knights of the Golden Circle] in Texas, 1860-1861." *SHQ,* LXX (April, 1967), 543-573.

Elliott, Claude. "Union Sentiment in Texas, 1861-1865." *SHQ,* L (April, 1947), 449-477.

Ewing, Floyd F., Jr. "Origins of Unionist Sentiment on the West Texas Frontier." *WTHAYB,* XXXII (October, 1956), 21-29.

Faulk, Odie B. *The Last Years of Spanish Texas, 1778-1821.* The Hague: Mouton & Co., 1964.

Fehrenbach, T. R. *Lone Star: A History of Texas and the Texans.* New York: The Macmillan Co., 1968.

Fehrenbach, T. R. "Seven Keys to Understanding Texas." *Atlantic Monthly,* 235 (March, 1975), 120-127.

Floyd, Jennie W. "An Annotated Bibliography on Texas Found in American Periodicals Before 1900." M. A. Thesis: Southern Methodist University, 1927.

Fornell, Earl Wesley. *The Galveston Era: The Texas Crescent on the Eve of Secession.* Austin: University of Texas Press, 1961.

Fornell, Earl W. "Texans and Filibusters in the 1850s." *SHQ,* LIX (April, 1956), 411-428.

Frantz, Joe B. "The End of a Myth." *SSSQ,* LXV (June, 1964), 3-15.

Frantz, Joe B. "The Newspapers of the Republic of Texas." M. A. Thesis: University of Texas, 1940.

BIBLIOGRAPHY

Friend, Llerena. *Sam Houston: The Great Designer*. Austin: University of Texas Press, 1954.
Friend, Llerena B. "The Texan of 1860."*SHQ*, LXII (July, 1958), 1-17.
Fuermann, George. *Reluctant Empire*. Garden City: Doubleday & Co., 1957.
Gage, Larry Jay. "The Texas Road to Secession and War: John Marshall and the *Texas State Gazette.*" *SHQ*, LXII (October, 1958), 191-226.
Gailey, Harry A., Jr. "Sam Houston and the Texas War Fever, March-August, 1842." *SHQ*, LXII (July, 1958), 29-44.
Gambrell, Herbert. *Anson Jones, the Last President of Texas*. Garden City: Doubleday & Co., 1948.
Gambrell, Herbert Pickens. *Mirabeau Buonaparte Lamar: Troubadour and Crusader*. Dallas: Southwest Press, 1934.
Gambrell, Herbert, ed., *Texas: Today and Tomorrow*. Dallas: Southern Methodist University Press, 1961.
Gard, Wayne. *Rawhide Texas*. Norman: University of Oklahoma Press, 1965.
Garrison, George P. "The First Stage of the Movement for the Annexation of Texas." *AHR*, X (October, 1904), 72-96.
Gates, Paul W. "Frontier Estate Builders and Farm Laborers." In Walker D. Wyman and Clifton B. Kroeber, eds. *The Frontier in Perspective*. Madison: The University of Wisconsin Press, 1957.
German, S. H. and Vincent, Louella Styles. "Governor George Thomas Wood." *SHQ*, XX (January, 1917), 260-276.
Goldman, Eric F. *The Tragedy of Lyndon Johnson*. New York: Dell Publishing Co., 1968.
Graham, Harvey Lewis. "The *Northern Standard*, 1842-1848: A Texas Frontier Newspaper." M. A. Thesis: University of Texas, 1928.
Hamilton, Holman. *Prologue to Conflict: The Crisis and Compromise of 1850*. New York: W. W. Norton & Co., 1966. Orig. ed., 1964.
Harmon, George D. "The United States Indian Policy in Texas, 1845-1860." *MVHR*, XVII (June, 1930), 377-403.
Head, Nancy Ann. "State Rights in Texas: The Growth of an Idea, 1850-1860." M. A. Thesis: The Rice Institute, 1960.
Hendrix, Paul Leo. "A Historiographical Study of the Texas Revolution." M. A. Thesis: University of Houston, 1961.
Heroes of Texas. Waco: Texian Press, 1964.
Hershkowitz, Leo. "'The Land of Promise': Samuel Swartwout and Land Speculation in Texas, 1830-1838." *NYHSQ*, XLVIII (October, 1964), 307-326.
Hicks, Jimmie. "Texas and Separate Independence, 1860-61." *ETHJ*, IV (October, 1966), 85-106.
Hill, Watt Goodwin, Jr. "Texan Santa Fe Expedition of 1841: A Visionary Dream?" M. A. Thesis: St. Mary's University [San Antonio], 1965.
Hogan, William R. *The Texas Republic: A Social and Economic History*. Norman: University of Oklahoma Press, 1946.
Holden, William Curry. "Frontier Problems and Movements in West Texas, 1846-1900." Ph.D. Diss.: University of Texas, 1928.
Holden, W. C. "Immigration and Settlement in West Texas." *WTHAYB*, V (June, 1929), 66-86.
Hollingsworth, Harold M. and Myres, Sandra L., eds. *Essays on the American West*. Austin: University of Texas Press, 1969.
Hollon, W. Eugene. *The Southwest: Old and New*. Lincoln: University of Nebraska Press, 1968. Orig. ed., 1961.
Howren, Alleine. "Causes and Origin of the Decree of April 6, 1830." *SHQ*, XVI (April, 1913), 378-422.
Hughes, W. J. *Rebellious Ranger: Rip Ford and the Old Southwest*. Norman: University of Oklahoma Press, 1964.
Hunley, Josephine Keller. "A Documentary History of Texan Sentiment for Annexa-

BIBLIOGRAPHY

tion to the United States, 1835-1838." M. A. Thesis: University of Texas, 1937.

Hutchinson, W. H. "Bear Flag and Lone Star: Two Imperial Powers and Their Stereotypes." *SHQ*, LXXII (October, 1968), 141-151.

James, Marquis. *The Raven*. Indianapolis: Bobbs-Merrill Co., 1929.

Jordan, Terry G. "The Imprint of the Upper and Lower South on Mid-Nineteenth Century Texas." *Annals of the Association of American Geographers*, LVII (December, 1967), 667-690.

Jordan, Terry G. "Population Origins in Texas, 1850." *GR*, LIX (January, 1969), 83-103.

King, Alvy Leon. "Louis T. Wigfall: The Stormy Petrel." Ph.D. Diss.: Texas Technological College, 1967.

Koch, Lena Clara. "The Federal Indian Policy in Texas, 1845-1860." *SHQ*, XXVIII (January, 1925), 223-234; (April, 1925), 259-286; XXIX (July, 1925), 19-35; (October, 1925), 98-127.

Lamar, Howard Roberts. *The Far Southwest, 1846-1912: A Territorial History*. New Haven: Yale University Press, 1966.

Lathrop, Barnes F. *Migration into East Texas, 1835-1860: A Study from the United States Census*. Austin: The Texas State Historical Association, 1949.

Leach, Joseph. *The Typical Texan: Biography of an American Myth*. Dallas: Southern Methodist University Press, 1952.

Lewis, Victor Truman. "Texas and the Nation, 1845-1860." M. S. Thesis: East Texas State Teachers College, 1940.

Lord, Walter. *A Time to Stand*. London: Longmans, Green and Co., 1961.

Lowrie, Samuel Harmon. *Culture Conflict in Texas, 1821-1835*. New York: Columbia University Press, 1932.

McConnell, Weston Joseph. *Social Cleavages in Texas: A Study of the Proposed Division of the State*. New York: 1925.

McDonald, Archie P. "The Young Men of the Texas Revolution." *Texana*, III (Winter, 1965), 333-346.

McDonald, Johnnie Belle. "The Soldiers of San Jacinto." M. A. Thesis: University of Texas, 1922.

McMurtry, Larry. *In a Narrow Grave: Essays on Texas*. Austin: The Encino Press, 1968.

Maher, Edward R. "Secession in Texas." Ph.D. Diss.: Fordham University, 1960.

Marshall, Thomas M. *A History of the Western Boundary of the Louisiana Purchase, 1819-1841*. Berkeley: University of California Press, 1914.

Mayhall, Mildred P. *Indian Wars of Texas*. Waco: Texian Press, 1965.

Meinig, D. W. *Imperial Texas: An Interpretive Essay in Cultural Geography*. Austin and London: University of Texas Press, 1969.

Merk, Frederick. "A Safety Valve Thesis and Texan Annexation." *MVHR*, XLIX (December, 1962), 413-436.

Middleton, Annie Laura. "Studies Relating to the Annexation of Texas by the United States." Ph.D. Diss.: University of Texas, 1938.

Muckleroy, Anna. "The Indian Policy of the Republic of Texas." *SHQ*, XXV (April, 1922), 229-260; XXVI (July, 1922), 1-29; (October, 1922), 128-148; (January, 1923), 184-206.

Muir, Andrew Forest. "The Free Negro in Harris County, Texas." *SHQ*, XLVI (January, 1943), 214-238.

Myers, Elbert Jefferson. "Life of George W. Smyth." M. A. Thesis: University of Texas, 1931.

Nackman, Mark E. "Anglo-American Migrants to the West: Men of Broken Fortunes? The Case of Texas, 1821-46." *WHQ*, V (October, 1974), 441-455.

Nackman, Mark E. "The Making of the Texan Citizen Soldier, 1835-1860." *SHQ*, LXXVIII (January, 1975), 231-253.

Nance, John Milton. *After San Jacinto: The Texas-Mexican Frontier, 1836-1841*. Austin: University of Texas Press, 1963.

BIBLIOGRAPHY

Nance, John Milton. *Attack and Counterattack: The Texas-Mexican Frontier, 1842.* Austin: University of Texas Press, 1964.

Neighbours, Kenneth F. "The Expedition of Major Robert S. Neighbors to El Paso in 1849." *SHQ,* LVIII (July, 1954), 36-59.

Neighbours, Kenneth Franklin. "Robert S. Neighbors in Texas, 1836-1859: A Quarter Century of Frontier Problems." Ph.D. Diss.: University of Texas, 1955.

Neighbours, Kenneth F. "The Taylor-Neighbors Struggle Over the Upper Rio Grande Region of Texas in 1850." *SHQ,* LXI (April, 1958), 431-463.

Nevin, David. *The Texans: What They Are – And Why.* New York: William Morrow & Co., 1968.

Newcomb, W. W. *The Indians of Texas.* Austin: University of Texas Press, 1961.

Nordyke, Lewis. "The Truth About Texas." *The Rotarian,* XCII (February, 1959), 12 ff.

Oates, Stephen B. "Los Diablos Tejanos!" [The Texan Devils]." *AW,* II (Spring, 1965), 41-50.

Oates, Stephen B., ed. *The Republic of Texas.* Palo Alto, Cal.: American West Publishing Co., 1968.

Oates, Stephen B. "The Texas Rangers in the Mexican War." *TMH,* III (Summer, 1963), 65-84.

Oates, Stephen B. "Texas Under the Secessionists." *SHQ,* LXVII (October, 1963), 167-212.

Oates, Stephen B. *Visions of Glory: Texans on the Southwestern Frontier.* Norman: University of Oklahoma Press, 1970.

O'Faolain, Sean. "Texas." *Holiday,* XXIV (October, 1958), 34-49.

Ogier, William Calvin. "Settlement of the Texas-New Mexico Boundary Dispute." M. A. Thesis: University of Texas, 1929.

Paxson, Frederic L. "The Constitution of Texas, 1845." *SHQ,* XVIII (April, 1915), 386-398.

Paz, Octavio. *The Labyrinth of Solitude: Life and Thought in Mexico.* Translated by Lysander Kemp. New York: Grove Press, Inc., 1961.

Peevy, Lucien Elliot. "The First Two Years of Texas Statehood, 1846-1847." Ph.D. Thesis: University of Texas, 1948.

Pierce, Gerald Swetnam. "The Army of the Texas Republic, 1836-1845." Ph.D. Thesis: University of Mississippi, 1963.

Pierce, Gerald S. *Texas Under Arms: The Camps, Posts, Forts, & Military Towns of the Republic of Texas, 1836-1846.* Austin: The Encino Press, 1969.

Porter, Kenneth W. "Negroes and Indians on the Texas Frontier, 1831-1876." *JNH,* XLI (July, 1956), 185-214; (October, 1956), 285-310.

Potts, Charles S. "Early Criminal Law in Texas: From Civil Law to Common Law, to Code." *TLR,* XXI (April, 1943), 394-406.

Proctor, Ben H. *Not Without Honor: The Life of John H. Reagan.* Austin: University of Texas Press, 1962.

Ramos, Samuel. *Profile of Man and Culture in Mexico.* Translated by Peter G. Earle. Austin: University of Texas Press, 1962. Orig. ed., 1934.

Ramsdell, Charles W. "The Frontier and Secession." In William Archibald Dunning, *Studies in Southern History and Politics.* Port Washington, N. Y.: Kennikat Press, 1965. Orig. edn. 1914.

Ransom, Harry. "Spirit of Texas." *AH,* IV (Fall, 1952), 24-27.

Reese, James Verdo. "The Worker in Texas, 1821-1876." Ph.D. Diss.: University of Texas, 1964.

Richardson, Rupert N. *The Comanche Barrier to South Plains Settlement: A Century and a Half of Savage Resistance to the Advancing White Frontier.* Glendale: A. H. Clark, 1933.

Richardson, Rupert N., Wallace, Ernest, and Anderson, Adrian N. *Texas the Lone Star State.* Englewood Cliffs: Prentice-Hall, 1958.

Rippy, J. Fred. "Border Troubles Along the Rio Grande, 1848-1860." *SHQ,* XXIII (October, 1919), 91-111.

BIBLIOGRAPHY

Robertson, Robert J. "The Texas Delegation in the National Congress, 1851-1861." M. A. Thesis: Lamar State College of Technology, 1965.

Roland, Charles P. *Albert Sidney Johnston: Soldier of Three Republics.* Austin: University of Texas Press, 1964.

Roper, Laura Wood. "Frederick Law Olmsted and the Western Texas Free-Soil Movement." *AHR,* LVI (October, 1950), 58-64.

Sandbo, Anna Irene. "Beginnings of the Secession Movement in Texas and the First Session of the Secession Convention." M. A. Thesis: University of Texas, 1913.

Sawyer, William E., ed. "A Young Man Comes to Texas in 1852." *Texana,* VII (Spring, 1969), 17-37.

Schmitz, Joseph William. *Texan Statecraft, 1836-1845.* San Antonio: The Naylor Co., 1941.

Sholars, Fannie Baker. "Life and Services of Guy M. Bryan." M. A. Thesis: University of Texas, 1930.

Sibley, Marilyn McAdams. "The Texas-Cherokee War of 1839." *ETHJ,* III (March, 1965), 18-33.

Sibley, Marilyn McAdams. *Travelers in Texas, 1761-1860.* Austin & London: University of Texas Press, 1967.

Siegel, Stanley. "Anti-Annexation Sentiment in the Republic of Texas." Texas State Historical Association Meeting, May, 1968.

Siegel, Stanley. *A Political History of the Texas Republic, 1836-1845.* Austin: University of Texas Press, 1956.

Smith, Justin H. *The Annexation of Texas.* New York: Barnes & Noble, 1941. Orig. ed., 1911.

Smyrl, Frank H. "Unionism in Texas, 1856-1861." *SHQ,* LXVIII (October, 1964), 172-195.

Sonnichsen, C. L. *Ten Texas Feuds.* Albuquerque: University of New Mexico Press, 1957.

Spell, Lota M. *Music in Texas.* Austin: 1936.

Spence, Mary Lee. "British Impressions of Texas and the Texans." *SHQ,* LXX (October, 1966), 163-183.

Steen, Ralph W. "Analysis of the Work of the General Council of Texas, 1835-1836." *SHQ,* XL (April, 1937), 309-333; XLI (January, 1938), 225-240; (April, 1938), 324-348.

Stenberg, Richard R. "The Texas Schemes of Jackson and Houston, 1829-1836." *SSSQ,* XV (December, 1934), 229-250.

Stone, Maybelle Virginia Glasgow. "Immigration to Texas, 1836-1845." M. A. Thesis: University of Texas, 1938.

Swafford, Ralph R. "Anson Jones and the Diplomacy of Texas Annexation." M. S. Thesis: North Texas State College, 1961.

Taylor, Paul Schuster. *An American-Mexican Frontier: Nueces County, Texas.* Chapel Hill: University of North Carolina Press, 1934.

Turner, Frederick C. *The Dynamic of Mexican Nationalism.* Chapel Hill: The University of North Carolina Press, 1968.

Turner, Oreta. "Border Troubles Along the Rio Grande, 1848-1878." M. A. Thesis: East Texas State Teachers College, 1940.

Utley, Robert M. *Frontiersmen in Blue: The United States Army and the Indian, 1848-1865.* New York: Macmillan, 1967.

Vogt, Evon Z. "American Subcultural Continua as Exemplified by the Mormons and Texans." *American Anthropologist,* LVII (December, 1955), 1163-1172.

Walker, Daniel Gers. "The History of the Establishment of the Boundaries of Texas." M. A. Thesis: Southwest Texas State College, 1954.

Walker, Emma Jean. "The Contemporary Texan: An Examination of Major Additions to the Mythical Texan in the Twentieth Century." Ph.D. Diss.: University of Texas, 1966.

Wallace, Ernest. *Texas in Turmoil, 1849-1875.* Austin: Steck-Vaughn Co., 1965.

BIBLIOGRAPHY

Ward Forrest E. "Pre-Revolutionary Activity in Brazoria County." *SHQ*, LXIV (October, 1960), 212–231.

Webb, Walter Prescott. *The Great Plains*. New York: Grosset & Dunlap (n.d.). Orig. ed., 1931.

Webb, Walter Prescott. *The Texas Rangers: A Century of Frontier Defense*. Cambridge: Houghton, Mifflin Co., 1935.

Webb, Walter P. and Carroll, H. Bailey, eds. *The Handbook of Texas*. 2 vols. Austin: The Texas State Historical Association, 1952.

West, Elizabeth Howard. "Southern Opposition to the Annexation of Texas." *SHQ*, XVIII(July, 1914), 74–82.

Wharton, Clarence R. *The Republic of Texas*. Houston: C. C. Young, 1922.

Wheeler, Kenneth W. *To Wear a City's Crown: The Beginnings of Urban Growth in Texas, 1836-1865*. Cambridge: Harvard University Press, 1968.

White, William Wilson. "Migration into West Texas, 1845-1860." M. A. Thesis: University of Texas, 1948.

Williams, Amelia. "A Critical Study of the Siege of the Alamo and of the Personnel of its Defenders." *SHQ*, XXXVI (April, 1933), 251-287; XXXVII (July, 1933), 1-44; (October, 1933), 79-115; (January, 1934), 157-184; (April, 1934), 237-312.

Williams, Elgin. *The Animating Pursuits of Speculation: Land Traffic in the Annexation of Texas*. New York: Columbia University Press, 1949.

Williams, Robert H., Jr. "Travis – A Potential Sam Houston?" *SHQ*, XL (October, 1936), 154–160.

Winfrey, Dorman H. *Julien Sidney Devereux and his Monte Verdi Plantation*. Waco: Texian Press, 1962.

Winfrey, Dorman H. "Mirabeau B. Lamar and Texas Nationalism." *SHQ*, LIX (October, 1955), 184–205.

Wooster, Ralph A. "Early Texas Politics: The Henderson Administration." *SHQ*, LXXIII (October, 1969), 176–192.

Wooster, Ralph A. "Membership in Early Texas Legislatures, 1850-1860." *SHQ*, LXIX (October, 1965), 163–173.

Wooster, Ralph A. *The People in Power: Courthouse and Statehouse in the Lower South, 1850-1860*. Knoxville: University of Tennessee Press, 1969.

Wooster, Ralph A. *The Secession Conventions of the South*. Princeton: Princeton University Press, 1962.

Wooster, Ralph A. "Texas Military Operations Against Mexico, 1842-1843." *SHQ*, LXVII (April, 1964), 465–484.

Index

INDEX

constitution of 1836, 30, 60, 72, 78, 129; protection against imprisonment for debt, 145n.23
constitution of 1845, 108; guarantees of, 145n.23
Consultation of All Texas, 28, 66, 67
convention of 1832, 21, 22
convention of 1833, 22, 65, 66
convention of 1836, 30, 60, 61, 67, 83
convention of 1845, 62, 67, 68, 108, 116, 160n.53
Cooke, Philip St. George, 103
Cortina, Juan, 129; biographical sketch of, 128
Cortina's War, 128-29
Creeks, 65
Crockett, David, 9, 34, 87, 110, 131

Dallas, George M., 10
Daniel, Price, 132
Davis, Henry Clay, 7
Dawson, Nicholas, Moseby, 59
DeBow, J. D. B., 50
DeCordova, Jacob, 50
defense of frontier, 18, 42, 43, 56, 58-59, 78, 80, 91, 96, 117
Devereux, Julien S., 68
DeWitt, Green, 26, 35
Dill, James, 52
Donelson, Andrew Jackson, 107
Duerr, Christian, 106
Dunlap, Richard G., 96

empresario contracts, 14, 16
Eve, Joseph, 101-02

Fallersleben, Hoffman von, 46
Fannin, James W., 92, 110; surrender at Goliad, 57
Farias, Gomez, 23, 24
Felloseby, John, 35
Fillmore, Millard, 121-22, 124
Fisher, S. Rhoads, 73
Fisher, William, 93
Force, William A., 40
Ford, John S. (Rip), 68, 118; in Cortina's War, 128, 129
Forsyth, John, 94
Franco-Texienne bill, 43, 45
Freeman, Ira M., 54

Gaillardet, Frederic, 86
Giddings, G. H. A., 58
Goliad, battle of, 30, 57, 110
Goliad Declaration of Independence, 29
Goodman, Christopher Columbus, 32
Gordon, T. G., 39
Gray, William Fairfax, 29, 33, 75
Grayson, Peter W., 61; biographical sketch of, 60; suicide note of, 60
Greeley, Horace, 10
Guadalupe Hidalgo, Treaty of, 89, 114, 128

Hale, Edward Everett, 94
Hale, William, 33
Hamilton, Alexander, 94
Hamilton, James, 38
Hamilton, Robert, 61
Hamilton, Vincent, 36
Hammeken, George L., 10-11

Harison, Jonas, 21, 22
Harris, John W., 95
Hassauex, Pierre, 43
Hayes, Rutherford B., 11
Headright system, 34, 40, 44, 73
Heintzelman, S. P., 129
Henderson, James Pinckney, 68, 73, 76, 105, 106; as diplomat in England and France, 77, 80; description of, 110; as governor, 110, 113; in Mexican War, 111-12
Holland, Benjamin J., 34
Holley, Mary Austin, 37, 42, 73
Homestead Law of 1839, 145n.23
Hone, Philip, 10
Houston, Sam, 9, 28, 32, 35, 60, 61, 62, 65, 66, 68, 81, 92, 95, 114; at battle of San Jacinto, 30; as president of Texas, 43, 59, 71, 80, 90, 93, 94, 97, 100-106; sense of humor of, 55; biographical sketch of, 64; description of, 72-73; on annexation, 74, 80, 104-07, 110, 159n.43; reaction to Mexican invasions, 101, 102, 104; as U. S. Senator, 115, 121; as governor, 128-131; characterization of, 146n.37; on protectorate over Mexico, 129, 163n.7
Howard, Volney E., biographical sketch of, 67-68
Hunt, Memecun, 94, 152n.17
Huston, Felix, 101; description of, 93
Hutchinson, Anderson, 158n.24

Immigration law of 1830, 19, 20, 22, 23
imperialism, 89, 92-96, 97, 98-100, 101, 102-03, 106, 108, 125-26, 128-29, 130
Indian hostilities, 3, 6, 8, 15, 22, 42-43, 47, 54, 56, 68, 70, 71, 77, 91, 96, 102
Ingram, Ira, 23, 35
Irion, Robert A., as secretary of state, 76, 77, 80, 89-90, 94
Iturbide, Agustin de, 15

Jackson, Andrew, 28, 36, 73, 90; on annexation, 74-75, 152n.17; on Santa Fe Expedition, 100
Jefferson, Thomas, 94
Jenkins, John H., 58
Johnson, Lynda Bird, 132
Johnson, Lyndon Baines, 132
Johnston, Albert Sidney, 5, 42, 68, 93; on love of Texas, 138n.5
Jones, Alexander, 38
Jones, Anson, 68, 80, 104; on reputation of Texas, 9; biographical sketch of, 62, 65-66; suicide of, 62; as president of Texas, 107, 108, 109; opinion of other presidents, 150-51n.37
Jones, John R., Jr., 42

Kaufman, David S., 78, 81
Kearny, Stephen W., 112, 113
Kennedy, William, 84
Knights of the Golden Circle, 129

INDEX